Physical Universe

Virtual God

Exploring the Mystery of the Virtual Inner World

By Ramesh Kushwaha, Ph. D.

Published by

Abhasi Publishing,

Published 2025

ISBN – 13: 979-8-9923369-3-1

Library of Congress Control Number: 2025900172

Dedication

To my Parents who brought me into this world!

Disclaimer

The content presented in ***Physical Universe - Virtual God*** represents the author's personal research, interpretations, and perspectives on topics such as science, religion, consciousness, and metaphysics. It is not intended to promote or challenge any particular religious or scientific belief system but rather to encourage thoughtful exploration and dialogue.

Readers are advised to approach the material with an open mind, recognizing that interpretations of the physical universe, spirituality, and theology may vary greatly. The ideas and theories discussed are speculative in nature and should not be considered definitive or absolute.

This book does not provide professional advice in scientific, religious, philosophical, or medical domains. Readers are encouraged to consult experts in their respective fields for professional guidance. The author and publisher disclaim any liability for decisions made by readers based on the information presented in this book.

All references, quotations, and citations used are acknowledged, and every effort has been made to ensure accuracy. However, any errors or omissions are unintentional, and feedback for corrections is welcome.

The purpose of this book is to inspire inquiry, debate, and personal reflection, promoting an understanding of the potential connections between science and spirituality.

Contents

Preface

My curiosity about God lit up in my early childhood—somewhere between folding my hands at the temple and wondering if He was actually listening. What started as a simple interest soon turned into a passion, and eventually an acute obsession. I consumed books on the subject, browsing through arguments that both convinced me to believe, not believe, and everything in between.

I was privileged to take part in research in the field of unconscious brain processes, where I discovered that science is also wrangling with the mystery of consciousness. The timeless debate between the physical universe, God, the brain, and the mind has always fascinated me.

During the years of social isolation brought on by COVID-19, the term 'Virtual' hit the headlines. This got me thinking - why not apply the concept of 'Virtual' to God and the mind? I penned an article on 'Virtual Physicalism', asserting that 'Virtual' could be a more acceptable explanation for the mind and consciousness in the scientific community, as it is cemented in the physical reality. So, I decided to apply the term 'virtual' to God and the Soul.

In Chapters 2 through 5, I have provided some background information. One major point of contention that I have addressed is the ongoing controversy between science and religion. Scientists and atheists often find themselves at odds with religion, arguing that the two are incompatible. In a different light, theists believe that science and religion can peacefully coexist. However, individuals like Chris Hedges and James Lindsay have taken a different stance, claiming that both sides are mistaken.

In my opinion, both theists and new atheists are falling wide of the mark. I have defended my reasoning for why I believe that science and religion, or human nature, are different.

In this thought-provoking analysis, I propose the existence of not one, but two worlds - the physical external universe and the virtual inner world. I claim that everything we experience is 'virtual', and by applying this concept, we can gain the flexibility needed to understand the complexities of the mental world.

One core point I make is that the laws of physics simply do not apply to the virtual inner world. Through writing this book, I have caught on to a unifying principle that surpasses religious experiences. It explains the miraculous healing powers of prayer and the subtle impact of faith and belief on the physical body. These attention-grabbing topics are further presented in the following chapters.

It is clear that science falls short in interpreting the phenomena of the virtual inner world, as these experiences are inherently subjective and deeply personal.

I urge that if we entertain the idea of the universe being eternal, as some religions and astrophysicists suggest, then the concept of God is no longer needed. This could potentially put an end to the long-standing debates between theists and atheists. Furthermore, it may provide answers to other questions commonly used to prove the existence of God.

In my writing, I describe the creation of the Virtual Inner World within our brains, where the real God resides for me - present in all living creatures. This Pure Consciousness is required to generate awareness and phenomenal consciousness within us. It is only through our more evolved brains that humans can leverage this Pure Consciousness, a practice that mystics have been mastering for centuries. I propose that by adopting this concept, humans can find happiness in their daily lives as well.

Chapter 9, titled 'Consciousness,' may be a bit dense for some readers. If you find yourself weighed down by the theoretical aspects, feel free to skim through the basics. After all, understanding the inner workings of our minds should be an enlightening experience, not a harrowing task.

Drawing from my Indian heritage, I have incorporated examples and references from a multitude of religions. In addition to Christianity, Judaism, and Islam, I have pored over the teachings of Hinduism, Buddhism, Jainism, and Taoism. I intend to offer you a global perspective on faith and belief systems.

Along the course, I have shared my observations, which you may or may not vibe with. These are just my takes based on my experiences. I do not mean to stir the pot or question your beliefs, so please approach this with an open mind. Take what resonates with you and leave what does not - let's agree to disagree!

My aim is not to force my opinions on you but rather to kindle some introspection and a deeper appreciation for the various spiritual paths that have influenced human thought and culture. Let's walk through these teachings together, broaden our horizons, and nestle a sense of respect for the diverse belief systems out there. I highly recommend keeping it light and nonjudgmental.

The cover of this book features AI-generated artwork created with 'AI Image Generator'.

Before I conclude this section, in response to feedback from some beta reader friends, I have used gender-neutral pronouns such as 'He/She' and 'His/Her' when referring to God. They questioned why I exclusively used 'He' and 'His' for God and how I knew if God is a male. After all, who are we to assume God's gender? So, let's keep it open-ended.

About the Author

Dr. Ramesh K. Kushwaha holds an M.S. in Electrical Engineering and an M.S. and a Ph.D. in Bioengineering from the University of Michigan, Ann Arbor. He works as Sr. Engineer and Staff Specialist in the Neurology department at Michigan Medicine, the University of Michigan. Dr. Kushwaha has spent more than three decades in the trenches of Conscious and Unconscious Brain Processing research. He has worked with Dr. Howard Shevrin at the famed Ormond and Hazel Hunt Laboratory in Michigan's Psychiatry department—because the unconscious mind does not clock out, and neither does Dr. Kushwaha.

He lives in Ann Arbor, Michigan. He lives with his wife and has three grown-up children. He likes to think and read about mind, brain, God, and Consciousness when alone.

A deep-seated childhood passion to seek the truth about God has set the course for his career, the essence of his life, and the soul of this book.

Chapter 1

Introduction: My Search for God

Early Religious Experiences

I grew up in a traditional Hindu family in Northern India. In my days of yore, I regularly attended temples, participated in Hindu rituals, read the holy scripture Ramayana, and prayed daily. Just like any typical kid, I used to frequent temples with a never-ending list of wishes. From acing exams to scoring a dream job, from snagging a promotion to owning a house - you name it, it was on my list. It was all part and parcel of growing up in my neck of the woods. I was a theist - one who believes in God.

As we enter our teenage years, our logical mind tends to take over. We may start questioning our beliefs and rituals. Therefore, around the age of 10 or 12, I found myself questioning the purpose of temple visits and reciting prayers. I mean, could those God idols help me ace my exams and make it rain money? And what about getting sick - could the temple Gods formulate a cure for that? I could not help but wonder if there was a higher power pulling the strings behind all the disasters in the world - floods, hurricanes, tornadoes and earthquakes. Did God also decide when we enter and exit this planet called Earth?

Naturally, I turned to the wise sages around me for answers. And, surprise, surprise, they proposed the same solution - "Yes, there is a God." Their reasoning? "Just like a chair does not magically appear out of thin air, this world must have been created by someone. And that someone, is none other than God."

I was told that my life was completely controlled by God. Every event, every swirl and spin, was already written in the stars by a higher power. According to Hindu beliefs, my Karma from past lives determined my fate in this one, and my current actions would shape my future. Occult sciences such as palmistry, astrology, and numerology are like a crystal ball to catch a glimpse of my future. It was like living in a cosmic choose-your-own-adventure book.

But then in middle school, my young ears were often fed with Gandhi ji's famous words, "God helps those who help themselves." And suddenly, I was faced with a dilemma. If I am the one responsible for my actions, then what is the role of God? It is like trying to solve a puzzle with missing pieces - only one of these theories can be true.

I quickly noticed that simply praying to God was not going to magically fill my pockets with cash or miraculously complete my homework. So, being the curious youngster I was, I decided to experiment on myself. I kept a diary to document the events of each day, noting when I half-heartedly skipped my prayers.

Astonishingly, for a couple of weeks, it seemed like God was keeping score and dishing out rewards or punishments accordingly. But as time went on, the correlation between my prayers and my life events started to fade. It became clear that my little experiment had run its course, and I decided to call it quits.

My Quest for Evidence

As I entered my teenage years, a rebellious phase, if you will, I decided to stop attending temples and participating in worship. I asked the ones around me to provide concrete evidence of a higher power's existence. My peers labeled me as an atheist - one who does not believe in God. I relished debating with friends and family on this controversial subject. Despite my best efforts, no one could provide me with a convincing response. Eventually, I grew weary of my persistent questioning.

I kept my search for God to myself, fearing the consequences of straying from religious guidelines (Dharma) and neglecting prayers. The threat of punishment not only in this birth but in many future lives started to haunt me.

It is a common belief that misfortunes in this life are a result of past wrongdoings. When I saw my uncle's 2-year-old son suffering from a serious illness, I could not help but question the fairness of it all. What kind of sins could a toddler possibly commit to deserve such pain?

The responses I received were always the same - his suffering was attributed to his actions in a past life. I could not help but wonder about the timeless nature of karma, as it seemed to be punishing a child for crimes he could not possibly have committed. Is karma truly blind to innocence, or is there a deeper lesson to be learned here?

Despite the explanations, I could not shake the feeling that there had to be more to it. Maybe the universe was just having a bad day, or perhaps karma was simply a misunderstood concept. Either way, it left me questioning the rationality of it all.

I always had this thought in the back of my mind that if billions of people believe in God and pray to God for their happiness, there must be some truth to it. This perception and fear of punishment made me 'agnostic'. This is a term introduced by Thomas Huxley (1825-1895) which means, 'One who does not have an opinion if God exists or not.'

At one point, I was so bent on seeking spiritual enlightenment that I considered walking into the woods or trekking a mountain in search of a divine connection. I was curious about the awakening Buddha experienced under the Bodhi tree in Bodh Gaya, India. However, I believe, life had other plans for me.

I questioned if there is only one God. But then, why is there a separate God for each religion: one for Christians, another for Islam, yet another for Sikhs, Jews, and many for Hindus? There are a multitude of Gods in the Hindu religion - a polytheistic religion. Hindus also worship idols – a pantheistic religion. In Hinduism, there are numerous Demi-Gods such as Lakshmi, the Goddess of Wealth; Saraswati, the Goddess of Education; Hanuman, the God of Power; Krishna, the God of Love; Durga, the Goddess of Power; and Indra, the God of Rain, among others. Similar to Pagans and Romans, Hindus worship natural elements including rivers, mountains, trees, earth, soil, wells, lakes, sky, sun, moon, stars, planets, rain, wind, cows, and more.

The Forage Continues

Growing up in India, I had great plans to conduct research to bring to light the truth about the existence of the Gods. I was convinced that I could finally put an end to the debate once and for all. However, as I studied other religions, I realized that this question was not as earth-shattering as I had initially thought. After all, trying to change the beliefs of billions of Hindu followers seemed like a futile endeavor.

Instead, a more intriguing question began to occupy my mind: Does a higher power truly exist, the one that created the universe and oversees its workings? And what about the concept of the soul - does it transcend the physical body and undergo reincarnation?

As I immersed myself in research, my focus shifted yet again. Rather than mulling over the existence of God, which is a debate that may never reach a definitive conclusion, I found myself drawn to a more gripping inquiry: What is the essence of the God that theists place their faith in, and how does it differ from the concept of God that atheists strongly deny? And what about the soul - what is its true nature, and what does the idea of rebirth or reincarnation truly mean?

In the quest for answers, one thing became abundantly clear - the mysteries of the universe are vast and endlessly engrossing. As I continue to analyze these philosophical questions, I am reminded that the pursuit of knowledge is filled with wonder and discovery.

Sinking My Teeth into Religious Philosophies

Like an eager-beaver, I began reading books about religious philosophies in the hopes of finding answers to my questions about the existence of God and the true nature of God. I wanted to know what God looks like, whether

God is male or female, and what it means to meet, see, or talk to God in person. I always wondered what I would ask God if I ever had the chance to meet Him. I read books by spiritual leaders like Swami Vivekananda, Acharya Rajneesh, Ramakrishna Paramhansa, Paramhansa Yogananda, and many others that I found in bookstores and libraries. I also came across the idea that God is within each of us, although I did not fully understand what that meant at the time.

In Hinduism, the concept of reincarnation is a fascinating belief that adds depth to the understanding of life and death. It is said that every individual strives to accumulate good karma in their current life to secure a more favorable existence in their next life. According to Hindu teachings, the soul is eternal and transcends the physical limitations of the body, persisting through multiple lifetimes.

The idea of karma, or the deeds one performs in this life, is thought to determine the form one takes in the next life. So, depending on your actions in this lifetime, you could come back as a noble human, a sharp-witted rat, a majestic elephant, a peaceful cow, a graceful fish, or even a tiny insect. It is like a cosmic play, where your choices today shape your destiny tomorrow.

Christians believe that our actions in this life determine whether we end up in heaven or hell. According to Christian doctrine, we are all born sinners and only Jesus can help us cleanse ourselves of our sins, paving the way for our salvation.

Islam believes that our actions in this life will determine whether we end up in heaven or hell, where we will be rewarded or punished by Allah.

Buddhism and Jainism, offshoots of the Hindu religion, reject the notion of a creator deity. Yet, they both follow the concepts of a soul and the cycle of rebirth or reincarnation.

This implies that there is a part of us that transcends the physical body, moving on to the afterlife and potentially being reincarnated.

I continued inquiring into the concept of the soul. Where does the soul reside in the body? How does it transfer from one vessel (body) to another after death? Can the soul exist independently of the physical body? Is the soul non-physical? Can it be passed down through genes? But genes are physical. I read many accounts of reincarnation that suggested the existence of past lives. Despite numerous stories supporting life after death, there is still no concrete scientific evidence to confirm it.

Before I continue sharing my quest, let us take a moment to marvel at some astonishing theories chronicled in the annals of history.

In 1907, Dr. Duncan MacDougall of Harvey Hill, MA, made headlines by weighing patients dying of TB and claiming they lost ½ to 1 ounce at the moment of death. He believed this weight loss was the soul leaving the body. The New York Times even ran a headline on March 11th, 1907, declaring, "Soul has weight, Physician thinks." However, this theory is now considered flawed (McGrath, p. 131, Note 1).

One of the most famous researchers in this area was Dr. Ian Stevenson, a psychiatrist at the University of Virginia. He investigated over 2,500 cases of children who claimed to remember past lives. Dr. Stevenson documented specific details in some of these cases, such as children recalling names, places, and events that they could not have known through normal means. Some of these recollections were later verified, which Stevenson argued could not be easily explained by chance, suggestive of reincarnation.

Despite these intriguing cases, the scientific community remains skeptical. Critics threw shade, suggesting these memories were nothing more than suggestibility, false memories, or plain old coincidences. Others proposed the idea of inherited memories, which sounds exciting but lacks scientific credibility.

Therefore, despite the tempting tales and a few studies here and there, there's still no smoking gun proving reincarnation is the real deal. So, for now, it's all just a fun topic to debate over a cup of tea, rather than a proven fact (Note 2).

Ghosts, Spirits, Possessions and OBE

In the 19th century, the belief in ghosts and spirits became popular in society based on the idea that the soul can exist outside the physical body. Practices like Planchette and Ouija were common pastimes during this time. Spiritualist gatherings, known as 'seances', as well as national conventions and summer camps, were also popular. There were over 200 journals dedicated to these topics. Spiritualism revolved around the belief that the soul is eternal and that the deceased can communicate with the living. From 1850 to 1930, spiritualism was a global phenomenon, with even famous figures like Edison and Tesla working on machines to communicate with the dead.

Notable scientists like Nobel Laureate Pierre Currie, Alfred Thomas Nikola, co-discoverer of Evolution Russel Wallace, and Harvard Psychologist William James were also drawn to this movement. Sir Arthur Conan Doyle, the renowned English novelist and creator of Sherlock Holmes, frequently presented psychic evidence at Carnegie Hall. Stefan Bechtel and Laurence Roy Stains have written detailed accounts of the spiritualism movement in their book, 'Through a Glass, Darkly' (2017).

I heard many stories of people whose bodies are hijacked by someone else's spirit (living or dead person's soul). The person possessed can then speak in the same manner or language as the deceased individual. Many movies are still being made in various cultures today that revolve around ghosts, spirits, and reincarnation.

One piece of evidence supporting the existence of a soul can be found in Out of Body Experiences (OBEs), where individuals witness or experience their own bodies from an external perspective. This phenomenon challenges conventional notions of consciousness and raises intriguing questions about the nature of the self. Susan Blackmore has deeply examined OBE, Astral projection, and 'doubles' in depth in her book, Beyond the Body, (1992). After eliminating various paranormal phenomena like ESP and PK with imagination for the explanation of OBE, she concludes that nothing leaves the body. OBE can best be understood as an Altered State of Consciousness (ASC) and is a product of memory and vivid imagination.

An Altered State of Consciousness (ASC) is when your mind takes a little detour from its usual route of awareness and perception. In this altered state, your thoughts, feelings, and senses can go on an unusual ride, making reality, self-awareness, and time feel like they are playing a game of hide and seek. It is like your brain decides to take a spontaneous vacation from the everyday grind.

Recent breakthroughs in neuroscience have illuminated the complex workings of human consciousness and perception. Out-of-body experiences (OBEs) have fed the curiosity of researchers and individuals alike, often linked to spiritual or near-death experiences. However, scientific inquiry has solved the mysteries behind these phenomena, attributing them to the brain's intricate mechanisms. One notable pioneer in this field is Dr. Josef Parvizi, a distinguished professor of Neurology at Stanford University.

Dr. Josef Parvizi, a professor of Neurology at Stanford University and a team of researchers have found a sausage-like brain structure between two hemispheres called precuneus. This is responsible for the OBE type of experience because this centre gives a sense of inhabiting their own body or bodily self (Note 3).

Pursuing Higher Studies in Canada

After earning my undergraduate degree in Electrical Engineering from Allahabad University, I was presented with the opportunity to pursue my studies in Canada. Instead of sticking to the traditional path, I decided to step into the then-emerging field of Biomedical Engineering in the 1980s - the perfect blend of science and engineering applied to the human body.

My research project focused on the early detection of heart disease, but it was the classes and conferences that truly opened my eyes to the enticing field of brain and mind research. The idea of examining the complexities of the mind, brain, and consciousness was like a magnet pulling me in.

So, off I went to the University of Michigan to pursue my Ph.D. in these mind-boggling topics. It was an episode filled with excitement, curiosity, and endless possibilities.

Backtracking to my 'Search' for God and the Soul

During the course, my hibernated interest in God and the soul was re-awakened. Immersed in the vast reservoir of knowledge housed within the University of Michigan's libraries, I studied intently various domains that have captivated the Western world for the past century. These included religion, God, the Soul, Ghosts, Spirits, Metaphysics, Occult Science, and Paranormal Research.

There were five graduate students in my group who had similar interests and curiosity about these topics, and we often discussed these things. It seemed as though mystics struggled to articulate their experiences in scientific terms, while science faltered in decoding the mysteries of the mystical realm. The lack of connection between spiritual wisdom and factual awareness has led to extensive revelations being overlooked and disregarded. This disconnect has created a gaping chasm between our understanding of spirituality and our comprehension of tangible facts.

Therefore, in this book, I have tried to bridge this gap by sharing the observations I have gathered over time. My objective is to demystify the experiences of mystics in a clear and accessible manner.

History of Research on Mind and Consciousness

I learned about Abrahamic religions like Christianity, Judaism, and Islam, which I did not have much exposure to in India. Christianity has had a pronounced influence on science in the Western world for the past few centuries.

There has not been much research done in the field of mind, brain, and consciousness for the last 200 years, even though Descartes brought up the idea of a non-physical nature of mind during the 17th century in his book,' Discourse and Method and Meditations' (translated in 1960). People were afraid that it would encroach on religion and God and anger Christians.

It was not until the early 20th century that society finally started to openly discuss and research the complexities of the mind and consciousness. Mental hospitals opened during the 19th century, treating mental illnesses much like physical ailments were cured. Before that, mental illnesses were often addressed within the confines of churches. Even today, in small towns and villages in India, Gurus and Tantriks (exorcists, occultists, or sorcerers) continue to treat mental illnesses, including epilepsy.

Research and debate on mind, brain and consciousness gained momentum at the end of the 20th century and into the 21st century. In the USA, the 1990s were dubbed the 'Decade of the Brain'. A new group of mostly scientists grew with the name 'New Atheists'. The Spiritual but not Religious (SBNR) group saw a surge in followers, and more recently, the NONES (Note 4) group has formed, with members proudly declaring they do not belong to any group at all. The ranks of Atheists and Skeptics groups also surged.

Buddhism has become more popular in the West because it does not believe in a creator God and mainly focuses on meditation for better mental health. Religions, especially Christianity, are being challenged by scientists in the West. Of course, there are more books written and published today on Christianity than all other religions and Atheism combined.

Pew-Templeton Global Religious Future Project surveyed 200,000 people from 95 countries with 130 languages and found: 31.4% Christians, 23.2% Muslims, 15% Hindus, 16.4% Religiously Unaffiliated (SBNR and NONES), 5.9% Folk Religions, 7.1% Buddhists, 0.8% others, 0.2% Jews. (Note 5).

We will learn more about theists, atheists, and agnostics and their varying interpretations of the elusive concept of God. It's a symphony of beliefs, doubts, and uncertainties as we investigate whether God exists, controls our lives, or created the universe. Well, there is no definitive answer!

New Atheists believe that religion is the cause of all the problems in the world including most fights and wars. Crooked people who claim themselves to be agents of God cheat and exploit good people by scamming their money and respect in the name of religion and God.

Now, let me give you a preview of what lies ahead in the upcoming chapters.

What Awaits You in The Pages to Follow

A truckload of books has been written arguing for and against the existence of God, with theists holding onto their faith like a lifeline and atheists standing firm in their disbelief. Agnostics, on the other hand, are just chilling on the fence, unable to commit to a side. But who can blame them? We are just a bunch of agnostics at heart, unsure of what lies beyond.

So, let's size up the old-as-Adam question of God's existence. After all, who knows the truth? It is all just a matter of belief, not certainty.

I sift through the idea that the root of all problems lies not in science, religion, or God, but in the insatiable human nature of greed. It seems that people are always looking to score something for themselves from a higher power - whether it is a new house, a job promotion, better health, or even a visa to a foreign land. This desire for personal gain is what drives individuals to flock to temples, churches, and mosques, hoping that their prayers will be answered.

We examine how this relentless greed can lead people down a path of wrongdoing, serving as the catalyst for a myriad of other human evils. Interestingly, there are eight temples in India known as 'Visa Temples,' where worshippers seek divine intervention in securing visas for foreign countries. This evinces how people will stop at nothing to fulfill their desires, even if it means turning to a higher power for a little extra help (Note 6).

I then present my idea about God. There are two realities, not one – External physical objective reality and Internal virtual subjective reality. The physical Universe is out there, doing its thing, completely independent and eternal. It is like a cosmic mechanism that never ends.

The Universe is constantly expanding and contracting, like a cosmic accordion. The Big Bang? Just one epic moment in this never-ending cycle. It's like the Universe is throwing a massive party, then cleaning up the mess, only to start the party all over again. Some astrophysicists are even on board with this idea (Note 7).

Living creatures perceive the external Physical Universe through sense organs and the brain. Each one of us makes a virtual model of the external physical Universe in the brain to best fit it for our survival. This is the virtual Universe that we create in the brain. In this sense, we are the creator (God) of our internal virtual universe.

We do not have any other way of knowing the external physical universe except through our perception. However, the external physical universe always exists, even if no one is observing or perceiving it. One proof of the independent existence of the external physical universe is that we all see the same tree and moon at the same time in our internal virtual world. I explain the 'virtual' term, virtual objects, and virtual world in detail with many examples.

When it comes to measurements and observations, things get a bit tricky. The external physical world offers objective and public data, while the internal virtual world is all about private and subjective experiences. There is no easy way to translate or map one to the other. It's like trying to turn a cat into a dog - it's just not going to happen.

I propose that physical laws, such as Quantum Mechanics (QM), Entanglement theory, String theory, and the Theory of Relativity, only apply to physical objects in the external physical universe. These laws cannot be directly applied to virtual objects like visual images, sounds, smells, tastes, touch, feelings like greed, intention, desire, hate, empathy, happiness and sorrow, and all the other intangible goodies that make up our internal virtual universe - our 'virtual self' or Virtual Empirical Self (VES).

In simpler terms, you cannot use physics to explain why you love chocolate, hate Mondays, or feel a deep connection to your favorite TV show. Those are all part of the mystery tour that is our internal world, where physics dares not tread.

The Virtual Empirical Self (VES) is like the key to unlocking the mysteries of the phenomenal virtual world, but it is also the root of all evil and goodness. It is a real double-edged sword. I will discuss VES from the perspective of Eastern and Western philosophy.

I touch on the properties of virtual objects in the virtual world. Virtual objects can be given any meaning by VES without following any rigid physical laws or rules. Virtual objects are perceived only when attention is paid to them. Virtual perception, even for the same object and by the same person, may be different at different times, places and situations. One's thoughts can change perception. This has deep consequences for all perceptions, including the perception of pain.

However, I am going to blow your minds with the revelation that there is something even more vital than VES when it comes to experiencing virtual objects.

That is Virtual Absolute Self (VAS) or Virtual Core Self (VCS) or Pure Consciousness (PC). VCS is the fundamental feature of living creatures, and it is needed for creating and knowing the virtual world, including virtual objects and VES. Further, VCS is the ultimate reality and true nature of the creator God from the perspective of living creatures.

I believe that by viewing God in this manner, we can finally put an end to the old-as-the-hills argument between believers and non-believers. Let us bring some closure to this theological tug-of-war.

I decode the practical phenomenal consciousness that we experience every day when we listen to music or taste food versus fundamental Pure Consciousness (PC or VCS).

The crux of the matter lies in the distinction between sentient beings, such as ourselves, and non-sentient entities like stones and robots. Sentient beings have the remarkable ability to perceive and attribute relevance to their surroundings, all in the name of ensuring their survival and reproductive success. Humans have the added ability as they are aware of perceived things.

On the other hand, stones and robots lack this capacity. Robots simply operate based on their programmed instructions, offering a limited semblance of "meaning." As we stew over further, it becomes evident that the notion of conscious robots remains a far-fetched dream. Even the most brilliant AI scientists are facing numerous hurdles in their quest to create conscious machines.

Therefore, the essence of consciousness transcends mere programming and algorithms. It is a complex fusion of awareness, intentionality, and subjective experience that cannot be replicated by artificial means. So, while robots may excel in many tasks, true consciousness remains an elusive prize beyond their reach.

I want to make it clear that VCS or PC is a fundamental principle of Consciousness, much like the principle of Gravity, rather than a tangible object or person. All religious philosophies around the world assert that Pure Consciousness (PC) or VCS (VAS) is the Ultimate Reality, Absolute Truth, or the creator God of our Virtual world. In Vedanta, it is referred to as Brahman (Atman for individuals). VCS or PC serves as the foundation of spirituality and the pinnacle of happiness.

We walk through how virtual beliefs and faith can bring about changes in our experiences, minds, brains, and physical bodies. This fact may leave physicalists and mechanists wondering in disbelief but I will provide relevant citations to help you wrap your head around it all. This phenomenon forms the basis of spiritual experiences and faith healing, which cannot be explained by the laws of Physics.

Lastly, I attempt to shine the torch on some perplexing questions about life, such as heaven and hell, the soul and reincarnation. This also comprises the purpose of the universe and life, the meaning of life, our existence, our purpose, and our destination. Is there life after life?

Chapter 2

The Discord Between Science and Religion

The ongoing debate between science and religion is like a winding river, constantly shifting course through uncharted territories—sometimes calm, sometimes turbulent—each curve revealing new depths yet always leaving much unknown.

Science relies on observation, experimentation, and empirical evidence to crack the secrets of the universe. Conversely, religion offers a perspective on existence, analyzing faith, spirituality, and the search for meaning beyond the physical world.

At the heart of this conflict is the timeworn question: Does the universe operate only on natural laws, or is there a divine power guiding its course? It is a duel between facts and beliefs, where logic and faith come together in a cosmic clash of titans.

The Agnostic Paradox

Since childhood, the question that has transfixed me the most is the mystery of God's existence. It's like a distant star on my horizon, always shimmering just out of reach. I have spent years at the crossroads of belief, a curious agnostic traveler, constantly seeking the elusive truth that seems to slide through my fingers.

There was a brief period during my teenage years when I considered myself an atheist, but looking back, I realize it was just my arrogance speaking. The truth is, no one can definitively answer this question. Theists argue that atheists must prove that God does not exist, while atheists argue that it is impossible to prove the non-existence of something that is not there, and that the burden of proof lies with theists to prove God's existence.

Atheists often claim that because there is no concrete evidence of God's existence, they choose not to believe. They maintain that the responsibility to provide proof lies with believers, as it is impossible to prove the non-existence of something that is not there. For example, just like no one can prove that my imaginary creature 'Zellephant' does not exist, other mythical beings like Unicorns, the tooth fairy, Santa, and angels also cannot be proven to not exist. The search for answers may continue indefinitely, but it is unlikely to ever be conclusive or definitive.

While religion may not illuminate every shadow, science too often finds itself amidst a fog of enigma. The existence of God remains a mystery, as no one has seen or heard directly from the divine being. However, God is just one piece of the religious puzzle. From rituals to miracles, art to politics, religion encompasses a wide array of aspects that shape our beliefs and practices. In this chapter, we venture into the topic of God and His/Her existence. The next chapter plumbs the depths of the many other facets of religion that make it such a magnetic and complex subject.

Let's now time-travel to the genesis of humans and try to gather the source of the beliefs that have gained mass over time.

Early Human Civilizations and Belief in Supernatural Powers

In my humble opinion, it seems that early civilizations, with their limited understanding of the world, may have conjured up the idea of a higher power - perhaps God - to explain the mysteries of life. The existence of Homo Sapiens, or true humans, can be traced back hundreds of thousands of years. It is believed that Homo Sapiens may have evolved from hominids who roamed the earth some 600,000 years ago.

Back in the day, our ancestors were more into gathering food than growing it. They spent their days fishing, hunting, and foraging for wild fruits. It was not until the Neolithic Age, around 10,000 to 3,000 BC, that agriculture and animal domestication became a dilemma.

Even in this modern age, there are still groups of people who continue to live off the land through food gathering, hunting, and fishing. From the

Kalahari bushmen to the Australian aboriginals, Alaskan Eskimos to the Red Indians in America, and even the central African Pygmy tribes, there are countless communities around the world who maintain a lifestyle reminiscent of the pre-Neolithic era.

These tribes, along with others like the Andaman and Nicobar islanders, the Lakshadweep islanders, and the Daman and Diu islanders, have managed to preserve their traditional ways of life despite the ever-changing world around them. Even the Ainus of Japan and the Nuer of South Sudan are holding onto their ancient customs and beliefs.

What sets these groups apart is their deep connection to the spiritual world. They believe in unseen forces, which they refer to as 'Mana,' spirits, or Gods. Magic and supernatural powers are a central part of their existence, defining their daily lives and interactions with the world around them.

Imagine a time when humans roamed the earth, clueless about the mysteries of nature. Storms, diseases, and disasters struck without warning, leaving our ancestors scratching their heads in confusion. Without the luxury of Google or weather apps, they turned to the only explanation they could think of: magic and supernatural beings.

People believed that by connecting with or pleasing these higher powers, they could secure their place in the universe and maybe even score some protection or prosperity along the way.

These beliefs were not just superstitions - they were the building blocks of early societies. They laid the groundwork for the religions and mythologies that would shape civilizations for centuries to come.

In Sir James Frazer's distinguished work, "The Golden Bough" (1890), he proposed that ancient civilizations initially turned to magic as a way to make sense of and manipulate their surroundings. When magic did not quite cut it, they shifted their focus to the concept of spirits and deities to explain the mysteries they could not quite grasp.

Alternatively, Bronisław Malinowski's Functionalism theory suggested that primitive societies developed beliefs in supernatural forces as a coping mechanism for dealing with life's uncertainties - especially when faced with hazards like illness or natural disasters. These beliefs provided our ancestors with a sense of comfort, control, and emotional stability in an otherwise cryptic world (Note 1).

Different Religions, Different Beliefs

The Hindu religion believes in many demigods such as Brahma, Vishnu, Shiva, Ganesh, Kali, Lakshmi, Durga, Saraswati, and more, whom Hindus worship. They also worship nature, including trees, rivers, fire, rain, the earth, the moon, planets, and the sky, similar to Pagans and Romans. The four Vedas, the oldest holy scriptures of Hindus, outline rules, rituals, and ceremonies for daily life.

Hindu priests explain these teachings to ordinary people during ceremonies like birth, weddings, and others. As worship and rituals are a part of daily life, there is no questioning of God's existence, and therefore no debate against science. Rituals involve worshiping demigods for various reasons like money, food, housing, success in exams, marriage, job promotions, and more (Note 2).

Buddhism and Jainism do not have a belief in a God as the creator of the universe (Atheistic Religions). They do not discuss how the universe was created and assume that it always existed. These religions do have a concept of soul and rebirth. They do not use the term reincarnation, though. The main hallmark of Buddhism is meditation and how to eliminate sorrow (Dukkhham).

Taoism and Confucianism, mostly found in China, both share the unique characteristic of not believing in a higher power. These traditions are more about guiding social behavior rather than focusing on religious beliefs. Contrarily, Marxism, born in Russia, is more of a political ideology than a traditional religion. All three of these belief systems fall under the category of atheistic religions.

Interestingly, figures like Tao, Confucius, Buddha, and Mahaveer (from Jainism) never intended for their teachings to be considered religious. Buddha and Mahaveer never claimed to be messengers of a divine being. Buddha was all about that minimalist lifestyle - no temples for him, just open-air sermons. It was his followers who took the teachings and ran with them, turning Buddhism into a full-fledged religion, complete with temples, rituals, and prayers.

Buddha's first sermon was delivered in Sarnath, near Varanasi in India. A stupa (pillar) was erected in Sarnath, which has since become an iconic symbol of India, adorning everything from rupee bills to government documents.

These religions disregarded other facets of religion and instead fixated solely on the personal aspect that aligned with William James's definition of religion from 1887. James believed that religion should be a deeply personal experience:

"'Religion' means the feelings, acts, and experiences of individual men in their solitude, so far as they apprehend themselves to stand in relation to whatever they may consider the divine...the belief that there is an unseen order, and that our supreme good lies in harmoniously adjusting ourselves thereto ..."

In my opinion, this sounds more like a description of the Spiritual But Not Religious (SBNR) movement of our time. Atheism, as it has evolved in the West, goes by various names such as Secular Humanism, Pragmatism, Effective Altruism, Atheistic Communism, Existentialism, and New Atheism.

Christianity, Judaism, and Islam are more structured religions compared to others, collectively known as Abrahamic religions. These three religions all indicate a belief in one all-powerful creator God, making them monotheistic religions. In Islam, Allah is the Almighty, with Mohammad as the prophet. In Judaism, Yahweh (or Jehovah) is the God described in the Old Testament as a superhuman figure - powerful, omnipotent, jealous, and wrathful. Both Judaism and Islam strictly forbid any depictions of God.

Approximately one-third of the world population (31.4%) is Christian, as per Pew-Templeton Global Research (Chapter 1, Note 4, 2022). According to the 'World Christian Encyclopedia', there are 45,000 Christian denominations and rites in the world (Note 3).

As we weigh the multitude of belief systems that have molded human history, it is evident that our quest for meaning, purpose, and understanding of the universe has manifested in countless ways. From ancient rituals to modern spiritual practices, we have always yearned to form a connection with forces beyond our existence.

The Apple of Content Between Science and Religion

After completing my Engineering in Canada, I migrated to the USA in (1983) for further studies. When I arrived in the USA to pursue my Ph.D., I studied in depth numerous books on the relationship between science and religion. It seems that the contest between the two (especially Christianity) has been raging on for centuries.

The clash with science often aims to discredit scientific findings or claim that everything science has discovered was actually written in the Bible ages ago. New Atheists such as Victor J. Stenger, Sam Harris, Christopher Hitchens, Richard Dawkins, Daniel Dennett, Jerry A. Coyne, James T. Houk, and many others have penned books fervently debunking the existence of a God resembling the Christian deity.

The controversy is not about religion versus science. However, it is about religion versus scientific materialism, as explained in the book 'Modern Physics and Ancient Faith' by Stephen M. Barr. Materialists argue that there is nothing else other than matter that exists, and all laws of physics and mathematics can explain all the phenomena in this universe. Religions assert that there is a God who is beyond this material world and who created the universe. He is the one who controls all events that happen in it every nanosecond.

Believers claim that although God cannot be physically seen, His creation and power are evident and can be experienced. Christianity follows the belief in the Trinity, consisting of the Father, Son, and Holy Spirit. The Spirit is said to reside within each of us, while Jesus is considered the Son of God within this divine trio. According to the New Testament, God is described as omniscient, omnipresent, and omnipotent - the ultimate all-knowing, everywhere-at-once, all-powerful being. He is like the architect of the universe, creating everything and anything within it.

Christianity took a dig at Pagan religions, labeling them as atheistic for worshiping everything in nature - from trees and the sun to rivers, air, and fire. Jews and Christians, on the other hand, mulled over the question of who created all these natural wonders and concluded that they were just simple material things. They then introduced the concept of a single, all-powerful God who created both the material world and all living creatures. It was like they were trailing the mystery of 'Who's Your Creator?' and came up with the ultimate answer.

The Christian God is often described as a compassionate, merciful, and forgiving deity. Jesus's crucifixion and resurrection are the main events in Christianity. According to Christian belief, Jesus was sent by God to cleanse humanity of their sins, with his resurrection serving as evidence of God's existence and Jesus's role as the ultimate savior. Christians firmly hold on to the belief that Jesus will return for a second coming to deliver them, with Jerusalem being the anticipated location for his grand entrance.

Many American policies, planning, and politics seem to take into account the belief that Jesus will come back to save them. For instance, Israel was founded, and in line with the Christian belief of salvation, the capital of Israel was officially moved from Tel Aviv to Jerusalem on December 6th, 2017, under the administration of former President Donald Trump (Note 4). Further, some believe that even the Holocaust was created by God, so Israel could be created in 1945, as claimed by Bart Ehrman in his 2023 book, Armageddon.

The Jewish religion considers the first five books of the Bible as the 'Torah', which means 'The Law', the master plan that God followed to create the universe and to guide the people of Israel.

The three Abrahamic religions all share the common belief in the existence of heaven and hell. In Christianity, the passage to the heavenly gates is faith in Jesus and the Christian God. The Book of Revelation, penned by John, is chock-full of tales about the afterlife. As for Islam, the golden ticket to paradise is earned through prayer to Allah and strict adherence to His commandments.

It describes events leading up to the final judgment, where the righteous are rewarded with eternal life in heaven, and the sinners are cast into hell. The book also provides descriptions of heaven as a place of peace, beauty, and eternal worship of God, while hell is portrayed as a place of eternal punishment and suffering. This revelation has been influential in shaping Christian eschatology, the study of the end times, and the afterlife.

Christianity is an organized religion that has put up continued fights against science. I was surprised to see, for the first time, a two-minute advertisement promoting Jesus and Christianity on TV during the Superbowl LVIII on Sunday, Feb 11th, 2024. The cost of this advertisement must have been around $14 million.

As I traverse the familiar route between Chicago and Ann Arbor on I-94, I cannot help but notice the numerous billboards proudly proclaiming the existence of Jesus. One particular billboard boldly states, 'Beyond Reasonable Doubt, Jesus is Alive, Call 83 TRUTH'. It begs the question - why does Jesus need such aggressive advertising? Who is funding these campaigns, and who stands to benefit from them?

I briefly present below the main points of contention between religion, especially Christianity and science, and arguments given for and against the existence of God.

In his latest book, 'Is God Real: Exploring the Ultimate Question of Life' (2023), renowned author Lee Strobel presents this gray-haired discussion with a fresh perspective. Through many interviews with experts in the field, the New York Times bestselling author, Strobel presents a thought-provoking case for the existence of God from a Christian standpoint.

1. **Cosmological Argument:**

A powerful 'Being' who created the universe and operates it in detail. He is the God of theism and not Deism. The concept of Creationism in Christianity posits that God created the world in a mere six days at the beginning of time, as detailed in the book of Genesis. This standard answer was also given to me when, as a young person I asked for proof of God's existence from acquaintances in India. The answer had this form: If there is a chair, someone must have made it; if there is a radio, someone must have made it; similarly, the sun, moon, trees, birds and humans are also created by someone – the almighty God. Believers of all theistic religions, including Islam, Judaism, and Christianity, also believe that if there is a universe, it must have been created by someone – God. This also implies that the universe has a beginning as compared to Greek, Pagan and Hindu religions which believe that the cosmos always existed. Buddhism and Jainism do not deal with the creation of the universe, instead assuming it has and is always existing.

According to Biblical scriptures (Genesis), the universe was created some 6000 years ago. So, churches were very happy to learn that the Big Bang was proposed in 1927 by Father Georges Lemaitre as the beginning of the universe. It was confirmed in 1965 that the universe is 15 billion years old (Note 5). Another big question arose as to who created the Big Bang and what was there before the Big Bang. Christian believers have the answer: God created the Big Bang – The first cause - the beginning of Time and Space. But who created God then? Christian Theology says that God is uncaused. God does not need to be created. Scientists do not feel comfortable with this discovery of the Big Bang because it means there is a purpose as defined by the Christian God (Teleology) rather than a mechanistic explanation. Scientists are still on the lookout for a satisfying explanation of how the Big Bang went down.

Back in the day, there was this theory called the Steady State theory, claiming the universe was unchanging across all of time and space. Well, turns out that theory got debunked in 1948 when we found out the universe is actually expanding. So, what's the deal now? Will it keep expanding forever? Who knows! One thing's for sure though, the universe is not going to remain the same and last forever. Just like that table you have had since college; everything eventually breaks down and decays. The universe had a start with the Big Bang and as with everything else, the universe will decay and die, and the sun will lose its energy and die. The earth will die. It's all part of the grand scheme of things, following the laws of Thermodynamics. So, what's next for the universe once everything in it dissolves?

The Greeks and Hindus both have their unique take on the universe. The Greeks think it has always been around, just doing its thing in a never-ending cycle. Hinduism features belief in a cyclical universe with the Big Bang as just one important event in it and at some point, the expansion may stop, and the universe will start to shrink (big crunch). Some scientists are even jumping on board with this whole expansion and contraction idea (check out Chapter 1, Note 2 for more details).

But these are all just theories. Personally, I am putting my money on science to eventually crack the code. And Genesis was way off the mark with that whole 6000-year-old universe claim. Science has come through with the receipts, showing us that our universe has been orbiting for at least 15 billion years.

One of the most heated debates of the past revolved around the belief that the Earth was the center of the universe, with the sun orbiting around it. According to Biblical scriptures, man was considered the focal point of creation, distinct from all other living and non-living entities. This belief was so ingrained that when Galileo dared to suggest otherwise in the seventeenth century, the Catholic Church condemned him and placed him under house arrest. It was not until overwhelming scientific evidence supported Galileo's heliocentric theory that the Church reluctantly accepted the truth. It's one thing to deny reality, but punishing someone for speaking the truth? Now that's just plain baffling.

2. Evolution:

As previously mentioned, according to Biblical scripture, God created the universe and humans in just six days. However, in 1859, Charles Darwin thunderstruck everyone with his book 'Origin of Species'. Darwin's theory of Natural Selection shook things up by showing how traits are passed down through DNA and genes, with random mutations causing small changes over time. Basically, it's survival of the fittest out there - only the strong survive and pass on their genes, while the rest bite the dust. It's a slow process, though, taking millions of years and countless generations for creatures to adapt and evolve.

Renowned author Richard Dawkins has eloquently conveyed in his leading-edge works, 'The Selfish Gene' (1976) and 'The Blind Watchmaker' (1986), the concept that nature operates blindly in the domain of evolution. This means that nature does not have foresight when it comes to designing organisms. The result is unpredictable, and the timeline for creation is uncertain. In fact, there may not even be a definitive 'final product' in evolution's grand scheme. Evolution is a work in progress, with no end in sight. Genes, in their quest for survival, can be considered rather selfish in their motives.

According to Hindu beliefs, human life is just one stop on a lasting 8.4 million species ride through reincarnation. It's like evolution, but with a spiritual whirl! Hinduism rejects the idea that humans are a special creation separate from the rest of the animal kingdom.

Christian theologians respond, suggesting that as with everything else, God guides evolution as well. This is also called 'Theistic Evolution' and it claims to support 'Darwinian Evolution'. That is the version of evolution that finally was accepted by the Catholic Church. The Vatican accepted on Oct 27, 2014 (Note 6).

Pope Francis, the head of the Roman Catholic Church, said that Darwinian evolution is real, and so is the Big Bang, according to the *Telegraph*. Elsewhere in his speech to the Pontifical Academy of Sciences, the Pope said:

"When we read about Creation in Genesis, we run the risk of imagining God was a magician, with a magic wand, able to do everything. But that is not so."

He added: *"He created human beings and let them develop according to the internal laws that he gave to each one so they would reach their fulfillment."*

Darwin and modern scientists do not see any role for God in evolution. Christians and Jews believe that humans (Homo Sapiens) are different from other animals and plants and that humans were made in God's image. There have been many court cases for teaching evolution in schools, especially in the southern states of America. John Scopes was convicted in Dayton, Tennessee, in 1925 in the 'Monkey Trial' for teaching human evolution, which violated the Butler Act (Note 7). Islam allows evolution to be taught in schools but believes that humans were created by Allah.

Was the evolution of humans inevitable? No one can say for sure unless we can recreate the whole of evolution from scratch again, which is not possible. It might have taken a different route if something else might have happened, e.g. if the destruction of dinosaurs had not occurred by a meteorite.

3. Argument from Design - Intelligent Design:

From the Theistic view, all things in this universe are created by God. All laws are made by God. The sun, the moon, the earth, and the other planets move according to the laws made by God. All living creatures, from birds to fish to insects to flowers to trees, are created by God. Their sophisticated body parts are like works of art fantastically crafted by the divine hand. But have you ever stopped to wonder what kind of design laws govern the wings of birds, the fins of fish, or the internal ears of monkeys? It's a mystery that even the most brilliant minds have yet to solve.

For those who are skeptical of evolution, the idea that random chance could have produced such perfectly adapted body parts is mind-boggling.

It's as if nature itself is a master sculptor, creating beauty and functionality out of tumult.

William Paley, an Anglican Archdeacon, was not knowledgeable about evolution. In his Natural Theology (1802) book, he argued that a wristwatch, so complex that it could not just happen, as say a simple stone, it must have been designed by an Intelligent designer. Likewise, the human eye could not just happen by random chance of evolution. It is so complex that it must be designed by an intelligent designer – God.

Darwin's theory delivered a knockout punch to the argument about design and the existence of a divine designer - God. He explained how complex life forms could evolve naturally over millions of years through the process of natural selection. In his atypical book, 'The Blind Watchmaker', Dawkins dismantled Paley's Watch riddle by asserting that nature itself is the blind watchmaker responsible for creating complex living beings.

Victor Stenger, in his attention-grabbing book 'Not By Design' (1988), boldly declared that the universe is nothing but a cosmic accident. And in 'The First Three Minutes' (1977), esteemed particle physicist Steven Weinberg wrote:

"The more the universe seems comprehensible, the more it also seems pointless."

Dawkins also seems to italicize the same pointlessness in his paper titled 'Science and God: a Warming Trend' (August 1977).

4. Anthropic Principle and Fine Tuning:

Another big question that is not answered yet by science is how life started – the Origin of Life puzzle. It is believed that it started with a single cell, Amoeba.

But how was the first Amoeba created? Darwin's evolution and natural selection theories cannot explain this. Scientists have attempted to recreate the perfect conditions for single-celled life to emerge, but their efforts have been as fruitful as trying to grow a garden in a desert. It seems we must come to terms with the fact that the universe is playing a game of chance, like a never-ending lottery where the odds are stacked against us. It's like winning the mega jackpot with a one in 750 million chance - talk about luck! Some may call it fate, others may call it destiny, but science simply shrugs and says, "Hey, it's all just a roll of the dice."

For life to blossom on our lovely planet Earth, there are certain physical characteristics that must be in place. This concept is known as the Anthropic Principle. But have you ever stopped to wonder why electrons, protons, neutrons, and other elements have the charge and mass that they do? I mean, why does a carbon atom have 4 electrons in its outer orbit? Could it have been different? And what about the head honchos of organic life - Carbon, Hydrogen, and Oxygen? Could life have existed if these atoms were swapped out for something else? The laws of Physics are set in stone, but could they have been different? Would we still be sipping our morning coffee if things were altered? Please refer to the below references for a more detailed analysis – 'Modern Physics and Ancient Faith' by Stephen M. Baar (2003) and 'The Big Question' by Alister McGrath (2015).

I have briefly mentioned the core physical forces and parameters that govern our universe and have allowed life to flourish on Earth (Baar and McGrath).

There are four fundamental forces in nature- the Strong nuclear force between proton and neutron, Gravity, Electromagnetism, and the Weak nuclear force responsible for radioactive decay. Other important factors are – a constant (v, read as Nue) that determines masses of all particles known as the 'Vacuum expectation value of the Higgs field', the Cosmological constant in Einstein's equation of Gravitational force (lambda), the quantum nature of the universe, the number of dimensions of space, the flatness of space, the neutron being heavier than proton, and the stability of proton.

This so-called Fine Tuning of these fundamental cosmological constants is supposed to have been orchestrated by God (of course), such that if those were different, life would not have been possible on earth. This view is referred to as 'Teleological', in other words, there is a purpose – one that is as it is as defined by God. Scientists who have written on the Anthropic principle do not like the idea of attaching any religious value. Noble prize-winning physicists, Steven Weinberg and Stephen Hawking were atheists.

Scientists address these matters by saying that life might have been different or might already be there different on different solar systems and planets. We do not have any way of predicting. Religious believers object and say that God had no choice to make because God had to make the universe and all matters and living creatures, including humans, the way it was made. Atheists may argue that God could choose whatever God wanted. Why is omnipotent God limited? I think theists would say that God knows that these are the only parameters that produce life.

There are approximately 100 billion galaxies and 100 billion stars in a galaxy, with most of them having some planets attached. Some hold that there must be some planets with conditions right for life and human life. To increase the chances of this happening, scientists bring the idea of the multiverse (Baar). The diversity of laws in each universe enhances the likelihood of life sprouting up in numerous universes. It would be quite a cosmic blunder if God were limited to creating life solely on Earth, wasting precious mass, energy, and divine effort.

5. Argument from Miracle:

In his book 'Licensed Insanities' (1987), John Bowker discusses religions and belief in God in today's world. As we cannot see God in person, the only evidence for His existence would be through miracles, supernatural powers, creation, magic, and divine power. This includes *superstitions*, extrasensory perception (ESP), clairvoyance, premonition, psychokinesis (PK), remote viewing, spiritual healing, astrology, Tarot reading, wearing stone rings for healing, better health, and prosperity, magnetic healing, horoscopes, Tantrik effects, charms, out-of-body experiences (OBE), near-death experiences (NDE), miracle healing, ghosts, demons, devils, spirits, apparitions, ectoplasm, haunted houses, rebirth, Heaven and Hell, communication with the dead, planchette, dowsing, Ouija, poltergeist, possession by spirits, seances, and other supernatural and paranormal phenomena. These are also known as occult science or pseudoscience.

Superstitions

When bad things happen to someone three times in a row within a short period, they often look for a supernatural explanation. If they find or are suggested one, they tend to believe in it. If no other explanation is found, they may attribute it to something bad they did to others in the recent past. Even today, people believe in wearing a stone ring to ward off negative supernatural influences on their health, wealth, and overall well-being. These stones are chosen by astrologers based on the wearer's birthdate and the positions of stars and planets at the time of their birth. Some examples of these stones include ruby, onyx, quartz, diamond, pearl, amethyst, garnet, and more.

Faith Healing:

Many faith healings are described in the New Testament. Christians believe that Jesus cured leprosy and re-enlivened dead people, made deaf people able to hear, and cast out evil spirits. During the 16th and 17th centuries, Satan, ghosts, witches, and ghouls were popular in Christianity. It was thought, for example, that witches affected peoples' daily lives and misfortunes, epidemics, natural disasters, and crop losses.

Many other spiritual healers claimed to have healed people in all parts of the world. Recently, Hugging Amma in Kerala state in India is very popular. People claim that their pains are gone after she hugs them (Note 8).

Sathya Sai Baba in India also had healed people from many diseases. To his disciples, he claimed that he could get diamonds and ashes from the air. He was challenged by some university physicists once, but he never accepted that. His disciples mentioned to me that they witnessed ashes mysteriously appearing on his photographs in their homes. However, no one was willing to provide me with concrete evidence of this peculiar phenomenon (Note 9).

Miracles

Many times, we read that Mary's or Jesus's image is seen on an oil spill on a highway due to the light scattering effect.

In Mumbai, in 1912, it was discovered that Jesus's feet were oozing water (Note 10). People gathered to visit this site. It was discovered later that there was some plumbing problem from beneath.

In Sep 1995, we heard that the Ganesha idol made from stone in all Hindu temples all over the world suddenly started drinking (absorbing) milk that are poured on it for worshipping (Note 11). When it was scientifically checked, it was found that in most places it was not true, but some idols made of porous materials were absorbing milk (Note 11).

It is believed that bread and wine will become skin and blood during the Eucharist. It has been tested and nothing like that happens (Note 12).

I have read and heard many such miracles, but I have never witnessed one with my own eyes.

Paranormal Phenomena

Diverse experiments were conducted at Duke University on ESP, PK, Clairvoyance, and Telesthesia, also known as remote viewing. The US Government even threw some cash into the mix, trying to outdo Russia in the early 20th-century race to master remote viewing of Russian space. One key person in these experiments was Israel's very own Uri Geller. Unfortunately, despite all the effort and funding, no legitimate findings were ever established, leading to the abrupt halt of research funding.

Many theories have been given to explain paranormal phenomena such as electromagnetic waves communicating directly from the brain without going through any sense organs. Proponents of this idea were/are I. M. Kogan (1966) from Russia, Michael Persinger (1975, 1985, 1989) from Canada and Robert Becker (1992) from America. These scientists believe that the waves in question are such Extra Low Frequency waves (ELF) that no buildings can stop them. Energy Field Theory (Wassermann, 1956) holds that quanta of energy are so small that they cannot interact with matter. In Japan and Eastern Europe, this mind control was known as Psychotronic.

The American Physicist Evan Harris Walker (1975) explained that consciousness or what he calls 'Intention' is responsible for the collapse-like observation seen when a physical system collapses to one of the many potential states. Skeptics have an opposing view, believing there is no need for any scientific theory, as the data can be explained and attributed to misinterpretation, misperception, chance and inaccurate recall.

Evil Spirits Cause Mental Diseases

In the 19th and 20th centuries, many mental diseases were considered to be acts of God or rather the devil, Satan, ghosts, witches, jinns (or Djinn: supernatural beings as termed in Islamic tradition) and the mentally ill person was said to be possessed by an evil spirit. Every village in the USA used to have a medium (Tantrik, Exorcist, Occultist, Sorcerer) to treat sick people during the 19th century.

Many movies, both in the East and the West, have featured this idea. Around 50 years ago, when I was a young lad in India, one of my pals was believed to be possessed by an evil spirit because he had epilepsy. Ignorance was rampant, and I had no clue about epilepsy myself. It was not until I sought my studies in the Neurology department at the University of Michigan Hospitals that I finally learned the truth about this misunderstood condition.

Prophecies

None of the prophecies in the Bible have turned out to be true. The Apocalypse as predicted has not occurred (so far). Some other predictions also have failed: –The Nile would dry up, Egypt would be deserted, Damascus would no longer be a city (Page 182, Stenger). Jesus told his followers that he would come back again within a generation and establish His kingdom. Believers are still waiting. The Exodus, Jesus's birth, death and resurrection have not been proven to be true, either as predicted or as detailed in the Bible.

Jesus did not come back. He did not end slavery, prevent World War I or II, or the American Civil War. He did not save Jews from Hitler, nor he protected Gazans from Israeli's disproportionate killings. Jesus has, moreover, not saved believers from COVID-19.

6. Argument from Evil:

Here are some mind-bending questions: Why does the all-powerful and kind-hearted God allow pain and suffering to exist in the world? Why did He not make everyone equal from the start? Why do some people hit the jackpot while others struggle to make ends meet? And why did COVID-19 wreak havoc across the globe, claiming countless lives in its wake? Why do diseases like TB, pneumonia, cancer, and heart disease continue to plague humanity? If God is so loving, why does He not put a stop to all this suffering?

What about wars, hatred, and senseless violence that tear communities apart? Natural disasters like earthquakes, hurricanes, floods, droughts, and tornadoes also take their toll on innocent lives each year. This may make you wonder if God is really in control of it all.

Recent earthquakes in Turkey, Syria, and Afghanistan killed several thousand people (Note 13). It was felt in New Delhi and the surrounding regions. Some people in India believed it was due to the anger of an Indian goddess – the goddess of Wrath - Kaali. Indian people around New Delhi did mass prayers and worship so it would not happen again.

Deadly hurricane Katrina in 2005 killed thousands of people in Louisiana and Mississippi (Note 14). Christian clerics blamed it on the parade of LGBTQ on the same Monday that Katrina landed. Some Christians felt that Katrina was revenge for the evacuation of Jewish settlers from the Gaza Strip. Others believed the wrath owed to an attack on Iraq.

Kedarnath, one of the four religious temples for Hindus in the northern Indian state of Uttarakhand, was flooded with serious landslides, destroying many buildings, roads and bridges. Thousands of people died, and hundreds of visitors were stranded for many weeks (June 13, 2013), (Note 15).

A Sunami on Dec 26, 2004, killed more than two hundred thousand people in several neighboring countries in the Indian subcontinent (Note 16).

Hurricane Maria landed on Sep 7, 2017, and fully devastated Puerto Rico (Note 17).

How could God simply keep watching His/Her people's suffering? In the jungle, more powerful animals eat smaller animals. Did God make it that way? Does God like killing His/Her own creatures? Millions of fish are eaten right away in the ocean as soon as they are born.

We read each day in the news about shootings in schools, colleges, shops and offices, not so different from jungle life and death. How could God allow Putin of Russia to kill thousands of people in Ukraine in the recent war he started in February 2022 (Note 18)? Why does God not stop all these killings and suffering?

One point worth mentioning is that during natural disasters, it seems like the poor always get the short end of the stick. It's like they are playing a game of survival with one hand tied behind their back, while the rich have all the cheat codes and power-ups. Some people say it's because God has a soft spot for the underprivileged and wants them to come chill with Him/Her in the afterlife. Hindus, on the other hand, blame it on some bad deed from a past life. And then you have got the atheists, who are like, "God, where are you?" They think either God does not care, is not strong enough, or is just a figment of our imagination.

The theists, though, have got a different take on things. They say, "Hey, it's not God's fault! It's that sneaky devil causing all the trouble." Apparently, Satan is like a rebellious teenager who does not listen to their parents (aka God). But then the question arises, if God is all-powerful, why can He not reign in the devil? Some believers argue that maybe God has a reason for allowing evil to exist. Like, how can we appreciate the good without a little taste of the bad, right? It's like going to a buffet and only eating dessert - you must have some veggies in there somewhere.

Perhaps through suffering, we learn to be better humans. It's like the universe's way of teaching us some moral values. Who knew that calamities could be part of a divine plan? In the Old Testament, God admits that He is the source of evil:

"I form light and create darkness, I make weal and create woe, I am the Lord, who do all these things." (Isaiah, 45:7), (Note 19).

Believers often argue that everything that happens is part of God's mystical plan, and we mere mortals cannot possibly comprehend His/Her divine intentions. When faced with tragedy, some may suggest that God has something better in store for us, hidden within His/Her grand design. But seriously, what kind of plan involves so many people succumbing to cancer, heart attacks, strokes, Covid-19, and various other diseases? Why could God not just hit the pause button on all these deaths?

I remember speculating a similar question as a young whippersnapper. I was taught that the heart was the weakest link in our bodies, and if we decided to throw in the towel, we were done for. So, I asked God: "Why do we not have two hearts, like we do with other important organs (except for the liver, which apparently has some magical regenerative powers)?" What's the deal with that? And do not even get me started on all the natural disasters causing havoc and taking lives.

Now, Hindus, Buddhists, and Jains have a pretty straightforward explanation for all this suffering and joy in life - it's all about that good Karma from past lives. So, the question to meditate over is: Should we blame our past selves for our current problems?

7. Argument from Morality:

Do we need God to be morally good? Where do moral values come from? Who is the final authority, telling us what is morally good and what is bad? Theists answer that God is the final authority we should trust. Some people believe that's true because God teaches us what is morally good vs bad. Others behave due to fear of punishment from God, either in this life, in hell or the next life. Dawkins compares the Fear of God to the fear of the police, needed to stop or discourage crimes. Dawkins in 'God Delusions', (2006), 'Outgrowing God', (2019), Stenger in 'God - The Failed Hypothesis', (2007), and Harris in 'End of Faith' (2004), point out in their books that God is not needed to behave. Note that many of the ten commandments of the Old Testament are not illegal in today's society, e.g. taking the Lord's name in vain, working on Sabbath, cursing one's parents, adultery, and so on. Punishment, according to the Old Testament for these, is Death (Harris).

Buddha did not believe in God but gave 10 moral teachings that are more practical in society today – no killing, no stealing, no telling lies, no speaking ill of others, not being angry, and so on. Jainism provides similar moral teachings.

Jainism is very strict about not killing any animals, including viruses and bacteria. Dedicated followers of Jainism comply with a strict code of conduct to avoid causing harm to living beings. They do not wear shoes to prevent inadvertently squashing insects, dine before it gets dark to avoid accidentally ingesting bugs, and steer clear of foods that may harbor bacteria, such as yogurt and root vegetables like potatoes, beets, ginger, garlic, and onions. Their commitment to non-violence extends even to the tiniest creatures, making their dietary choices as pure as their intentions.

Stenger and Harris have written that the Ten Commandments are not followed even in these religious scriptures, and killings were done with God's orders. Jesus allowed slavery. Krishna advised his disciple, Arjun, to fight and terminate his immoral cousins, the Kauravas, during the Mahabharat War. Dawkins cited several examples in his book 'The God Delusion' to show that even moral values can be traced back to Darwin's theory of evolution. Stenger, in his book 'God - The Failed Hypothesis,' also explains natural morality by using animal behaviors as examples.

8. Religion Brought Science:

In Europe, under the mantle of Christianity, Natural Theology-the study of things in nature created by God—included the study of planets and stars. At this time during the 18th, 19th, and 20th centuries, everyone, including all scientists, was religious as nothing else was known. God, as the cause of all natural phenomena, was the only explanation. However, India, Greece, the Middle East, and China were more advanced than Europe. Moreover, Christians have argued that science is based on faith, notwithstanding the fact that science has contributed to undisputed "bad things" like the atomic bomb, biological and chemical weapons, and guns.

9. God is Transcendental and Immanent:

This section is short. It asserts the view that, above all, God is beyond the physical world and does not need a creator. His/Her divine power and creation are expressed in the universe.

10. Why Does God Not Show Up? - Freedom:

Atheists are always asking, "Where's God?" Theologians have a clever response - God's playing hard to get. He/She wants us to have the freedom to choose whether or not to believe in Him/Her. But let's be real. God wants us to believe in Him/Her. Some religious people swear they can feel God's presence, like He/she is their hotline. Me? I have never got a call. Maybe it's a believers-only club. Others argue that God is just too mysterious for us mere mortals to comprehend. Some even assert God is unknowable, ungraspable, ineffable, incomprehensible - basically, a gigantic question mark.

The battle between science and religion boils down to their contrasting approaches to resolving the mysteries of the universe. Science puts its trust in hard evidence, experiments, and logical thinking to decode the natural world, while religion leans on faith, divine revelations, and spiritual convictions to tackle the big questions about life, purpose, and ethics.

The clash erupts when these two worldviews collide like mighty forces contending over the origins of existence, the vastness of the cosmos, and the influence of unseen forces. It's a vibrant mix of ideas, circling the ancient riddles that have bedazzled humanity for countless generations.

Chapter 3

Why Are Atheists and Scientists Against Religion?

"Men never do evil so completely and cheerfully as when they do it from a religious conviction."

Pascal, Blaise, Pensees, (Note 1A)

In this chapter, I zoom into the long-existing clash between science and religion, analyzing various perspectives beyond the divine. This includes economic, historical, psychological, philosophical, political, and sociological viewpoints, as well as ritual practices. Let's begin with a little help from the Oxford English Dictionary's definition of 'religion':

"Action or conduct indicating belief in, obedience to, and reverence for a god, gods, or similar superhuman power; the performance of religious rites or observances."

The reason for sharing this definition is to establish a clear and foundational understanding of what 'religion' comprises before moving forward.

Atheism: the art of just living this life without expecting any divine sequel. Science: the ultimate quest to figure out how the universe works, like a never-ending episode of "Cosmos" but with fewer aliens. Atheists reject the idea of any Gods, while scientists are like professional truth-seekers, always probing, questioning, and searching for evidence.

The Conflict Between Science and Religion

When science and religion walk into a conference room, it's like a collision of beliefs and facts. From Copernicus to Darwin, there has been a long history of arguments over who gets to decide how this whole universe thing happened.

Scientists have been called misbelievers, and some religious people have a habit of getting defensive when their beliefs are questioned. It's like a non-stop debate of "He Said, She Said," but with more telescopes and fewer love letters. From debates over how we got all these fancy species to disagreements on who created the world in seven days (and if the creator took a coffee break on the eighth), science and religion have some serious barbeque stuff that's been marinating for centuries.

Rationality vs. Faith: The Atheist Perspective

Atheists believe in using reason, evidence, and a healthy dose of skepticism to sift through life. They are like the kids at the science fair who question everything and do not take 'Because I said so' as a valid answer. Atheists are not necessarily quick-tempered nihilists who hate joy and puppies. They just prefer a universe where things make sense without needing a divine rulebook. Atheists are not shy about pointing out flaws in religious teachings. It's like the quiz of 'Spot the Plot Hole' where they are the expert fact-checkers, and the religious texts are the scripts that keep getting revised.

Scientific Methodology and Religious Beliefs

In the battle of evidence vs. faith, science brings its A-game with facts, experiments, and peer-reviewed studies. It's like a courtroom drama where the burden of proof is on the universe, and science is the judge, jury, and executioner. Science demands evidence like a detective demands clues. Meanwhile, religion asks you to take a leap of faith, like a trust fall exercise with the cosmos. It's a showdown between cold, hard facts and warm, fuzzy feelings.

Science cannot answer every question, and religion cannot prove everything it claims. It's like a Venn diagram where they overlap in some areas but stay firmly apart in others. At the end of the day, maybe they both have something to offer in the grand quest for understanding the universe.

Let's pore over this with more wit and some 'may-be-bitter but factual' analysis.

Religious Groups Based on Belief in God

Most people, with the exception of devout theists and atheists, can be found in a variety of professions - from engineers to plumbers to homemakers. And guess what? They are all religious in some way or another. Their level of religiosity may vary on a scale from 1 to 10, with some being more into rituals than others.

These people keep their religion and profession separate, unlike those who love to argue about religion and science. Even if they have a college education, they are probably not experts in Theology or Quantum Mechanics - they just go to their place of worship, perform their ritual, and then get back to work.

Such people do not question the existence of God or the authenticity of their scriptures - they just believe. Of course, who has time to scrutinize ancient texts when there's work to be done? They simply accept that their scriptures are the word of God, passed down from generation to generation.

Most of these followers were born into their religion, but there are some converts floating around. They could also be referred to as Accommodationists or followers of NOMA (Non-Overlapping Magisteria), a concept introduced by Stephen J. Gould. According to Gould, science and religion can peacefully coexist as long as one does not put his feet on other's toes (1999).

NOMA is the idea that science and religion should just stay out of each other's business like nosy neighbors in a sitcom. Science deals with the "is" - you know, facts and evidence and all that jazz - while religion deals with the "ought" - morality, meaning, purpose, all those big questions that cannot be neatly solved with a Bunsen burner and some pipettes. So basically, NOMA is like saying to science and religion, "You do you boo, just make sure you are not stepping on each other's toes." It's a way of keeping both sides happy without causing too much of a ruckus at the dinner party of life.

A very small percentage of these people are spiritualists who seem to be following the definition of religion as was defined by William James in his book (1918):

"Religion' means the feelings, acts, and experiences of individual men in their solitude, so far as they apprehend themselves to stand in relation to whatever they may consider the divine...the belief that there is an unseen order, and that our supreme good lies in harmoniously adjusting ourselves thereto ..."

Today, this definition matches SBNR (Spiritual but Not Religious). SBNR is like ordering a cappuccino with extra foam - it's a personal twist on spirituality without the traditional religious ties. This modern movement is all about seeking a higher power or connection to the universe outside of organized religion. SBNR individuals often find peace and purpose in meditation, yoga, nature walks, or even crystals and astrology. They exhibit an eclectic mix of beliefs and practices that resonate with their inner truth rather than following strict dogma or rituals. It's like having a spiritual salad bar where you can pick and choose what feels right for your soul quest. This group is growing.

There is a small but vocal group of hardcore Atheists out there. They are mostly scientists who are dead set against the idea of religion and the existence of God. Not all scientists fall into this category, though. Some of them just cannot wrap their heads around the whole God concept and find religion to be a bit of a snooze fest. The likes of Hitchens, Harris, Stenger, Dawkins, Dennet, Houk, and Coyne make up this crew of New Atheists.

On the flip side, there is a minority group of uncompromising religious enthusiasts. These people are all about using God and religion for their personal gain or to push their political agendas. A tiny fraction of them are so obsessed with their God and religion that they cannot stand the thought of anyone else's beliefs. They are the fundamentalists, the extremists, the terrorists, and the suicide-bombers. These individuals are willing to kill and die in the name of their God, which is pretty intense.

Of course, not everyone in this group is a total nut job. Some are just in it for the money or have been brainwashed into thinking that violence is the answer. Others have simply hit rock bottom and see terrorism as their only way out.

For instance, I came across a TV interview featuring a poor teenage boy who was being trained to participate in the tragic Mumbai 11/26, 2008 attack (Note 1). This young lad was promised a ticket to heaven, complete with a harem of beautiful girls awaiting him. On top of that, he was told his parents would be given enough money to live happily ever after without him, and they too would be granted entry into paradise. However, when he found that no money had been given to his parents, he made a run for it.

Then there are the 'Agnostics' - those who do not care about whether God exists or not. Then there is the rapidly growing group known as the NONES, who proudly declare their independence from any religious affiliation (Chapter 1, Note 1).

James A. Lindsay, in his enlightening book 'Everybody is Wrong About God' (2015), introduced the term 'Ignosticism'. This is a fancy way of saying, "I have no idea what you are talking about." So, whether one is chasing virgins in heaven or simply shrugging shoulders at the existence of a higher power, there's a label for everyone in this diverse world of beliefs.

Gods of Abrahamic Religions Do Not Exist

Over the past 15-20 years, a pile of books has emerged aiming to challenge religious beliefs and the existence of God. These books use various arguments such as the argument from design, cosmological and teleological arguments, personal experiences, and scriptures to dismantle the notion of God and religion.

The majority of these literary works specifically target the Gods of Abrahamic religions, attempting to prove their non-existence. Despite the relentless efforts of Western scientists to scientifically disprove the teachings of Abrahamic scriptures, religious beliefs have managed to stand their ground.

In Victor Stenger's book "Has Science Found God" (2003), he thoroughly dissects the supposed proofs of God's existence and finds them lacking. In his subsequent work "God, The Failed Hypothesis - How Science Shows That God Does Not Exist" (2007), Stenger examines in greater depth the subject, utilizing modern scientific theories to argue that God is nothing more than a figment of our imagination.

In "Faith vs. FACT- Why Science and Religion Are Incompatible" (2015), Jerry A. Coyne provides a comprehensive analysis of the irreconcilable differences between religion and science. Coyne asserts that scientific facts are alike religious beliefs found in ancient scriptures, advocating for the abandonment of irrational religious beliefs in favor of rational scientific truths.

In a world where science and religion clash like two stubborn goats on a narrow bridge, these authors offer a refreshing perspective on the magnitude of choosing reason over superstition.

God is the Cause of Most Wars and Terrorism

In the New York Times bestseller, 'God is not Great: How Religion Poisons Everything' (2007), the renowned author Christopher Hitchens meticulously dismantles the foundations of religion. Similarly, Sam Harris, in his book 'The End of Faith: Religion, Terror, and the Future of Reason' (2004), boldly points fingers at religion as the root cause of numerous conflicts and wars around the world. For example, Jews vs. Muslims in Palestine, Protestants vs. Catholics in Northern Ireland, Hindus vs. Muslims in Kashmir, Muslims vs. Christians in Nigeria and many more. The latest fight in Gaza between Hamas and Jews that broke out on Oct 7th, 2023, is another example that may be added to the list (Note 2).

According to the State of Religious Atlas, there were 18 active wars in 1992-93 where religion played a significant role or was directly involved (Page 329, Houk).

Harris and Hitchens argue convincingly that all religions serve no purpose other than to sow discord and lead to unnecessary loss of human life. Hitchens, in 'God is not Great' (2007), provides a chilling list of locations where religious animosity has led to bloodshed - Bethlehem, Bombay, Baghdad, Belgrade, Beirut, Belfast, Gaza Strip, Kashmir, Lebanon, Palestine, Serbia, Croatia, Estonia, Iran, Iraq, India, Sri Lanka, Burma, Indonesia and many countries in African continent (e.g. Rwanda, Uganda and Sudan) and so on.

No religion is spared in this savage critique - Muslims, Christians, Jews, Buddhists, Sikhs, Hindus, you name it. The infighting among different sects within these religions only stirs the pot. Shia vs. Sunni, Catholic vs. Protestant, Sikh vs. Hindu - the list goes on.

In 1981, the world was shocked when Indian Prime Minister Indira Gandhi was assassinated by her own Sikh bodyguard. This tragic event was a result of Gandhi's controversial decision to launch 'Operation Blue Star' in 1984, targeting the Golden Temple, the holiest shrine of Sikhs, in an attempt to flush out terrorists (Note 3). The aftermath of Gandhi's death led to violent clashes between Hindus and Sikhs, culminating in the bombing of Air India Flight 182 from Canada to India in 1985, killing 329 innocent people, including many Sikhs by Sikh terrorists (Note 4).

The cycle of religious violence continued in Sri Lanka, where Buddhists and Hindu Tamils engaged in deadly conflicts, ultimately resulting in the assassination of Rajeev Gandhi, the then prime minister of India and the eldest son of Indira Gandhi, by a Tamil suicide bomber in 1991 (Note 5).

The spread of violence was not limited to India, as reports emerged of Buddhists targeting Muslims in Burma, Sri Lanka, and Indonesia, contradicting their reputation for non-violence (Note 6).

The devastating attacks of 9/11/2001 on the Twin Towers in New York City (Note 7) and the Mumbai Taj Hotel on 11/26 in 2008 (Note 1), both carried out by Muslim terrorists, underlined the global impact of religious extremism. More recently, the ongoing conflict between Israel and Hamas has claimed the lives of thousands, with a disproportionate number of casualties among Palestinians (Note 2, and 8).

The reference of religion to justify acts of terror is a disturbing trend that author Sam Harris explores in his book 'The End of Faith- Religion, Terror and Future of Reason'. From suicide bombings to targeted attacks, the manipulation of religious beliefs for violent ends continues to pose a threat to global security.

Harris and Hitchens famously argued that throughout history, religion has been the primary instigator of wars. For example, in 1994, the horrific genocide in Rwanda was carried out in the name of faith (Hitchens, p190-192). Then there was the despicable actions of the Lord's Resistance Army in Northern Uganda in late 2005, where innocent children were abducted and subjected to unspeakable brutality and misery in the name of religion (Hitchens, p188).

Moving on to Kashmir, India, where Muslim terrorists destroyed a city that was once considered 'heaven on earth'. The violence forced thousands of Hindus to flee for their lives, leaving behind their homes and livelihoods. Thankfully, the pro-Hindu Indian government took a bold step by removing the restrictive ruling of 370, allowing progress and development to flourish in Kashmir once again (Note 9).

Hitchens also points out the irony of even peaceful Hindus and Buddhists committing acts of violence in the name of God, despite their religions preaching non-violence. It's a head-scratcher, to say the least. Then there was another disturbing trend of killings justified by all three Abrahamic religions, starting with Abraham's sacrifice of his son and a lamb. Sacrifices that, thankfully, no longer involve humans but are still carried out annually on Passover and Eid.

But how can any killing be justified, whether it's Putin's actions in Ukraine, the atrocities of the Holocaust, or the killing of Palestinians in the Gaza Strip? These are not religious-based killings, but rather senseless acts of barbarity that defy all logic and morality. It's time to put an end to the madness and switch to peace and understanding instead.

Exploitation by Cult Leaders

In his eye-opening book, 'Lies Upon Lies – God, Authority, and How Your Faith is Used to Control You' (2023), Daniel Warren analyzes further the dark world of exploitation and oppression driven by fear, illiteracy, and blind faith. It's no secret that religious cult leaders have taken advantage of the faithful, swindling them, and even resorting to violence in the name of God. Warren provides terrifying examples to drive this point home.

CBS News (among many other news agencies) has described many cults and their abuses of women and children. (Note 10).

Take, for instance, the infamous 'Branch Davidians' cult, led by David Koresh, which ended in tragedy when the FBI and ATF raided their compound in 1993. Eighty-two innocent members were coerced into drinking poison by their deranged leader. The 'Branch Davidians' started in 1955, established by David Koresh in 1987 in Mount Carmel, Waco, TX.

Besides, there was the harrowing Jonestown Massacre in Guyana, in South America on November 18, 1978, where over 900 members of the 'Peoples Temple' cult perished in a mass suicide engineered by Jim Jones. He started this cult in Indiana in the 1950s and then moved to California in the 1960s and to Guyana in 1970.

These real-life horror stories are a severe reminder of the dangers of blind faith and unchecked authority. Warren's book investigates more extensively these dark corners of society, urging readers to question and challenge the status quo. After all, as history has shown us, blind faith can lead to devastating consequences.

Other cults which exploited people are:

1. The 'Love Has Won', with Carleson Amy known as Mother God in Moffat, Colorado.
2. The 'School of Prophet', a polygamy cult led by Ron Lafferty killed his brother's wife because she did not follow polygamy and he claimed that he had the revelation to do this.
3. 'NXIVM' led by Keith Rainere, who operated an abusive sex cult from his Albany-based seminar business. He ran DOS and VOW cults in which female cult members were used as sex slaves. Allison Mack, an actor recruited falsely young girls under the women empowerment group.
4. Bhagwan Rajneesh had an Ashram in Wasco County, Oregan, which functioned as a cult. I remember his interview on ABC News where he was asked why his followers donated 100 Rolls Royce to him. His answer was that they liked him.
5. The 'Angel's Landing' led by Daniel Perez, ran for 15 years. He led a group of mostly women, and moved from state to state, claiming he had visions. He collected the life insurance money of the young women when they died.
6. The 'Heaven's Gate' cult – in 1970, 42 innocent people died.
7. The 'Mansion Family' cult was started in California by Charles Mansion in 1960, as Mansion claimed he was the reincarnation of Jesus. He attracted mostly young women.
8. The 'Children of God' cult, also known as Family International, started in Huntington Beach, California, in 1968.
9. The 'Matamoros' cult for human sacrifices.
10. The 'Aum Shinrikyo' cult, a Japanese Dooms Day cult led by Shoko Asahara in 1984, convinced members that the Apocalypse was nearby.
11. 'The Order of the Solar Temple' cult in 1984 led by Joseph D. Mambro and Luc Juret in Canada.

12. The 'Russian Doomsday Cult' led by Pyotr Kuznetsov split from the Russian Orthodox church and asked his members to wait in a cave as the end of the world was coming in 2008.
13. The director of the 'Movement for the Restoration of the Ten Commandments of God' cult in Uganda, declared that Apocalypse was coming on Dec 31st, 1999. When it did not happen, he declared a new date of March 17, 2000, and arranged a big party on this day in a church in a remote jungle. When members were there, a deliberate fire broke out (or was arranged) and 530 members died in the fire and 924 died from poison.

All these directors of cults were finally caught and punished or died.

Many such cults are operating around the world and within India also and control people, brainwash them, sexually abuse them, and rob them financially. One such cult was run by a spiritual leader, Asaram Bapu in Western Gujarat since 1970, and was sentenced in 2018 on multiple rape charges.

In India, there is a spiritual cult called 'Dera Sacha Sauda' led by Gurmeet Ram Rahim Singh. In 2019, he was convicted for the murder of a journalist who had exposed the mistreatment of women in his group. Following his sentencing, riots broke out among his followers, resulting in the tragic deaths of 36 individuals (Note 11).

Therefore, it's time for these shady cult leaders to pack up their bags and take a long-overdue vacation to reality. Let's shut down this circus of manipulation and exploitation once and for all. Instead of blindly following the pied piper of brainwashing, let's start thinking for ourselves and reclaim our autonomy. Just because someone claims to have all the answers, does not mean they actually do. It's time to close the book on this chapter of manipulation by cult leaders – after all, life is too short to be living in someone else's shadow.

Religion is Misused to Treat Mental Diseases

In ancient African tribes, each society had a medical doctor who was believed to have the power to expel demons from the bodies of the afflicted. Hysteria and epilepsy were viewed as diseases caused by evil spirits taking hold of a person. Symptoms such as grinding teeth, foaming at the mouth, and loss of bodily control were seen as signs of possession by malevolent forces seeking to punish the individual.

Mystical individuals known as Tantric people, occultists, exorcists, or sorcerers, would treat these ailments in churches and temples. Surprisingly, these beliefs and practices persist even today. During the Covid lockdown in 2020, a lady from Australia sought special permission to visit a Tantrik at the Ganga Ghat in Varanasi, India, in hopes of communicating with her deceased husband.

Even in modern times, some people in India attribute diseases like smallpox to curses from deities. I once heard a story from the elder brother of a man with epilepsy, who believed his brother's seizures were caused by a Hindu God, Hanuman, punishing him for some misdeed. Despite my advice, he refused to seek medical treatment for his brother.

In some African countries, strict adherence to Christian beliefs prohibits the use of condoms, leading to the spread of HIV, AIDS, and other sexually transmitted diseases, resulting in countless deaths. Mother Teresa once stated in her Nobel Prize speech that "Abortion is the main cause of killings." It seems that superstitions and religious beliefs continue to influence people's lives in unexpected ways (Note 12).

Discrepancies in the Stories of Scriptures

In his book, 'The End of Faith- Religion, Terror and Future of Reason' (2004), Sam Harris fearlessly delves into scriptures, dismantles their arguments and boldly declares them wrong. He boldly asserts that faith is simply human ignorance and irrationality that needs to be corrected. According to Harris, wealth and education alone cannot guarantee rationality. He argues that religions are inherently hostile towards each other, leading to violence and that secular knowledge is the only solution.

On the other hand, Daniel K. Chaney ventures deeper into the world of religion in his extensive 461-page book, 'Religion Refuted – Debunking the Case for God' (2023). Chaney carefully dissects arguments such as the first cause, contingency, ontological, and transcendental arguments, along with other religious concepts like biblical inerrancy, fine-tuning, and Pascal's wager. He leaves no stone unturned in his quest to disprove the case for God.

Harris, Hitchens, and Houk are on a mission to find the discrepancies and conflicts within the stories of the Old Testament, New Testament, and Quran. From Exodus to Adam and Eve, Noah's Ark to the creation of the world in 6 days, and even the proof of Jesus's resurrection, they argue that these tales do not hold up to scientific scrutiny. It seems that even the divine cannot escape the critical eye of modern science.

In his book 'The Illusion of Certainty- How the Flawed Beliefs of Religion Harm Our Culture', author James T. Houk (2017) takes readers through the wacky world of religious beliefs. Using examples from scriptures, Houk exposes the absurd and irrational things people believe in the name of faith, God, and religion. Religious Fundamentalists cling to these beliefs as if they were the gospel truth.

For example, Houk refutes the religious belief that the universe is only 6000 years old, with 12 technical reasons. He points out that we can see lights from stars and galaxies that are millions of light years away, meaning they existed millions of light years ago. Fossilized bones and rocks have been dated to be much older than 6000 years, and the process of evolution takes longer than a mere 6000 years. But true believers will argue that anything is possible for God, right?

Houk does not stop there. He also draws attention to 48 contradictions and 24 mistakes in the Old and New Testaments (p. 230), showing that even the holy scriptures are not immune to errors. And do not even get him started on how women were treated in the Bible. According to Houk, women were treated like second-class citizens, just a commodity for men, with no voice in public and subject to being stoned for adultery. The Bible even condones the killing of female sorcerers (witches) during 1400-1600 CE- talk about a rough time to be a woman!

In the end, Houk paints a picture of a world where absurd beliefs are not only accepted but fiercely defended by believers.

Houk boldly asserts that fundamental religion, particularly the three monotheistic religions, is to blame for a laundry list of societal ills including slavery, misogyny, homophobia, xenophobia, the Holocaust, anti-Semitism, racism, white supremacy, and numerous wars. He argues that religious fundamentalism gives a divine stamp of approval to these harmful beliefs, such as guardian angels, resurrection of the dead, virgin births, heavens, hells, witches, demons, possessions, and creationism. Houk takes issue with the notion that faith is the ultimate truth, calling it a misguided foundation for knowledge. In his eyes, the illusion of religion is a dead end.

In their latest literary offering, 'Guessing About God – Ten Tough Problems in Christian Belief, Book1', David Madison and Tim Sledge (2023) make a shocking revelation by suggesting that Jesus may have been nothing more than a mythical figure, rather than a historical person. They point out discrepancies in the Gospels of John, Mark, Matthew, and Luke, arguing that these accounts, penned long after Jesus's time, cannot be considered accurate.

Jesus's whereabouts between ages 13 and 29 are unknown. According to a BBC documentary, Jesus may have spent his missing years in Kashmir, India, with records indicating his travels throughout the country (Note 13). Madison and Sledge boldly claim that the Bible is not the word of God, but rather the work of fallible humans. They question the invisibility and silence of God, dismissing traditional methods of knowing God as ineffective. The authors poke holes in the Bible, labeling it as a collection of outdated ideas and contradictions, casting doubt on the validity of divine revelations.

Below are some books that question the existence of God, particularly the Gods of Abrahamic Religions: "Illusion of God's Presence" by John C. Wathey (2016), "How We Believe – Science, Skepticism, the Search for God" by Michael Shermer (2000), "The God Delusion" (2006) by Richard Dawkins, "Breaking the Spell" by Daniel Dennett (2007, and "Letter to a Christian Nation" by Sam Harris (2008). These authors, along with many other atheists, are often referred to as the 'New Atheists'. So, if you are looking to test your beliefs and venture deeper into some thought-provoking literature, these books might just be your cup of tea.

Discrepancy in Scriptures of Other Religions

I am sure there are many disparities in the scriptures of other religions, like Hinduism, Buddhism, Jainism, Sikhism, and Taoism as well. I have shared below the discrepancies within the Hindu religion, as it is the area in which I am most knowledgeable. Take, for example, the tale from the Ramayana where God Hanuman, leader of Rama's army, uprooted the entire Kishkindha Mountain and transported it to Sri Lanka. Why, you ask? Well, because he could not quite identify which magical plant or herb was needed to heal Rama's brother, Lakshman, who was injured in battle with the dastardly Ravana. You see, Ravana had snatched Rama's wife, Sita, and all hell broke loose.

Then, there is a reference to the construction of a bridge between India and Sri Lanka for the sole purpose of launching an attack on Ravana. According to the Ramayana, when Lord Rama laid his divine hands on heavy stones, they miraculously became light as a feather and floated in water to form the bridge. Quite the engineering feat, would you not say?

Now, Hindus also believe in the Nav-Grah, or nine planets, which include the sun and moon. Hindu priests dutifully offer prayers to these celestial bodies in all their rituals. These stories may defy logic and science, but they are followed by billions of Hindus without question. Not even Indian scientists dare to dispute these chronicles.

It seems that Hindus have mastered Gould's rule of NOMA, expertly keeping science and religion in their respective lanes without any overlap. They have truly perfected the art of balancing faith and reason, never allowing one to encroach upon the other.

I have not come across anyone from the East or West who dares to criticize the tales of Hindu mythology. Even if I were to demonstrate that no stone on this earth can be lifted by a mere touch, who among the devout Hindus would be persuaded? Even if I were to prove that mountains cannot be transported from one country to another, as evidenced by the absence of a said mountain in Sri Lanka, who among the faithful would be convinced?

How does one go about lifting an entire mountain, you ask? Take, for example, the tale of Lord Krishna effortlessly hoisting Mount Govardhan in Mathura with just a flick of his finger to shield the people of Vrindavan from torrential rain. During my recent visit to Mathura and Vrindavan, the birthplace of Lord Krishna, my guide narrated to me even more enchanting stories of the deity. According to him, Lord Krishna still visits a small orchard at night to play his flute, much to the delight of those who have been fortunate enough to witness him. These stories, along with countless others found in Hindu scriptures, are fervently believed by billions.

Then there's the tale of Lord Hanuman, who supposedly revealed the sun in his mouth to his mother. How one could swallow the sun is beyond me, yet countless Hindus accept this story as truth. We may choose to view these stories as allegorical or metaphorical rather than literal truths, remaining neutral in our beliefs. Some may believe in these tales wholeheartedly, while others may question their validity. Personally, I have no intention of engaging in battles with believers, attempting to disprove their cherished myths, or investing time and resources into debunking these stories.

Folklores passed down through generations are like a game of Chinese Telephone - you know, where one person whispers a message to another and by the time it reaches the end, it's completely different. I experience my version of this play every day at home when I mishear my wife over the noise of the kitchen fan. Luckily, she is quick to set me straight and prevent any misinformation from spreading within our family.

It's not just in our personal lives where stories can get twisted. News headlines often sensationalize scientific research, leading to misunderstandings. Take, for example, the time a local newspaper claimed scientists would soon be able to read minds based on our group's research on the unconscious mind. Trust me, it is not as easy as it sounds.

Nowadays, everyone is buzzing about AI and ChatGPT potentially creating conscious robots. But those of us in the field know that is a far-fetched idea. So, next time you read a headline about mind-reading or sentient robots, take it with a grain of salt. After all, the truth is often more complex than it seems.

Why Godly People Have Unnatural Births?

Why are Western scientists so fixated on disproving the birth of Jesus from the Virgin Mary when we all know how babies are actually born? It's like trying to convince a toddler that storks do not deliver babies - they just do not get it yet! There are countless versions of Jesus's birth story in religious texts, with some claiming he was born in Nazareth to Joseph. But let's not forget the Hindu myths, like when King Dasharatha fed his queens magical mangoes and ended up with four sons.

Then there's Karan, the Sun God's son found floating down a river by Queen Kunti in the Mahabharata. Even Nataputra Vardhamana (Mahaveer Jain) and Gautama (Buddha) were supposedly born of virgin mothers in special circumstances.

Hitchens in his book, 'God is Not Great' (Page 23) has given many other examples of such virgin births in history, e.g. Genghis Khan was born of a Mongol king's daughter when she awoke one night and was flooded with miracle light. Horus was born of the virgin Isis; Mercury was born of the virgin Maia and Romulus was born of the virgin Rhea Sylvia.

It's like a virgin birth trend that's been going on for centuries! So why all the fuss about Jesus's birth? Why not read these as mythological stories?

Why is NOMA Not Followed by Followers of Abrahamic Religions?

Why is NOMA not followed by Christians in America? Why are Western scientists so much after proving that the resurrection of Jesus did not occur? Maybe, it occurred that he went into shock, and then due to some physiological reasons, he recovered from shock after some time (resurrection). I have heard a couple of stories in India that a dead person woke up while he was taken to a riverbank to be cremated or when he was set on the pyre to be burned. A long time ago, there was no accurate method to declare if someone was physiologically dead. Pulse and breathing were the only way to declare if someone was dead. Today, someone is declared objectively that he/she is dead when brain waves (EEG) are shown to be flat (no activity) continuously for 30 minutes.

I have not seen any books written in India criticizing the Indian scriptures of Vedas, Puranas, Ramayana, and Mahabharata. One reason may be that believers also do not claim that things written in these scriptures are scientifically accurate or they contradict scientific truths. In modern times, with many TV serials with video effects and dramatization, these religious mythological stories have increased their credibility (belief factor) much more. Vedas are full of rituals and rules written thousands of years ago for people at that time to follow. Most of those rituals and rules may not make sense in today's world, and not many people follow them today. But I have not seen any books written criticizing them. I notice that people who do not believe in them slowly keep dropping them and do not follow them but do not make any noise about them.

Why do Western scientists feel the need to pore over the scriptures of three Abrahamic religions with a fine-tooth comb, expending so much time and energy trying to debunk them? Meanwhile, religious believers are busy trying to prove that every word in those scriptures is gospel truth. It's like a continuous battle of one-upmanship that's causing more conflict than a family reunion at Thanksgiving.

Take the story of Adam and Eve, for example. Scientists have dug up fossils and run DNA tests, all in an attempt to prove that these two were not the original power couple. The 'Turin' cloth has been proven that it's not Jesus' handiwork. As for Jesus' resurrection? Well, let's just say scientists have been trying to debunk that one for years. Noah's Arc has not been found.

But why do Christian believers cling so tightly to the Bible's tale of creation, insisting that the world is a mere 6000 years old and that God created humans like a batch of cookies? Evolution and global warming are dismissed as hogwash, yet the Big Bang theory gets a thumbs up. It's like they are picking and choosing which scientific facts to believe in - a practice that Dawkins aptly calls cherry-picking.

In India, they have got this thing called NOMA - a hands-off approach to religion and science that keeps everyone in their lane. But here in the West, it's like science and religion are constantly stepping on each other's toes. Believers want scientific proof to back up their beliefs, while scientists are busy trying to prove those beliefs wrong with cold, hard facts.

I find myself brooding about why Western scientists and individuals in the West do not follow NOMA as they do in India. Luckily, Coyne refers to this in the final chapter of his book, 'Faith vs. Fact'. It seems the main issue lies in science and religion constantly stepping on each other's toes. Believers insist that scientific truths, like the origin of the universe and life, can be found in the Bible, while also claiming that God created everything. On the contrary, religious followers argue that science falls short when it comes to answering questions about morality, love, beauty, and the purpose of life.

Why Religious Christians Oppose Medical Care?

More tangible crimes that religious people are blamed to do are to reject medical care and rather do prayer and miracle healing for their children. I read that Mother Teresa, in the Indian city of Calcutta (now known as

Kolkata), forced sick people to suffer pain while waiting for miracles and prayer to work. So many people died during COVID-19 because they did not choose to get the vaccine due to religious reasons. I cannot shake off the memory of a heartbreaking news story about a mother on her deathbed, pleading with people to vaccinate her children after losing her brother and sister to preventable diseases just days before. It got me thinking - if we can make education mandatory from kindergarten to 12th grade, why can we not have laws in place to ensure children receive necessary medical care, even if their parents object for religious reasons?

Coyne is even pushing for laws that would hold parents accountable for neglect or even homicide if their child dies due to lack of medical treatment. It's like playing medical roulette, where some parents rely solely on prayers and miracle healing, hoping for divine intervention while neglecting modern medicine. Or follow Indians' strategy to get medical treatment along with prayers and miracle healing in parallel, hoping one would work.

Of course, they give more credit to God and prayer than to the doctors and medicine that actually save lives.

Scientists point the finger at religious individuals who oppose Embryonic Stem Cell Research, a groundbreaking field with the potential to cure numerous diseases by cultivating tissues and organs from unused frozen embryos leftover from in-vitro fertilization. These embryos are viewed as full-grown humans by religious groups, who accuse scientists of committing murder. While Presidents Clinton and Bush failed to sign a bill supporting Stem Cell Research, President Obama stepped up and secured funding for this vital work.

On the topic of vaccinations, religious believers shun them, fearing impurity from viruses. Despite the Center for Disease Control's recommendation, they refuse to allow vaccination against human papillomavirus (HPV), a leading cause of cervical cancer. Assisted dying is also a no-go for most religions, with only five states in the USA permitting it – Washington, Montana, Vermont, Oregon, New Mexico. Interestingly, even many atheists are not keen on the idea.

Christian believers deny the existence of global warming, believing that God will take care of the Earth without human intervention. However, the scientific truth is that excessive carbon dioxide emissions from burning fossil fuels are causing temperatures to rise, leading to melting polar ice caps, rising sea levels, mudslides, flooding, and devastating natural disasters.

Scientists are up in arms against these irrational religious beliefs, as they hinder funding for crucial research. The First Amendment to the Constitution clearly advocates for the separation of state and church, a principle that should be upheld to ensure progress and innovation in the scientific community:

"Congress shall make no law respecting an establishment of religion or prohibiting the free exercise thereof."

As per this, one is free to follow any religious belief in his/her private life and at home but not to use religion for making laws. But how can someone stop somebody's personal beliefs from affecting/biasing his or her decision-making anywhere? Strangely, the religious biases of different congressmen and Supreme Court judges are clearly known to the public – right or conservative, left or liberals and center or moderate. It is also known that most Republicans are religious Christian believers (strong or moderate) while most Democrats are liberals. Of course, congressmen have to answer to the people of the constituencies they represent.

Religion is Used for Personal and Political Gains

It has become all too common these days to hear about shootings happening in schools, colleges, malls, offices, and shops across the USA. According to NPR news (5/4/23), there have been a staggering 190 mass shootings in the first 4 months of 2023 alone (Note 14). So, why hasn't Congress taken action on gun control?

The National Rifle Association (NRA), known for its strong lobbying efforts in Congress, argues that it's not the guns that kill people, but rather people who kill people. The right-wing in Congress seems to hide behind the First Amendment as an excuse for their inaction. Similarly, religious believers claim that it's not religion that leads to killings, but rather people's actions.

After checking out the history of religious wars, conflicts, and killings, it's clear that many of these acts were politically and economically motivated, driven by personal ego and selfishness. God and religion have often been used to incite people and justify violence. Theists may point to atrocities committed by atheists, like the Holocaust in Germany by Hitler, wrongdoings in China by Mao, and in Russia by Stalin, but that does not make religious wars any more acceptable.

In the fleet-footed world of American politics, it's all about securing those precious votes and saving those cushy seats for the next election. Well, it's not about religion or God - it's about playing the game to win. Religion is just a tool used to manipulate the masses and achieve those political goals.

You can practically map out the political landscape based on which states lean Republican (hello Alabama, Arkansas, Mississippi, Indiana, Missouri, Tennessee and Texas) and which ones lean Democratic (looking at you, California and New York). Of course, there are those swing states that keep us on our toes, but - it all comes down to the Christian majority in each state.

From elected officials to policies on hot-button issues like stem cell research, abortion, vaccination, and LGBTQ rights, you can bet your bottom dollar that Christian beliefs play a major role. It's as predictable as the sun rising in the east.

Take Michigan's Democratic Governor Gretchen Whitmer, for example. Just last week, (Nov. 21, 2023), she made waves by signing a bill that removed the 1937 law so that abortion can never be challenged (Note 15). Let's also bear in mind the never-ending battle over Roe vs. Wade, where the outcome hinges on the political leanings of the Supreme Court justices at that time which is controlled by the President at that time.

In Texas, the drama never ends. Demonstrations are in full swing over a new drug ruling on April 15, 2023, showing just how high the stakes can get in the political arena (Note 16).

Pew Research Center reports that 53% of Americans said they would not vote for an atheist in political office (p. 269, Houk) This is one of the reasons for the fight by scientists.

Politics worldwide often capitalize on divisive factors such as race, caste, and religion to gain power and control. In India, caste and religion are shamelessly exploited to secure victories in both local and national elections. The pro-Hindu BJP party has gone to great lengths to construct temples in areas where there have been disputes over mosques. I had the chance to visit the glorious Shiva temple in Varanasi in 2022, which was still in the process of being built. The reconstruction of the Kashi Vishwanath temple in Varanasi was truly impressive (Note 17).

In a grand display of political gambit, Prime Minister Modi inaugurated the Rama temple in Ayodhya, U.P. state, just before the 2024 general elections (January 20, 2024). Despite not being fully completed, the temple holds relevance as the supposed birthplace of Rama as described in the Ramayana epic (Note 18). Despite the fact that Hindus make up eighty percent of the Indian population, the BJP did not secure a majority vote in the 2024 general election (Note 19).

Coyne's argument that religion is not necessary for art, literature, music, and morality is quite intriguing. He believes that without religion, we could see a decrease in opposition to things like euthanasia, condom use, vaccination, stem cell research, divorce, and LGBTQ rights. This could potentially save lives and eliminate superstitions like ESP, astrology, faith healing, acupuncture, and homeopathy.

However, I must respectfully disagree with Coyne when it comes to homeopathy being labeled as superstition. In India, millions of people rely on homeopathy for the treatment of simple diseases and health maintenance, especially for those who cannot afford modern medicine. Baba Ramdev has even popularized Yoga, helping millions maintain good health. While homeopathy may not cure serious diseases like cancer, it still has its benefits.

When it comes to the dialogue between science and religion, Coyne believes it would be more of a 'monologue' by science. He argues that religion should learn from science about the evolutionary, psychological, and cultural basis of religious belief. He points to Northern Europe as an example, where nontheistic spirituality seems to be working just fine. Countries like Norway, Sweden, and Denmark even outrank the USA in terms of people's well-being which includes divorce rate, homicide, incarceration, poverty, and so on.

When it comes to the debate of whether religion is a positive force in people's lives, the renowned Daniel Dennett has some interesting acumen. According to Dennett, the evidence is a bit of a mixed bag - sure, there may be some health benefits to be gained from religion, if those benefits cannot be found through other means. Dennett boldly asserts that religion does not hold a monopoly on moral values and that good people do not need the promise of heavenly rewards to do the right thing.

In fact, Dennett argues that faith does not necessarily have to be grounded in truth to be beneficial - he calls this concept 'belief in belief'. He advocates for further research into the evolutionary roots of religion and stresses the import of educating society, especially children, to dispel ignorance surrounding religious faith.

While some may argue that science and religion can live together gracefully, others believe that faith is nothing more than an obstruction to progress and critical thinking. So, whether you are team Dawkins or team Pope Francis, one thing's for sure: when it comes to the ancient rivalry of faith versus reason, there's never a dull moment.

In the next chapter, (Chapter 4), let us find out the perspective of a group of authors who believe that science and religion can coexist peacefully. So, stay tuned as things are about to get even more interesting!

Chapter 4

Are Science and Religion Compatible?

Flipping the Coin

In the previous chapter, we wrapped our minds around the battle royale known as The Conflict Between Science and Religion.

Sure, science and religion have often been portrayed as mortal enemies, but there is a whole crew of people out there who believe science and religion can play nice together. Science is all about poking and prodding the natural world to figure out how it ticks, while religion is more interested in the big questions like why we are here and what it all means. It's like they are two sides of the same coin, each offering a unique perspective on life.

The notion that science and religion can coexist without throwing punches suggests that they are like the ultimate power couple. Science is the brains of the operation, using evidence and experimentation to discover the mysteries of the universe. Meanwhile, religion is the heart, immersing in the depths of meaning, morality, and spirituality. Instead of butting heads, they can team up to give us a more multi-faceted view of the world. Science tells us how stuff works, while religion helps us figure out why it all matters. It's like a match made in intellectual heaven.

Contrary to Coyne, Harris, Hitchens, Houk, and Dawkins, numerous authors have penned works that interpret the relationship between science and religion, ultimately finding common ground and compatibility between the two. These 'accommodationists', as their name suggests, argue that religion should coexist with science for the betterment of humanity. Believers (Theists) point out that science has also been the cause of numerous societal issues, conflicts, and wars. So, who is really to blame for all the drama?

Science and the Bible Agree

In the book 'Amazing Truths – How Science and Bible Agree,' Michael Guillen (2015) breaks down ten mind-boggling truths in a way that even our grandma could understand. He shows us that science and scripture (Bible) get along pretty well, like two old pals sharing a meal at the restaurant. Guillen argues that faith is the Midas touch that makes both science and Christianity tick. The author compares concepts like space, time, and instantaneous communication in science with religious conceptions and claims that they are very similar, even for how they are written in the Bible as well.

Meanwhile, in 'The Serpent's Promise - The Bible Interpreted Through Modern Science,' Steve Jones (2012) claims that many stories from the Bible, Genesis, and Revelation, such as Exodus and Adam and Eve, might have some real-life parallels. He suggests we read these tales as symbols and myths, rather than taking them as gospel truth. Alluding to the need for religion, Jones reminds us (2012, p.416), *"Illness, depression, and greed are still with us, and mathematical biology will not cure them."*

Many believers claim that Natural Theology has its roots in Christianity. Notably, religious figures such as Kepler, Newton, and Copernicus were instrumental in cracking the laws of nature, positing that these laws were manifestations of the divine handiwork of God.

Science and Religion Agree

In 'The Big Question – Why We Can't Stop Talking About Science, Faith, and God' by Alister McGrath (2015), the author fearlessly takes on Richard Dawkins and the New Atheism movement. With clever analogies, McGrath expresses how science and faith can complement each other, rather than clash. He argues that reality is not just a cold, hard fact, but more like a gripping story, a beautiful picture, or a detailed map - all different ways of understanding the world around us.

McGrath points out that there are countless interpretations of reality, each with its unique perspective. Unlike the rigid rules of Mathematics, even science is constantly evolving. For McGrath, faith is a guiding light, helping him find meaning and purpose in life, maneuver through tough times, and develop a strong moral compass.

In the end, McGrath reminds us that while science can provide valuable judgments about the workings of the universe, it falls short when it comes to answering life's biggest questions about meaning and purpose.

More examples can be found in 'From Science to God', in which Peter Russel (2002), writes of his conversion from Atheist and Physicist to a spiritualist. By plunging into the heart of Eastern religions like Hinduism and Buddhism, he noted that consciousness is the ultimate mystery and reality.

Similarly, John Polkinghorne, also a physicist and student of Paul Dirac, compares science and religion and explains in his book, 'Exploring Reality – the Intertwining of Science and Religion' (2007) that both are similar and needed.

In his book 'Waking Up – A Guide to Spirituality without Religion' (2014), Sam Harris argues that the ultimate questions of life posed by religion are poorly framed and unnecessary to answer. According to Harris, these questions may be great, but they are ultimately false (p. 102).

Physics and Religion Agree

Another like-minded book comparing science and religion is 'The Tao of Physics: An Exploration of the Parallels Between Modern Physics and Eastern Mysticism' by physicist Fritjof Capra, (2010). This book will have you questioning the very fabric of the universe in a way that only a physicist can.

Krista Tippet's book 'Speaking of Faith – Why Religion Matters – and How to Talk About It', (2008) is a must-read for anyone interested in researching the connections between science and spirituality. Tippet has interviewed some heavy hitters in the world of religion, including Thich Nhat Hanh,

Karen Armstrong, and Eli Wiesel, to provide a bird's-eye view of this complex relationship.

In her follow-up book, 'Einstein's God', (2010), Tippet takes her expedition even further by chatting with physicists like Freeman Dyson, V.V. Raman, and Paul Davies, as well as other luminaries such as Mehmet Oz, John Polkinghorne, Sherwin Nuland, Darwin's biographer, James Moore. These interviews bring to the forefront the deep connections between science and religion, drawing examples from a wide range of belief systems.

Take 'Dark Matter' for example - it's like the ultimate cosmic force, lurking in the shadows where we cannot see it, but its impact is undeniable. Just like God, who operates in a stealthy manner, leaving only clues of His presence through the wonders of nature.

And then there's the head-turner question of whether light is a particle or a wave. Back in Einstein's day, this was the ultimate brain teaser. But Paul Dirac (teacher of John Polkinghorne) sprang into action like a scientific savior and revealed that light is actually both! Thanks to Quantum Mechanics, we now know that these particles (of EM waves including light and electrons) are playing a contest of hide-and-seek all around us, only revealing themselves when we are watching (detected by a detector).

Tippet (2010) climaxes the value of integrating both science and religion when probing the complexities of human existence. By solely relying on one perspective, conflicting answers may arise. She proposes that scientific experiments can measure the impact of meditation and prayer on the human brain and body and asserts that prayer and meditation can alleviate stress and other mental ailments.

In a similar vein, Moore eloquently describes:

"To treat Genesis as a commentary on science is to ignore its cogency as text and teaching, just as to read a poem as prose is to miss the point. It is more complicated than that, but it is also that simple." (Quoted by Tippet, 2010, p. 6).

These books all touch on similar themes: Elizabeth Gilbert's 'Eat, Pray, Love' (2007), Stephen Prothero's 'Religious Literacy' (2008), Andrew Solomon's 'The Noonday Demon' (2002), Yossi Klein's 'At the Entrance of the Garden of Eden: A Jew's search for God with Christians and Muslims in the Holy Land' (2002), and Khaled Abou El Fadl's 'The Great Theft: Wrestling Islam from the Extremists' (2005). It's like a literary buffet of deep thoughts and spiritual study.

World Religious Philosophies Agree

In the riveting book, 'Talking God – Philosophers on Belief' (2017), Gary Gutting features interviews with twelve esteemed philosophers from various religious backgrounds, including Christianity, Islam, Hinduism, Buddhism, Judaism, as well as atheists and agnostics. Originally featured in the 2014 'The Stone' column of 'The New York Times', these interviews include the opinions of Alvin Plantinga, Jay Garfield, Philip Kitcher, Sajjad Rizvi, Michael Ruse, Jonardon Ganeri, John D. Caputo, and more.

Rizvi astutely explains that religious faith devoid of critical reasoning veers dangerously into fanaticism, while Kitcher mentions the sense of community lacking in atheism. After all, we all crave something to believe in that guides us through life, and for many, that sense of belonging is found within a community (Gutting).

In a world where religious beliefs often divide us, it's refreshing to see these diverse perspectives coming together to shed light on the common threads that bind us all.

Here are just a taste of the many books out there that seek the existence and influence of religion and God: 'The Future of God' (2014) and 'The Souls Journey into the Mystery of Mysteries – How to Know God' (2000) by the one and only Deepak Chopra, 'Myths of Light' by Joseph Campbell (2012), 'How God Becomes Real – Kindling the presence of invisible Others' by T. M. Luhrmann (2020), 'My Adventures with God' by Stephen Tobolowsky (2017), 'Goddess Spirituality for the 21st century' by Judith

Laura (2008), and 'Religion as We Know it' by Jack Miles (2019). These books will have you deliberating the divine in no time!

In his 2014 book, 'The Future of God - A Practical Approach to Spirituality for Our Times', Deepak Chopra takes aim at the new wave of militant atheists such as Dawkins, Hitchens, Dennett, and Harris. He daringly asserts that God is not some distant deity, but rather human awareness itself. According to Chopra, God is the higher level of consciousness that we all have the potential to tap into.

Chopra's argument is ingrained in the idea that reality is fundamentally tied to consciousness, a concept that aligns with the principles of Quantum Mechanics. He dismisses the notion that randomness alone can explain the complex evolvement of life on Earth. By drawing on both modern science and ancient Eastern philosophy, Chopra offers an interesting case for adopting a more spiritual approach to our daily lives.

Religion Improves Health

New atheists often reference various scientific experiments to allege that prayer and religious practices have no tangible impact on human well-being, particularly when it comes to the health of sick individuals. This topic is hotly debated, with some, like Coyne, even going so far as to label homeopathy as mere superstition.

In 1985, Marcia Angell, the former editor-in-chief of the prestigious New England Journal of Medicine, boldly stated, "Our belief in disease as a direct reflection of mental state is largely folklore" (p. 5, Koeing, 2007). So, it seems the age-old idea of mind over matter may not hold as much weight as we once thought.

Since then, numerous articles have been published in reputable journals to debunk the outdated notion that the mind and body are separate entities. The emerging field of Psychoneuroimmunology studies how every aspect of human life can impact physical health, proving that the mind truly has power over the body. In today's digital era, dominated by information technology and social media, this connection is more basal than ever.

The past couple of years during the COVID-19 pandemic have witnessed an upsurge in mental health issues due to increased loneliness. This spike in mental health struggles has led to a higher demand for Psychiatrists in the USA. Could the rise in mass shootings in America also be attributed to the effects of COVID-19 (Note 1)?

According to NPR on 5/3/23, there were a staggering 190 mass shootings in the first four months of 2023. While it's uncertain, it's possible that a combination of factors, including the pandemic, may be contributing to this alarming trend.

Mental health issues like depression, anxiety, ADHD, bipolar disorder, and even thoughts of suicide are becoming more prevalent in today's society. With the strain on our healthcare system due to financial pressures, rising healthcare costs, and an aging population with various health conditions, religious communities must step up and provide support and education on how to cope with these calamities.

In the book 'Medicine, Religion and Health - Where Science and Spirituality Meet' by Harold G. Koenig, MD (2008), the author refers to the positive impact that religious beliefs and practices can have on patients dealing with illness. Through various clinical trials, Koenig discovered that incorporating spirituality into treatment can lead to faster recovery and improved coping mechanisms for patients. He uses religiosity and spirituality in a very broad sense for these experiments.

Koenig shows that mental health, the immune system, the endocrine system, stress, behavior-related diseases, mortality and disability are affected. He examines the relationship between religion, immune and endocrine systems such as breast cancer, HIV/AIDS, and fibromyalgia. Additionally, Koenig investigates how religion impacts blood pressure, heart function, autonomic functions, and behavioral habits like smoking, diet, weight gain, exercise, diabetes, age-related memory decline,

Alzheimer's, outcomes after heart surgeries, and longevity across diverse populations in the US, Asia, and Europe.

He concludes (p. 53, Koenig, 2008):

"From this sample research on both animals and human subjects, it is clear that pathways exist through which attitudes, emotions, and social relations can have either negative or positive effects on physical health. Psychological and social stresses have been shown to have negative effects on immune, endocrine, and cardiovascular functions. Such physiological changes can, in turn, increase the body's susceptibility to metabolic, neurological, cardiac, and vascular diseases. Likewise, people under stress can fall into poor habits, such as excessive alcohol use, smoking, and inadequate exercise or weight gain, which can also affect their physical health and functioning.

In contrast, positive social interactions and psychological states may boost immune, endocrine, and cardiovascular functions, thereby protecting against disease or slowing progression. New research is also appearing that shows how prosocial health behavior, such as altruism and volunteering, may improve not only mental health but physical health as well."

Koenig claims that religious and spiritual involvement can immensely improve psychological health, social interactions, and even physical well-being. By turning to their faith, people are better empowered to handle life's stumpers, such as divorce, loss, or a serious illness like cancer. In fact, Koenig's research revealed that a colossal 80% of 100 studies proved that religious individuals reported higher levels of well-being compared to their less religious counterparts (Koenig, 2000).

He quotes:

"It may do so by fostering hope, optimism, and joy, by increasing social support, and giving life, purpose and meaning."

Optimism and hope are like the charismatic duo of positive emotions, leaping into action to save the day when stress comes knocking. Research has shown time and time again that meditation reduces blood pressure

(Wenneberg, 1997). Studies from the United States, Europe, and Asia have all pointed to the fact that attending religious services, prayers, and meditation can lower the risk of mortality.

Koenig, the crackerjack of all health-related aspects, suggests that health professionals should ask their patients about their spiritual needs. Why? Because it can help patients deal with their illnesses and improve medical issues. But no one's saying you have to start chanting "om" if you are not into it. So, spirituality should not be forced on anyone.

Koenig even wrote a whole book about it called 'Spirituality in Patient Care' (Koenig, 2007). And guess what? This whole spiritual care thing is catching on like wildfire in major hospitals across the USA. I mean, even I got asked if I needed some spiritual service when I was at the University of Michigan Hospital recently.

In 2003, Smith, McCullough, and Poll conducted a thorough evaluation of over 200 studies and made a headline discovery: high religiosity is linked to a decreased risk of depression, drug abuse, suicide, and overall greater satisfaction with life (p.156, Ward). Similarly, a study at the University of Pennsylvania Center for Research on Religion and Urban Civil Society reviewed 498 surveys and found a correlation between lower hypertension and depression, as well as a higher level of happiness (p. 157, Ward). It seems like a little faith can go a long way in improving both our physical and mental well-being!

Koenig, McCullough, and Larson have confirmed through diverse studies that religious individuals tend to live longer and lead healthier lives. Ward has cited several studies that evince a correlation between religiosity and happiness. This trend is not limited to America; countries like India also boast higher rates of life satisfaction among the religiously inclined.

People's Opinion Poll Shows that Science and Religion Are Compatible

In the book 'Religion vs. Science – What Religious People Really Think', the authors allude to the American beliefs surrounding science and religion. Through surveys and empirical evidence, they get to the bottom of controversial topics such as climate change, creationism, evolution, and stem cell research (Ecklund, 2018).

Contrary to popular belief, religious individuals are not averse to science. In fact, Jews, Muslims, and Christians exhibit similar or even higher levels of interest in science compared to their nonreligious counterparts. Even Evangelicals, who may show slightly less interest, are not anti-science. They simply prefer to see God take an active role in scientific explanations. Surprisingly, 60% of Evangelicals wish for miracles to be included in scientific theories, and 50% believe in Biblical miracles. Conversely, 15% of Catholics and 20% of Muslims claim to have witnessed miracles and physical healing. It seems that some religious individuals who appreciate science may not always see eye to eye with scientists.

Paradoxical to popular belief, scientists at US universities are less religious than the general US population. However, there are still some scientists in US universities who manage to balance their love for science with their religious beliefs. On the flip side, a massive 75% of scientists working outside of universities are religious - talk about mixing business with pleasure!

When it comes to the classic argument of young earth creationism, only 28% of evangelicals are on board with the idea that the earth is a mere 6000 years old. Jews and Muslims also believe in the role of God in creation, with some even accepting the idea that God set Earth in motion. It seems like most religious Americans are pretty chill when it comes to their views on evolution and creation - who knew they were so open-minded?

And let's demystify a myth while we are at it: not all religious people are climate change deniers. In fact, a sizable 72% of creationists believe that climate change is real and that we are the ones responsible for it.

Oh, and speaking of denial, it turns out that political conservatism is more to blame for climate change denial than religious beliefs. Who would have thought that politics could be more divisive than religion?

Many Evangelicals are on board with certain reproductive genetic technologies (RGT), like detecting genetic diseases, but when it comes to stem cell research and abortion, they hit the brakes. It's like they are saying, "Stop right there, science!"

Experts suggest that religious leaders should bring scientists into the fold to educate their followers on the wonders of science. Let's have some discussions about how scientific advancements can benefit humanity and the world around us.

In a study by John D. Miller, a Research Scientist Emeritus at the University of Michigan, it was found that Gen Xers' views on evolution change and solidify over the course of 30 years from middle school (Note 2). It's like they are evolving right before our eyes!

Religion Is Not the Root of All Evil

In 2006, British philosopher-theologian Keith Ward released his timely publication, 'Is Religion Dangerous?' This book was a direct response to the atheistic works of authors like Dawkins, Hitchens, and Harris, as well as Dawkins's British TV series, 'The Root of All Evil.'

Ward tackles the long-standing question of whether religion should be opposed due to its alleged corrupting influence on children and its potential to incite terrorism and violence. On the very first page of his book, Ward courageously asserts his stance on the matter:

"I will come clean at once - I think such assertions are absurd. Worse than that, they ignore the available evidence from history, from psychology and sociology, and from philosophy. They refuse to investigate the question in a properly rigorous way, and substitute rhetoric for analysis. Oddly enough,

that is what they tend to accuse religious believers of doing. There is something there, I think that needs to be explained." (p.7, Ward)

He asserts that the majority of religions denounce and resist the 'Hatred of life'. Hatred, thirst for power, and apathy towards others are often cloaked as virtues such as loyalty, patriotism, and honor.

"It looks as if religions are not the causes of evil, but they do naturally share in the general moral state of the societies in which they exist."

He intones that it's a mistake to label all religions as dangerous. Instead, each religion should be examined within its social, economic, political, and historical context. Violence and war would still exist even without religion, as seen with communism and fascism in the twentieth century.

When it comes to the topic of life after death, Ward makes it clear that thinking you will go to heaven by killing people of a different religion is just plain wrong. However, believing in life after death, whether it's real or not, can provide comfort, courage, and alleviate the fear of dying.

In his brief essay "Why I Am Not a Christian", philosopher Bertrand Russell boldly accuses Jesus of moral imperfection, violence, intolerance, and judgmental behavior, citing instances such as the cleansing of the Temple and references to the flames of hell (Note 3). However, Ward suggests that Jesus was not cruel, violent, or intolerant. Instead, he believes that Jesus's life should be viewed in the context of the entire Bible, portraying him as a figure of love and forgiveness.

Religion is Not an Irrational Form of Belief

When mulling over the centuries-old riddle of whether religion is simply a blind leap of faith, one must consider the intellectual heavyweights of history. Were Anselm, Aquinas, Kant, Kierkegaard, Hegel, Descartes, Spinoza, and Leibniz all just irrational people? Materialism and Idealism duke it out as competing worldviews, with the concept of a 'First cause' or 'designer' (God) at the center of it all. Plato and Aristotle were all about appearances, while Kant sent things spiraling by denying a designer but leaving room for 'faith'. According to Kant, reason can lead to contradictions if we take observed reality as the ultimate truth. However, Ward argues that religious beliefs can be just as logical and sensible as non-religious ones - so maybe blind faith is not so blind after all.

In conclusion, Ward answers the title question of his book, 'Is religion dangerous?':

"Sometimes, it is. But it is also one of the most powerful forces in the world for good." (p. 200, Ward).

His "Sometimes" is often attributed to religious fundamentalists. His descriptions and surveys center on the everyday religious individual, omitting the extremes of both devout believers and staunch atheists. In other words, he is all about the middle ground - no fanatics allowed!

Religious People are Not Mentally Sick

Ward explains that being religious does not equate to having mental illnesses such as epilepsy, schizophrenia, hysteria, or neurosis, as some atheists suggest that religious individuals hear voices. Mental illnesses are neurological in nature and are not within a person's control. Religion provides numerous positive health benefits. It is important to differentiate between mental sickness and spirituality or lack thereof, as mental illnesses originate from brain malfunctions. While religion can offer support and comfort, it cannot replace medical treatment for diseases. So, let's keep our faith in check and leave the brain stuff to the professionals!

Opposed to what some atheists may believe, religious individuals do not suffer from delusions. The Diagnostic and Statistical Manual of Mental Disorders (DSM) states that religious beliefs are not considered delusions because they are shared within a cultural context (American Psychiatric Association, 2022). So, sorry to burst the bubble, but just because someone does not see eye to eye with you does not mean they are off their rocker.

Disagreements happen all the time, whether it's about politics, philosophy, history, or even just what toppings to get on a pizza. Having a different religious belief does not automatically mean someone needs to be fitted for a straitjacket. Unless, of course, their beliefs are causing harm to others or are just plain wacky.

Some people argue that our brains are wired to believe in a higher power, kind of like how we are programmed to crave pizza at 2 am. So, maybe it's not so much about fear of mental illness, but more about our brains doing their thing. Who knows, maybe God created our brains to believe in Him. It's a chicken or egg situation.

In the end, religion is a complex and personal matter that cannot be boiled down to a simple equation like 3 + 3 = 6. So, let's not jump to conclusions about someone's mental state just because they have a different belief system. He claims that religion is not founded on fear, mental illness or because of worry about what happens to us after death.

All Wars and Killings Are Not Due to Religion

When weighing the timeless question of whether we should discard religion because of its violent history like the Crusades by Christians and terrorist organizations by Muslims, Ward brings up a valid point: politics has also been a major player in the episode of mass murder. From Russia to Cambodia to Korea, to China, to Ukraine, to Vietnam, politics has left a trail of destruction in its wake. Also, science is infamous for the creation of weapons of mass destruction and guns. So, should we toss politics and science out the window too?

Ward argues that it's not the tool itself, but how it's used those matters. Just like a hammer can build a house or bash someone's head in, religion can inspire both good and bad deeds. It's not fair to blame religion for all the bloodshed when it has also motivated great figures like Martin Luther King, Mahatma Gandhi, Mother Teresa, Jesus, and Buddha.

So, before we go pointing fingers at religion, let's remember that it's all about how you wield the power, whether it's political, scientific, or spiritual. Let's not throw the baby out with the bathwater.

Ward believes that atheists can also appreciate truth, beauty, and goodness, but what's lacking is the ultimate purpose behind it all. Both atheists and theists can be bad people. Just look at the mass murders by Stalin and Hitler who were atheists, and atrocities by the Aztecs and witch-burners who were believers.

More recently, there were two major domestic terrorist attacks on US soil that were not related to religion. There was a bombing in Boston during a marathon on April 15, 2013 (Note 4). There was a bombing on April 19, 1995, on Alfred P. Murrah federal building in Oklahoma City by Timothy McVeigh, William Krar, and Judith Bruey (Note 5).

In the span of the 16th to the 20th century, Europe was not busy waging wars over religion and superstition, yet somehow managed to engage in two world wars, numerous conflicts, and the expansion of slavery, which were not related to religion. Science advanced, but unfortunately, it also gave birth to weapons of mass destruction. The transition from religious superstition to Enlightenment and reason did not exactly bring about world peace either. Ward's stance is that both secularism and religion have their fair share of pros and cons.

So, it seems like humanity has a knack for messing things up, regardless of whether we are guided by faith or reason.

Differences Among Religions are Not the Cause of Fights

When four individuals cohabitate for an extended period, diverging opinions are bound to arise, leading to the inevitable formation of two factions. Disputes and conflicts will surely ensue, stimulated by a truckload of reasons. This is human nature.

Religions are like spices in the global stew of humanity - each one adding its unique flavor based on local cultures and society. Despite their differences, all religions have contributed something positive to the world.

Judaism, for example, aims to create a peaceful human community known as the 'Kingdom of God', where people can worship, respect, and love the creator of all the beautiful things in nature. It acknowledges the sinful nature of humans but also preaches the forgiveness of God, who never abandons anyone.

Christianity, on the other hand, believes in the divine manifestation of God in human form, as taught by the life of Jesus. His sacrifice, resurrection, and the concept of the Trinity, all parade the power of love over suffering.

Islam, with its mystical branch known as Sufism, punctuates the personal connection with a supreme reality. And let's not forget that idolism is a big no-no in Islam.

So, whether you are a believer or not, it's clear that each religion brings something valuable to the table. Just like a buffet of spiritual wisdom, there is something for everyone to savor.

Hinduism believes in Polytheism. They worship many idols of Gods and Goddesses in search of the one supreme reality, Brahman. According to Hinduism, you are not a sinner - you must keep coming back for more lives until you finally get woke to the truth. Conversely, Christianity is all about the resurrection of the body, no reincarnation is necessary.

Karma forms the core of Hinduism - what goes around, comes around. Buddhism is also on board with the whole rebirth concept, but they do not believe in a creator God. Buddha shared four noble truths and an eight-fold path to nirvana. These teachings are like a spiritual framework, guiding people towards enlightenment and liberating oneself from the cycle of rebirth.

Sure, there's bound to be some discord between religions with all these differences, but it's not the religions themselves causing the spectacle. It's those troublesome human believers with their egos, ignorance, greed, selfishness, and hatred.

Just as there are endless flavors of ice cream, there are also countless opinions among us humans on a wide range of topics. From religion to history, science to art, and everything in between, we all have our own unique perspectives. Take the cremation of the dead, for example - different religions have different practices. There have been heated debates over reincarnation vs resurrection, heaven and hell, or one God vs many gods. It's like a never-ending talk show of philosophical ping-pong!

But here's the thing - these differences of opinion should not lead to conflict. Nope, it's the nettlesome human nature factors, politics, economics, and social issues that tend to stir the pot. Whatever you believe in, whether it's the Bible, the Quran, or something entirely different, it should never be an excuse to harm or kill others. It should be for human respect, life, justice, tolerance, and happiness. Let's keep it classy, friends.

Then there's another form of religion out there that's all about connecting with the spiritual reality of supreme wisdom, compassion, and bliss. Sounds pretty groovy, right?

There are scores of realities in the world, each deserving of expedition. In their book 'Teachings from the American Earth – Indian Religion and Philosophy' (1975, 1992), authors Dennis Tedlock and Barbara Tedlock (editors) discuss how the universe model for American Indians differs from that of modern science, particularly when it comes to the Ojibwa tribe.

Blaise Pascal (1623-1662), a seventeenth-century French polymath, put forth his famous wager theory (Connor), suggesting that it's safer to believe in God. After all, if God does exist, you will be in good standing and head to heaven. And if God does not exist, well, no harm done. In contrast, not believing in God could potentially land you in hot water if you are wrong and God turns out to be real (Note 6). So, why not hedge your bets and believe? It's a long shot worth taking!

All in all, numerous authors have drawn parallels between science and religion, noting their similarities. Accommodationists such as Alister

McGrath, Deepak Chopra, and Peter Russel contend that both science and religion have had positive and negative impacts on society, and advocate for a cordial coexistence through compromise.

Chapter 5

Most Theists and Atheists are Mistaken about Religion, God, and Science

A majority of theists and atheists seem to be missing the mark when it comes to understanding religion, God, and science. Theists cling to their faith without questioning or seeking evidence, while atheists adamantly reject the existence of any higher power despite the absence of definitive proof. Perhaps the real answer lies somewhere in the middle of these polarized stances.

Let's take a closer look at these contrasting perspectives and try to unmask the answers through the following propositions.

Most People Do Not Question God's Existence and the Stories of the Scriptures

Many people follow a religious way of life without giving it much thought. Growing up in India, I noticed that people did not engage in deep discussions about Gods like Rama, Krishna, Lakshmi, Hanumana, or Shiva. They simply went to the temple, said their prayers, and then got back to the daily grind of college or work. This seems to be a common trend for people of all religions worldwide.

While most people do not question the existence of God, there are a few of us who cannot help but philosophize such deep mysteries. I count myself among those deep thinkers.

Whereas, there are those ultra-religious people who will go to great lengths to defend their beliefs in God's existence, especially when it comes to their specific deity. These are the fundamentalists, the ones who take their scriptures literally and live by them; hence, they are termed literalists.

Certainly, there are extremists and fanatics out there - individuals who are willing to sacrifice their own lives and take the lives of others in the name of their God, all in the hopes of scoring a VIP spot in heaven.

Growing up, I never came across any literature discussing the clash between science and religion in India. It was not a common topic of conversation, as the two were kept separate in Indian society. In schools, students are taught about various religions, including Hinduism, Islam, Christianity, Buddhism, Sikhism, and Jainism, alongside science. It's like a religious medley of knowledge! And with a federal holiday for each religion, you can bet there's always a reason to celebrate in India.

Education helps people distinguish between rational and irrational facts, but when it comes to the existence of God or the words written in the scriptures, many tend to take things at face value. Hindu religious fundamentalists, however, do not insist that every word in their scriptures is scientifically accurate. Conversely, strong atheists and scientists, known as New Atheists, do not waste their time trying to disprove religious texts.

When I was a wee lad, my dear mother used to regale me with tales of a seven-hooded snake named Sheshnaag, who supposedly held the earth on its head and caused earthquakes whenever it got a little antsy. Quite the riveting story, I must say. However, as I investigated the dimensions of science and learned about planets, gravity, and the true causes of earthquakes, the whole Sheshnaag theory quickly lost its charm. I bid adieu to that fanciful notion without so much as a second thought. No internal conflict, no existential crisis - just a simple shrug and a move on.

As I have written in Chapter 3, there are many such mythological stories in all religious scriptures and cultures.

Ah, the wonders of childhood stories that once seemed so plausible, only to be disparaged by the cold, hard facts of science. It's a tale as old as time, really. And yet, I cannot help but wonder how many people out there in all religions and cultures still hang onto these mythological beliefs, like a security blanket in a world of uncertainty. I will not judge those who still find solace in ancient legends, just as they do not try to convert me to their way of thinking. While I may not personally subscribe to these myths, I can appreciate the sense of community and tradition they bring to those who do.

During a weekend in 2023, I had the opportunity to partake in an Iftar feast (The meal eaten after sunset during Ramadan) in Dearborn, Michigan, home to the largest population of Muslims in the USA. The ambiance was buzzing with excitement as everyone, especially the younger crowd, indulged in a multitude of mouthwatering dishes.

Despite the religious undertones of the event, it felt more like a lively celebration than a solemn affair. In one corner, an elderly individual serenaded us with religious verses and imparted wisdom through a religious lecture. However, most attendees were too busy enjoying the delicious food and engaging in lively conversations to pay much attention to the spiritual teachings.

While Iftar is typically a time for spiritual reflection and reverence, at this particular event, the attendees seemed more interested in enjoying the delicious feast and mingling with each other than in participating in religious rituals, such as listening to the elders' recitations and lectures. This contrast shows how even the most sacred gatherings can transform into lively social occasions, where communal happiness often outweighs solemn devotion.

Most people in the world celebrate their festivals like Holi, Diwali, Eid, Kwanza, Hanukkah, Christmas, Easter, with the above sentiments of holiday, food and fun, even if the festivals may have some religious connotations.

Most People are not Qualified Enough to Fully Understand Religion, God, and Science

How many people worldwide have a college degree sophisticated enough to understand the finer points of scientific phenomena like evolution, the inner workings of the human body (medicine), or the principles of Physics such as quantum mechanics, theory of relativity, or string theory? Even a college degree may not be enough to decode these principles. And how many people hold a Ph.D. degree in this vast world? Yet, once you specialize in a very narrow field, you may find yourself bewildered about other areas of expertise. It's like being a genius in one room but lost in the rest of the house!

I still cannot get my mind around the concept of time dilation, despite countless discussions with my physics professor friend over the years. It's like trying to understand why people willingly eat pineapple on a cheesy slice- it just does not make sense to me. But not everyone can be an expert in everything, right? We just have to trust the experts in their respective fields, even if we would rather be weighing more urgent questions like why cats always land on their feet or why some people think it's okay to wear socks with sandals. So, while most people could not care less about living longer on a fast-moving planet or the workings of quantum mechanics and string theory, I will just be over here, sipping on my brew and thinking of the mysteries of the universe.

Most people are not exactly experts when it comes to religion, God, theology, or philosophy. They are too busy in their work, family, and the never-ending mayhem of daily life to worry about analyzing ancient scriptures. Most people just stick with the religion they were born into, follow a few basic rituals, and call it a day. Who has time for rigorous studies of religious texts when there are bills to pay and kids to raise?

I am sure most people have not read and understand fully the scriptures of their religion. I guess it's a good thing most people have not fully studied their religious texts - can you imagine the pandemonium if everyone started taking things literally? We would have a whole bunch of atheists and fundamentalists running around, causing a rampage. So maybe it's best to stick to skimming the hotel room Bible for now.

Now, do not get me wrong - I am not talking about the extremists and fundamentalists here. Those people take their scripture study very seriously. But for the rest of us mere mortals, we are content to just go with the flow and believe what feels right.

If someone does decide to scrutinize those scriptures, they better be prepared to do some serious research. No cherry-picking passages to fit your agenda - you must do a comprehensive analysis of the literal meaning and find examples that support your argument. It's not for the faint of heart, that's for sure.

Separation of State and Church Does not Work

The First Amendment of the US Constitution clearly states that there should be a separation of state and Church. So, why are we still seeing so many political scenes revolving around religion? From stem cell research to condoms, gay rights, abortion, and climate change, it seems like religion is always being used as a wedge issue.

Meanwhile, in Europe, countries like Sweden, Denmark, and Norway are much less religious. In fact, my friend from Sweden told me that Swedes pay a church tax that is automatically deducted from their salaries. It's a bit paradoxical - the state supports religion, but the people are not very religious. How does that work?

Well, according to my friend, because churches and priests have stable salaries paid by the government, they do not have much of an incentive to increase church membership. On the contrary, the members do not have much of an incentive to attend church regularly, except for major life events like baptisms, weddings, and... well, you get the idea. It's a strange system, but at least they are keeping things interesting over there!

I often find myself speculating: why is it that Americans struggle to adhere to NOMA, as suggested by Gould (1999)? Why do theists insist on interpreting the Bible literally, defending its stories as absolute truth? And why do new atheists feel the need to mock these stories as irrational and impossible? Could it be that these interpretations are driven by political and personal agendas, aimed at swaying the opinions of the masses? It seems that in the battle of beliefs, logic often takes a backseat to persuasion.

Atheists Exist Because Theists Exist

In his book, 'Everybody is wrong about God', (2015), the author, James A. Lindsay, claims that atheism exists because theism exists. If theism were eliminated, atheism would automatically not be required. He suggests adopting a post-theistic approach and eliminating both theism and atheism. If believers can receive the same benefits through alternative means rather than belief in God, then God becomes obsolete. He suggests that it is a psychological, moral, and social benefit that one gets from believing in God, which can be obtained without actually believing in God. He writes (p. 47):

"If theism were to go away, technically everyone would be atheists, so the term would be utterly obsolete because of its lack of providing useful information about anyone. If everyone on earth rejected theism, we wouldn't call anyone atheists because we wouldn't need to. We would just call them people. "Atheism," then is a word that shouldn't exist."

A similar idea was also echoed by Sam Harris, 'An Atheist Manifesto', published in 'Truth Dig' in 2005 (Note 1):

"It is worth noting that no one ever needs to identify himself as a non-astrologer or a non-alchemist. Consequently, we do not have words for people who deny the validity of these pseudo-disciplines. Likewise, atheism is a term that should not even exist. Atheism is nothing more than the noises reasonable people make when in the presence of religious dogma."

Lindsay suggests that religion fulfills three essential psychological needs: attribution, control, and sociality. He deftly likens God to a sound mixer board, with various knobs representing different aspects of belief and influence. The ultimate knob, the 'Master Volume,' is Transcendence, cranking up or dialing down all other factors. From Moral to Teleological, Psychosocial to Abstract, each knob is instrumental in shaping our spiritual experience. It's like crafting the perfect orchestra of faith and understanding.

But he criticized Richard Dawkin's view of people being delusional about God (p. 157, Lindsay):

"Religious belief, however, is not typically delusional belief. One somewhat unsatisfactory reason that delusion does not quite describe religious beliefs is that there is some relationship between them and social norms. Believing in God, lamentably, is still quite normal, and so belief isn't itself, an indication of mental illness so much as simply being mistaken."

Lindsay also asserts that if religious beliefs were truly delusional, over half of the world's population would be deemed mentally ill and in need of psychiatric help. It's safe to say that psychiatrists would have their hands full!

Lindsay further points out in the last paragraph on page 157:

"People who believe in God do so because they don't know how else to meet certain psychological and social needs. By labeling these people as delusional, we miss the opportunity to address the actual issues in play."

He proposes that rather than opposing theists and dismissing their core values, we should strive for a post-theistic society. Lindsay punctuates that Western Europe has adopted a post-theistic mindset, where religious beliefs have become largely irrelevant, rather than strictly atheistic.

He recommends dismantling people's religious beliefs using three methods. First, there's Street Epistemology (SE) by Peter Boghossian, outlined in his book 'A Manual for Creating Atheists'. Boghossian employs Socratic techniques, posing the "right" questions to sow doubt and encourage believers to keep an open mind. The second method is John W. Loftus's Outsider Test for Faith, where Christians try being Muslim and vice versa. The third method involves using satire, but Lindsay cautions against crossing the line into mockery.

In my opinion, while these methods show promise, implementing them in reality may prove tricky. One concern is the lack of education needed to grasp these concepts. Even with education, people may struggle to find emotional and psychological fulfillment outside of their belief in a higher power. It's a tough nut to crack, but at least we are trying to crack it!

Some authors, such as Chris Hedges, offer alternative perspectives to Lindsay's on why both theists and new atheists are mistaken about the intersection of religion, God, and science. In the upcoming Chapter 6, I have shared my viewpoint on why science and religion are fundamentally incompatible, and why both theists and atheists may be mistaken about science, God, and religion.

Human Nature and Not Religion is the Problem

Human nature is a multifaceted beast. It's not like your run-of-the-mill laws of Physics, such as gravity or the theory of relativity. Nope, science cannot just break an equation to explain why we feel love, loneliness, happiness, courage, suffering, good, evil, feeling, hate, hope, empathy, pain, sorrow, grace, like, dislike, desire, wonder, compassion, anger, greed, morality, intention, wish, preferences, motivation, or any of those other messy emotions.

Indeed, Evolution and the Big Bang are cool and all, but they do not have all the answers. They cannot tell us the purpose of life or why we do the things we do. That's where Social Science and Psychology come in, strutting their stuff and showing us that there's more to human nature than meets the eye.

Science and religion may be as incompatible as chalk and cheese. However, they can coexist peacefully as long as religion does not try to pull a fast one and claim it has all the scientific answers.

Humans have a self that is greedy, selfish and egoistic. This is the cause of many personal fights and wars. This is the reason why India was divided between India and Pakistan in 1947, Pakistan divided into Pakistan and Bangladesh, Islam was divided into Shia and Sunni, Jainism was divided into Digambar and Svetambara, Buddhism has so many different organizations in different parts of the world and Christianity has more than 1000 independent organizations within the USA alone (p. 15, Houk).

As the great thinker Augustine once lamented, humans are not exactly known for their gentle nature. When push comes to shove, we can easily revert to our primal instincts, acting like wild animals in the name of survival. Trying to preach honesty to someone who is starving or parched is like trying to teach a fish to climb a tree – it's just not going to happen. In times of crisis, when our very existence feels threatened, we may find ourselves resorting to violence as a means of self-preservation.

Chris Hedges, the brilliant mind behind the NY Times bestseller 'American Fascists' (2008), has once again graced us with his wisdom in his latest book, 'I Do Not Believe in Atheists' (2008). In this masterpiece, Hedges takes a critical look at both new atheists and religious fundamentalists, revealing the real culprits behind wars and conflicts - politics, power, ego, and personal gain.

Drawing from his debates with Sam Harris and Christopher Hitchens in 2007, Hedges demolishes the notion that religion is the root of all evil. He argues that blaming religion for global conflicts is a convenient scapegoat, when in reality, it is politics and economics that fuel the fire.

Hedges calls out Harris for unfairly demonizing one billion Muslims, when only a small fraction engage in extremist activities. He also shines a light on the dark side of institutional churches and organized religions, exposing their misuse of power to commit heinous acts.

But amidst the disarray, Hedges reminds us of the positive contributions of the Muslim world - from algebra, and geometry to printing paper, and books, their legacy is undeniable.

Now, here's where things get interesting. You have got your religious fundamentalists on one side, dreaming of a perfect world through the miracles of Jesus and Mohammad. Then you have got your science fundamentalists (aka the new atheists) on the other side, thinking they can achieve utopia through science and technology.

But here's the kicker - science, technology, reason, and knowledge will not magically turn us all into angels. Nope, according to the Psychoanalyst Sigmund Freud, we are still slaves to our unconscious desires and animal instincts. So, sorry to dissolve your delusions, but we are all a work in progress, friends.

Evil is like that annoying relative who just will not leave your house, no matter how many times you drop hints. It's always skulking around, causing lawlessness and destruction wherever it goes. From the dark days of slavery to the horrors of genocide and war, evil has left its mark on history in more ways than we can count.

Take a look at the gigantic list of atrocities: the African slave trade, the Holocaust, the bombings of Hiroshima and Nagasaki, the 9/11 terrorist attacks on the Twin Towers in New York, and the ongoing conflicts in Afghanistan, Iraq, Russia's attack on Ukraine, Palestine and Israel war that started on Oct 7, 2023. It's like evil has a premium entry ticket to all the worst events in human history.

And then comes fascism and communism, those two troublemakers who thought they could make humans perfect by any means necessary. Spoiler alert: it did not end well. Millions of people paid the price for their twisted ideologies.

But here's the twist: the real danger is not religion or science. It's fundamentalism, the belief that your way is the only way and everyone else can go kick rocks.

Chris Hedges takes issue with the new Atheists, arguing that the root of the problem lies not in religion, but in the inherent greed and selfishness that creeps within human nature. He contends that the new atheists unfairly judge the entire Muslim population, and their faith based on the actions of a few extremists. Therefore, Hedges believes that it's not the religion that's the problem, but rather the darker aspects of human behavior that we all have.

I once pointed the finger at science for creating a rift in close-knit middle-class families by inventing gadgets like fridges, ACs, cars, motorcycles, iPhones, dishwashers, washing machines, new homes, and more. I believed that people were sacrificing family unity in the pursuit of these luxuries they could not afford. Back in the day, when our needs were simpler, we were content. However, I have realized that it's not the fault of these gadgets or science, but rather our insatiable greed and desire that's to blame for our discontent. So, we should not blame the poor innocent gadgets for our shortcomings!

Science Has Done Both Good and Bad Things

Over the past four years (2020-2024), science has gifted us with life-saving inventions like the COVID-19 vaccine, which has rescued millions from the clutches of the pandemic. However, not all scientific creations have been so benevolent. Take the atomic bomb, for example, a devastating weapon that has brought about untold destruction and loss of life.

The horrors of World War I and II are grim reminders of the destructive power of human innovation. The atomic bombings of Hiroshima and Nagasaki in Japan left hundreds of thousands dead and countless others maimed for life. The atrocities of the Holocaust claimed the lives of millions, leaving a scar on humanity that can never be erased.

In his critique, Hedges maintains that some individuals have twisted the concept of natural selection to justify their selfish desires. The idea of 'survival of the fittest' has been perverted to oppress women and the less fortunate, all in the name of greed, capitalism, and imperialism.

So, while science has the power to save lives, it also has the potential to destroy them. It is up to us to ensure that our advancements are used for the betterment of all, rather than the detriment of many.

The industrial revolution in Russia was a real doozy, resulting in the unfortunate killing of many millions of people. Some New Atheists believe that we can achieve moral enlightenment through advancements in science and technology, but as Hedges points out, that's a load of baloney.

Evolution and genetics may offer some insight into human behavior, but it's a combination of nature and nurture that shapes who we are.

Unfortunately, the idea of collective progress produced Nazi and Hitler, the Communist sterilization program in China, the genocide of Pol Pot, fossil fuel and global warming. The forced sterilization program (aka 'Nasbandi') by India's then Prime Minister's son Sanjay Gandhi (1975 and Note 2) failed badly leading to the Emergency during 1975-77.

In his book "The Selfish Gene" (1976), Dawkins coined the concept of "memes" - thoughts, beliefs, rituals, and ideas that replicate in our minds much like genes do in our bodies. He equated religious ideas to diseased memes, spreading like wildfire. Dawkins even proposed the idea of memetic engineering, manipulating these memes for better or for worse.

However, not everyone is on board with this idea. Hedges raises a valid concern about who gets to decide which memes are good and which are bad. The process of memetic engineering would involve no natural selection, but rather forced conversion, repression, and even prosecution. It's a bit like playing God with our thoughts and beliefs.

Unlike genes, which remain constant as they pass from one body to another, memes are ever-changing as they travel from one mind to another. It's like an erratic telephone call, where the original message gets distorted along the way.

Fundamentalism means all other views are inferior and your views are superior. This is true for religion and science. Science defines the world as a binary world of good and bad. Unconscious intentions and desires, not science, are the basis of moral behavior. Global capitalism moved factories to China, Vietnam, Mexico, and the Philippines where labor is cheap, but workers are not given basic rights, health benefits and retirement benefits in those countries. New Atheists support such policies.

Science cannot generate a basis for moral behavior, as Hedges noted below:

"Neither science nor reason call on us to love neighbor as ourselves, to forgive our enemies or to sacrifice for the weak, the infirm and poor." (p. 89, Hedges).

Mahatma Gandhi supported such a view, which is the basis of spirituality. Hedges supports that we must realize that humans have limitations and should not try to become God to control other groups for the betterment of a specific group.

Pamela R. Winnick, an award-winning journalist and medical reporter for the Toledo Blade, presents the contentious relationship between science and religion in her book, "A Jealous God – Science's Crusade Against Religion" (2005). Through compelling examples in stem cell research, cloning, and Intelligent design, Winnick argues that science has not only eroded human dignity and moral values but has also launched a full-scale attack on religion, transforming itself into a rigid and dogmatic belief system. In a world where science reigns supreme, Winnick challenges readers to question whether we have unknowingly placed our faith in a new kind of deity - one that is cold, calculating, and devoid of compassion.

Greed and not Religion is the Cause of Fraud and Cheating

Atheists often assert that scammers and con artists have been taking advantage of people in the name of religion for centuries. However, the truth is, it's not the religion that's to blame, but good old-fashioned human greed. Cheating has been a favorite pastime of mankind since the beginning of time, and these days, it's easier than ever.

Scammers are now using the internet, emails, phones, and social media to pull off all sorts of tricks to get their hands on your hard-earned cash. They will hack into your accounts, steal your identity, and use your credit cards to make online purchases faster than you can say 'scam alert!'

In India, they will even try to sweet-talk you into giving up your OTP (One Time Password) so they can clean out your bank account. Forget about old-school ransom kidnappings - now they will just lock up your computer and demand a hefty sum to set it free.

And it's not just individuals who are at risk. Companies and institutions are also falling victim to these cyber crooks, with central computer systems being hacked and held for ransom. Personal data is being stolen left and right, all in the name of personal gain.

So, while the methods may have changed, the root of the problem remains the same - good old human greed. And let's be clear, these scams and frauds have absolutely nothing to do with religion.

Cheating knows no bounds - it does not discriminate based on religion, tribe, country, or race. It's a universal issue fueled by our innate greed and selfishness.

Let's set the record straight: religion is not to blame for cheating and wars. It all comes down to our avaricious human nature, with its insatiable appetite for greed, ego, and selfishness. History is chock-full of examples of cheating and wars that had nothing to do with religion.

When it comes to experiences, beliefs, and faith, logic and reason often take a backseat. The only person who can truly change themselves is, well, themselves.

Unconscious Human Desire Causes Greed

Hidden human desires are the source of greed and fundamentalism. As the wise James Luther Adams, an ethics professor at Harvard Divinity School, once put it, "The lust of the mind, the lust of the flesh, and the lust of power." (p. 78, Hedges)

Hedges argues that neither science nor religion can rid us of our innate lusts; they are just part of our genetic makeup. We cannot rely on reason or faith to save us - we just need to accept our human limitations and resist the urge to play God. While some people think evil is an external force that must be violently conquered, Hedges begs to differ.

According to Hedges, atrocities like the genocide of Native Americans, the Armenian genocide, the Nanking massacre, and the horrors committed by Hitler, Stalin, and Mao were all carried out in the name of some twisted version of "common good" or "universal happiness." It's like a messed-up utopian vision gone terribly wrong.

Augustine once contemplated the insatiable desire for power, wealth, and fame that drives individuals, groups, and nations to act like they are auditioning for a role as God's understudy. This lust for greatness often leads to violence and force, as seen in conflicts like the war in Iraq, the Mexican war, and the Cuban war. Even President William McKinley got in on the action, justifying the war in the Philippines as a mission to "civilize and Christianize" the Filipino people, resulting in over six hundred thousand deaths. Then there were the English settlers in Massachusetts Bay, who decided to seize Pequot land because it's in the Bible, right?

It seems that throughout history, political change in the name of religion, communism, fascism, or imperialism has been the go-to excuse for inbreeding violence in the world.

The two worst genocides of the 20th century include the massacre of over 250,000 Bosnian Muslims by Serbian Orthodox Christians. Another tragic event was the atomic bombing of Hiroshima and Nagasaki by the United States, following the Japanese attack on Pearl Harbor, which killed more than 200,000 people, mostly civilians.

Unconscious Mind Controls Human Nature

Sigmund Freud was the pioneering psychologist who introduced the concept that our unconscious mind has a considerable impact on our behavior and thoughts.

Nobel Laureate Daniel Kahneman sliced this idea further in his book "Thinking, Fast and Slow" (2012), indicating how people often make irrational economic decisions driven by their unconscious thoughts. For instance, someone may end up buying a car at the showroom, which goes against all the careful analysis and logic they had done at home beforehand.

It's a well-known fact that our stomachs have a direct line to our wallets. When we hit the grocery store on an empty stomach, suddenly everything looks appetizing, and we end up with a cart full of goodies we did not even know we needed. And let's not overlook the holiday season - December rolls around and suddenly our wallets are open wider than ever, all in the name of Christmas cheer.

But let's talk about the real kicker - the lottery. We all know the odds of winning are slim to none, yet we still fork over our hard-earned cash for a chance at that elusive jackpot. It's like we are all secretly hoping to defy the odds and become instant millionaires.

But perhaps the biggest con of all is the power of advertising. We know those commercials are just smoke and mirrors, yet we still find ourselves reaching for that product on the shelf. It's like we are under a spell, unable to resist the siren call of a frilly ad. Advertisements in the twentieth century made people, especially ladies to smoke cigarettes as it was advertised as 'Liberty Torch'.

The unconscious brain is like a tricky puppet master, pulling the strings of human nature to make us all a little greedy, selfish, and egotistical. It does not care if you are a devout believer or a card-carrying atheist - it's going to do its thing, regardless.

On one side of the ring, we have the Christian fundamentalists, waving their banners of faith and proclaiming that Jesus will swoop in and save us all from suffering. Meanwhile, the New Atheists are flexing their intellectual muscles, arguing that science and technology are the keys to unlocking a suffering-free future.

The New Atheists, with their groupie lineup of Hitchens, Harris, Dawkins, Stenger, Dennett, and Coyne, are like a band of merry skeptics on a mission to take down religion, especially the big three: Christianity, Judaism, and Islam. They are out to prove that God is just a figment of our collective imagination and that most of what's written in those ancient scriptures is about as reliable as a fortune cookie.

In their eyes, science is the dazzling symbol of truth in a world filled with superstition and fairy tales.

Both theists and new atheists may have got it all wrong when it comes to God and religion. They are too busy pointing fingers and taking scriptures literally. The real issue here is our pesky human nature - full of greed and selfishness which are coded in our genes and show up as behaviors from the unconscious mind. But we have the power to control these behaviors through conscious modifications.

Religion is more about politics, economics, culture, and community than about God. I have experienced internal politics firsthand in the management of many Hindu temples in India, Canada, and the USA. I am sure the same must be true for churches, mosques, and synagogues around the globe.

I firmly believe that the root of all evil (and good) lies in the 'self', the 'Ego-I'. We walk through the details in the next chapter.

I share my views on why both new atheists and theists are most likely way off-beam when it comes to God, religion, and science. Spoiler alert: science and religion are like apples and oranges - they just do not mix. They are different and answer different nature of questions. I introduce a fresh viewpoint on the concept of the "universe" and the "Creator God" that may leave you thinking. In this innovative approach, traditional arguments (as shared in Chapter 2) to prove the existence of God like the Cosmological argument, Intelligent Design, Anthropic Principle, and Fine Tuning will become outmoded. By redefining the universe and its creator, I aim to bridge the gap between theists and atheists.

Chapter 6

What is the Verdict about God's Existence?

In the previous chapters, I presented both perspectives: theists' arguments affirming their belief in God's existence and the value of religion in society, as well as atheists' counterarguments asserting that there is no such God and that religion is not only unnecessary but potentially harmful. Many atheists profess that religion has been the impetus for numerous conflicts and wars throughout history. There is a common belief among some, particularly theists, that science and religion can function in sync. They suggest that both disciplines provide meaningful perspectives on the mysteries of life and the universe, ultimately alleviating our suffering. Furthermore, they insist that while science may clear up the complexities of the physical world; it falls short when it comes to addressing moral questions—a task at which religion supposedly excels.

There is a common misconception among some, particularly new atheists, that science and religion cannot share space. Scientific skeptics argue that religion is incapable of addressing questions related to the physical world. However, spiritual thinkers believe that the true issue lies not with God or religion, but with the inherent flaws of human nature - namely, greed and selfishness. They insist that these traits must be acknowledged and managed through behavioral modifications.

To add to this, there are philosophers who propose that if the concept of theism were eradicated, atheism would naturally become obsolete. They suggest that theism can be eradicated through strategic training and education.

In this chapter, I share my viewpoint on why science and religion are fundamentally incompatible. What's more, I bring forth a concept of God that outshines religious and scientific confines. This inclusive understanding of God aims to ring true with people from all backgrounds — including theists of various religions, atheists, agnostics, the Nones (individuals who do not identify with any organized religion or religious affiliation), the spiritual-but-not-religious (SBNR), scientists, and others.

Science And Religion are Different

In my opinion, science and religion are different and should be kept separate. Each has its domain and should not put its feet on another's toes. It's like having two neighbors who respect each other's boundaries. People should follow the concept of NOMA (Non-Overlapping Magisteria) to manage the complexities of these two spheres.

Science may be able to explain the intricacies of the physical world, but when it comes to the big questions about life, the Universe, and everything in between, it falls short. Questions about the purpose of life, the existence of a higher power, heaven and hell, and what happens after we shuffle off this mortal coil are not easily answered by test tubes and microscopes.

While physics, chemistry, and biology are great at explaining the how and the what, they tussle with the why. The mysteries of happiness, empathy, love, suffering, good, bad, evil, grace, death, purpose, gratitude, beauty, forgiveness, compassion, existence, and all the other good stuff that makes life worth living are beyond the reach of scientific inquiry. Science may be morally neutral, but that does not mean it has all the answers.

To some, these questions may seem irrelevant in the macro framework of the cosmos. But for many, they are basic to understanding who we are and why we are here. Science does not study 'self'.

Science is a cold, hard truth-teller. It does not give a hoot about your feelings, whether you are as happy as a clam or as sorry as a dog with no bone. When tragedy strikes, like learning about a spouse's death in a car crash, science is there to inspect the physical reason for the accident. It can break down the whole shebang and explain exactly how one's better half met his or her untimely demise. But all the scientific jibber-jabber in the world will not heal the heartache her family is going through.

It's kind of like your employer handing you a pink slip the day after a tornado turned your house into a pile of toothpicks. The management could not care less about your personal woes, they are just focused on the almighty dollar. Science is all about the facts, the figures and the laws of physics. It's not in the business of handing out tissues for your tears.

Religion just cannot quite keep up with the speedy world of physics and medicine. While physics can explain how electrons do their little dance in an atom, and medicine can tell us all about how the unruly COVID-19 virus plagues our bodies, religion is left deep in thought.

Sure, religions have their unique takes on the universe - like Hinduism's belief in the eternal steady state nature of things or Christianity's firm stance on a 6000-year-old universe - but there is not a vast array of hard evidence to back up these claims.

Take, for example, the Hindu belief that our bodies are made up of earth, water, fire, sky, and air.

"Ath (Kshiti), Jal, Pawak, Gagan, Sameera; Panch Tatva Yeh Bana Sareera"

"Earth, Water, Fire, Sky, and Air;

These five elements form the body."

Well, science comes crashing in with its 118 elements and says, "Hold my test tube." Turns out, we are a bit more complex than just five elements.

While we were all taught there are seven colors in a rainbow, science giggles and says, "Oh, sweetie, there are billions of colors your eyes cannot even see."

Atheist philosopher, Alex Rosenberg, in his book, 'The Atheist's Guide to Reality', (2012), claims that reality can only be known by science and his answers to life's deeper questions are negative- no God, no purpose, and no meaning of life and universe, and there is no moral difference between good and bad or right and wrong.

Hedges claims:

"Human beings prefer hope, even absurd hope, to Truth. It makes life to bear." (Page 42, Hedges)

In his Ph.D. thesis, Harris explained that science can provide an objective foundation for human ethics, with the primary goal being to reinforce the "well-being" of conscious beings. However, I believe that the concept of "well-being" is subjective and influenced by various cultural, political, economic, and social factors.

Nature of God

Well, after sitting through countless debates, I still have not got a straight answer to my question: does God exist? This has been my continuing quest, my childhood dream - to find out the truth about God. Theoretical arguments and debates just are not cutting it for me. Theists believe, atheists do not, and agnostics are still sitting on the fence, unsure of which side to pick. But some of us agnostics are out here on a mission for the truth, the whole truth, and nothing but the truth.

To me, hitting up temples, churches, mosques, synagogues, Gurudwaras, and Buddhist monasteries, and browsing scriptures should be the first step in our research for enlightenment. These places should not be the final destination, but rather the kick-off point for our spiritual course. As Chris Hedges so eloquently put it, "God is a search - a way to frame the question."

No one has seen God or heard Him. Science and religion, theists and atheists - none of them can definitively prove or disprove His existence. Before we can confidently say whether God is real, we need to nail down the specifics of His nature. And no one can prove that God was out here in human form, pulling cosmic rabbits out of hats.

Both theists and atheists are wide of the mark when it comes to understanding God. Theists are too busy trying to take scriptures at face value, while atheists are on a mission to counter anything that does not align with their scientific beliefs. But here is the kicker - scriptures were penned by humans, so they are not the end-all, be-all truth about God. He did not ghostwrite the scriptures, friends.

I am enthused to present a fresh perspective on the nature of God and the creation of the universe. My idea is sure to strike a chord with both scientific and religious beliefs, offering a coordinated and logical explanation.

The Physical Universe Exists Eternally - A Creator God is Not Needed

If we cannot prove the existence of a creator God, it's pretty safe to say that the physical universe was not created by anyone. We know the physical universe is real because we experience it every day, so for all intents and purposes, it's here to stay forever. Humans did not draw up this external physical universe - we are just along for the ride. Actually, no one in this physical universe has ever created anything from scratch (nothing). We are all just master recyclers, taking one thing and remodeling it into something new.

Back in 1948, some smart physicists figured out that the external physical universe is not just chilling in a steady state but is rather dynamically cyclical. The universe is currently in expansion mode post-Big Bang, which went down about 13.4 billion years ago. But that's just one stop on the universe's never-ending cycle. After this expansion work, we might see a little shrinkage, a big crunch, and then boom - a brand new Big Bang to kick off another round of expansion. It's like the universe's version of an eternal story but with way more cosmic explosions. Some physicists are exploring this idea of an eternal cyclical universe to best explain observed data (Chap 1, Note 2).

If such a physical universe is assumed, it solves the perennial problem of the need for a creator God. It's like a plot twist that would make Abrahamic religions like Islam, Judaism, and Christianity do a double-take. These religions have always believed that God created the universe with a Teleological purpose, meaning everything is connected to God in the end.

But Eastern religions like Hinduism have been chilling in their steady-state eternal universe, unfazed by this revelation. Then there are Buddhism and Jainism, which never got into the whole God and creation of the universe thing, anyway.

So, in the broader context, whether there's a God who created the physical universe or not, it does not matter. We cannot confirm it either way, so why lose sleep over it? If we assume that the external physical universe is eternally there, then a creator and maintainer God will not be needed.

Two Separate Universes - Two Separate Realities (External and Internal)

What sets living creatures apart from non-living objects like stones? Well, living creatures have the ability to perceive the world around them through sense organs and the brain, giving meaning to their surroundings that is vital for their survival and reproduction. Humans take it a step further by being aware of this perception, making us quite the unique bunch.

Now, let's talk about reality. Scientists and atheists are all about the physical universe, while theists bring a non-material aspect into the mix, claiming it controls the physical universe. It's like an astral warfare of beliefs!

Both scientists and theists are wrong here. I assert that there are two independent realities- two independent worlds. There's the physical world out there, and then there's the inner world we create within ourselves using our trusty sense organs and the brain. Our inner world is our reality, unique to each of us. It's like we are all living in our little universes within the big one. Our inner world is the only world that we can know exists for us. The external physical world does not matter to us.

I am not saying the external physical universe is just a figment of our imagination like some idealists might suggest. The external world is always there, whether we are looking at it or not. It's our inner world that springs to life when we experience it, disappearing when we do not. Our inner world is where the wonder begins, where everything is more useful and important to us.

In the enormous expanse of the physical universe, physical objects dutifully adhere to the laws of Physics that have been discovered by scientists. These laws are the guiding light, illuminating the mysteries of the physical world. However, when it comes to the domain of virtual objects within our inner world, they are free from the constraints of these physical laws.

Our Virtual Inner Reality is where the alchemy takes place. It is the reality that truly matters to us, as it is through this internal world that we perceive and interact with the external physical reality. Our sense organs and brain act as the bridge between these two worlds, allowing us to handle the complexities of existence.

Living creatures, in their infinite wisdom, are the true creators of their perceived world. They hold the power to shape and mold their internal reality, crafting a world that is uniquely their own. Therefore, they are the Gods of their internal world, wielding the power to create and destroy with a mere thought.

In the upcoming sections and the next chapter, we will investigate the subtle nuances of this internal world, seeking the extensive impact it has on our perception of reality.

Objective and Subjective Universes

Observing phenomena in the external physical universe is like watching a movie - everyone sees the same thing, no matter who's in the audience. We all follow the same script, using mechanical tools to keep things consistent. It's like a well-greased machine, churning out objective data for all to see.

Compared to objective physical observation, we create and experience our inner world subjectively. For example, we can measure objectively the exact temperature of water with a thermometer. However, if we ask the same question from different people, we will get different responses from different people – cold, mild, too hot, very hot, very cold, blustery and so on. These answers are not the same for everyone, but the answer by scientific method is the same. The answers by people are individual subjective feelings of the temperature. No one can deny these responses.

The distinction between science and religion is crystal clear. Science is all about objectivity, while religion is more personal and subjective. They are like parallel lines, close but never touching - no overlap, no compatibility. It's like trying to fuse hot and cold in one space - just does not work. So, let's keep them in their separate lanes, shall we? Let's not step on each other's toes. It is better to follow NOMA.

The main question that should concern us then would be: How does our inner world come to be? Who's pulling the strings in there? The answer lies in the perennial question of 'Who am I or self?' Let's take the wraps off to this question in Chapter 8. Our inner world is virtual as I explain in the next chapter.

For now, let's bring up why theories of Physics cannot be applied to the Virtual Inner World. Let me further illustrate how the Virtual Inner World is created and describe its properties and theories that work for the Virtual Inner World.

Physics Theories Cannot be Applied to the Virtual Inner World

One of the biggest issues we face is the tendency for people to mix up the rules of the physical world with those of the virtual world, and vice versa. It's like trying to use a fork to eat soup - it just does not work. Take, for example, the idea that Consciousness is necessary for Quantum Mechanics to function and that Quantum Mechanics can somehow explain Consciousness. These claims are about as accurate as a blindfolded archer trying to hit a target.

Despite the lack of evidence, many authors love to reference these ideas to support their arguments about the soul, religion, God, miracles, spirituality, and consciousness. It's like they are into an intellectual hopscotch, jumping from one theory to the next.

Every time a new Physics theory pops up to explain something in the physical world, there's always a group of people who try to force it to explain the mysteries of the mind, God, Soul, Consciousness, miracles, and religion. It's like trying to impose a mismatched solution. From Schrodinger's Cat to Hologram, EPR, String Theory, Entanglement Theory, Dark matter, dark energy, Double Slit experiment, multi-Verse to the latest craze in Quantum Mechanics, they just cannot resist the urge to make everything fit into one neat little box.

But there is not just one reality that needs explaining. There are two: the external physical reality and the Virtual Inner Reality. And guess what? They each require their own set of rules and theories to make sense of them. It's like trying to steer a ship in a sea of options - you are just going to end up lost and confused.

Numerous theology authors attempt to tackle the enigmatic field of Physics by studying subjects like Quantum Mechanics (QM), String theory, Entanglement theory, and Dark matter to explain religion, God, miracles, mind, and consciousness. It is like trying to explain one complex phenomenon with another complex theory. It cannot be understood easily by ordinary readers. These authors assume that their explanation of religion and God will be more credible by using not easily understandable complex Physics theories.

Many authors use the Double-Slit Experiment of QM to give the impression to readers that consciousness is required even for determining the location of a particle, which is not true. Only a mechanical detector is needed for the detection of the particle. Conscious observation of the detected particle by a human is not needed for the detection or collapse of probability waveform. This fact has been mis-informed by many theology authors to show the importance of Consciousness for QM or that QM requires Consciousness to operate. It's like claiming a fire never happened just because you did not witness it - it still blazed on in the physical arena, regardless of your awareness.

The EPR theory, also known as the Einstein-Podolsky-Rosen Paradox, has been used by some to illustrate the miraculous, powerful, and divine existence of God. However, three brilliant Physicists - John Clauser, Alain Aspect, and Anton Zeilinger - have since demystified this theory and shared the 2022 Nobel Prize in Physics for their efforts (Note 1).

Theology authors often use the example of dark matter to illustrate the compatibility between science and religion, likening its invisibility but observable effects to the unseen yet omnipresent nature of God. It's a baked metaphor, but let's not get carried away. It does not reflect any compatibility between science and religion.

The Theory of Relativity cannot be practically applied to slow-moving objects and at lower heights, but some authors say things like jogging will make you live longer or your hair age more than your feet due to feet being closer to earth's gravity (Note 2).

Just as the laws of quantum mechanics govern the behavior of tiny particles like electrons and protons, they do not cut the mustard when it comes to dealing with big things like planets, apples, stones, livers, and neurons (brain cells) - let alone the complexities of the mind, God, religion, and Consciousness. These things are just too big and complicated for quantum mechanics to handle. It's like trying to fit the unfittable.

But let us give credit where credit is due - quantum mechanics is the bee's knees when it comes to understanding the nitty-gritty of the physical world. No arguments there. But can it tell us how to whip up a delicious meal, score a winning goal on the football field, or design a killer outfit? Nope, not a chance. And as for matters of the heart - why we love what we love, why we feel what we feel - quantum mechanics is as clueless as a goldfish in a bowl.

So, can quantum mechanics help judges dish out the appropriate punishment for society's wrongdoers, or determine whether something is good or bad, sweet or sour, pleasant or unpleasant? Can it reveal the secrets of happiness, empathy, forgiveness, compassion, love, beauty, suffering, good, bad, evil, presence, grace, hope, gratitude, purpose, and the enigma of existence itself? Can it show us how to ease shoulder pain and find true happiness? The answer to all these questions is a resounding 'Nope'. Quantum mechanics may be a ninja in the world of physics, but when it comes to the complexities of life, it's like a stranger in a strange land.

Physical theories, such as Quantum Mechanics, are like a strict bouncer at a club - they only apply to objects in the external physical world. Sorry, but they will not let you in if you are a virtual object trying to sneak into our virtual world. Physics theories draw the line at human nature, God, religion, mind, and consciousness. It's like trying to use a metal detector on a ghost - it just does not work.

Once we reach the function of the physical neuron level, physics theories throw up their hands and say, "Sorry, folks, we're out of our depth here." It's like trying to explain a magic trick with science - sometimes you just need a new explanation. This reminds me of the adage "Where Physics stops, Metaphysics starts."

I discuss in the next chapter that "Virtual objects" are represented by neurons, which are physical media. The virtual content represented by neurons (physical media) does not depend upon physical media at all. Virtual contents are independent of physical media.

How Virtual Inner World is Created

Let me paint you a picture of how we fabricate our inner world and experience the external physical realm through our senses and brain. Picture this: you are gazing at a majestic tree, and as light rays bounce off its leaves and into your eyes, your brain goes to work. It extracts data on the tree's height, width, branches, shape, and color, and voila! A tree is born in your mind's eye. But hold up - it's not the exact same tree that's standing outside.

Our inner world is not just a snapshot from a camera - it's a whole new creation, fresh from the data we collect. I mean, sure, the tree exists out there in the physical world, even when we are not looking at it. But in our inner reality, it's all about what our senses tell us. If you are not looking at it, that tree might as well be a figment of your imagination.

And it's not just trees - it's everything. From the taste of ice cream to the smell of flowers, we all experience things in our unique way. That pain in your shoulder? Totally different from the pain in someone else's shoulder. We are like little reality creators, each forming our own version of the world around us.

So, when you are savoring that ice cream or inhaling the aroma of coffee, remember: your experience is yours and yours alone. In a way, we are all like mini gods, shaping our Virtual Inner Worlds. And to me, that's the real essence of what it means to be a creator. This, my friends, is the ultimate reality.

The concepts of life's meaning, happiness, morality, beauty, suffering, compassion, hope, love, courage, empathy, forgiveness, presence, gratitude, good, bad, sorrow, evil, feeling of Touch, taste, smell, vision and sound, death, grace, pain, greed, anger, intention, right, wrong, distraction, attention, purpose, mystery of existence, and all that jazz belong to our Virtual Inner World, not to the external physical realm. That's why science cannot give us the straight dope on these deep questions.

Let us review the finer points of our Virtual Inner World.

Virtual Inner World is Different for Each Person -

Even for the Same Person, it is Different at Different Times and Places

Now that we have established that we all have our little virtual worlds inside of us, it's like we are all walking around with our own personal Sims game going on. And just like in the Sims, our reality is constantly changing based on our mood, experiences, and what we had for lunch.

For example, imagine eating a piece of candy and then biting into an apple - that apple just will not taste as sweet as it would if you had not indulged in that sugary treat first. It's like your taste buds are playing tricks on you, creating a whole new flavor experience. And let's talk about epilepsy patients - they are like real-life spellbinders, producing more seizures in the comfort of their own homes than in a sterile hospital environment.

Moving on to the blood pressure - it's always on its best behavior at home, but as soon as you step foot in a hospital, it's like, "Time to show off and make a scene!"

And spiders? Well, to arachnophobes, those eight-legged creatures might as well be the size of a house, while the rest of us are like, "Eh, just a tiny little bug."

Then there is the undeniable fact that children are always the cutest to their mothers - it's like they have a special cuteness filter that only moms can see through.

Attention is Required to Create/Perceive Virtual Inner World

The second intriguing aspect of biological creatures, particularly humans, is that our inner world is shaped by what we choose to focus on in the external world. If we do not pay attention to something, it does not exist in our minds. For instance, imagine chowing down on some grub while binge-watching your favorite show. You will not even notice the taste of the food, let alone if it's overly salty, because your attention is elsewhere. That's why we must stay present in the moment and avoid multitasking. Paying attention helps us remember things and is a central element in experiencing consciousness.

Let me share with you an incident from my time at the University of Saskatchewan in the frigid city of Saskatoon, Canada. Known as the second coldest place in North America after Alaska, Saskatoon is no joke when it comes to chilly temperatures. One day, I set off for class from my apartment, completely oblivious to the fact that it was a bone-chilling -20 degrees Celsius (-4 degrees Fahrenheit) outside. Lost in thought, I had forgotten to bundle up in my trusty parka. Strangely enough, I did not even feel the cold until a friend pointed out my oversight. Suddenly, the frosty air fell on me like a heavyweight, and I sprinted back to my apartment to grab my parka.

This concept applies to all forms of perception and experience. When you look at a painting, there are countless details to take in. You might miss something on your first glance, but upon revisiting, new elements may catch your eye. It's like a treasure hunt for artistic nuances! Do not take me wrong. You cannot create a mouse anywhere you like in the painting just by looking at the painting. You will need a physical paintbrush and paint to create a mouse on the painting.

Pain works in a similar tricky manner. If you ignore the throbbing ache of a cut in your hand, it's almost as if the pain does not exist. Medical professionals have caught onto this trick and now use distraction techniques to help manage pain. So, when you are experiencing pain, try watching a movie or reading a good book - it might just work wonders!

And speaking of disappearing pain, have you ever noticed how a sudden crisis can make your discomfort fade away completely? Like when you are clutching your hand in agony, but then hear about your son's accident and suddenly, you are racing to the hospital without a care for your pain.

This phenomenon has some appealing implications, which we venture into further in Chapter 11.

We create and perceive something in the brain/mind only when we pay attention to an external object in the external world or an internal object from memory. If we do not pay attention to the object, we do not create the object. Paying attention to an object is like the detection of a particle in a double-slit experiment in Physics (QM) (Note 3). Only when a detector is placed at a certain location, then only the particle gets detected at that location. We create an object only when we pay attention to it. We create only those aspects of the object that we focus on. For example, if you do not pay attention to a small rabbit in a painting, there will not be a rabbit in your virtual painting that you will have created consciously in your brain/mind.

Optical illusions work similarly. Examples include the Necker cube, duck and rabbit, and vase and face (Note 4) (Figure 1). You pay attention to only one aspect of the figure. In Figure 1A, you pay attention to one aspect of the cube. In Figure 1B, you see only faces or a vase. In Figure 1C, you see only a duck or rabbit.

Figure 1: Optical Illusions

Figure 1A: Necker Cube

Figure 1B: Face and Vase

Figure 1C: Duck and Rabbit

The presence of an object is contingent upon our focus, much like how the presence of a particle at a specific location relies on the placement of a detector. I have detailed this concept in my upcoming book, 'Physical Body-Virtual Soul'.

Let me make it clear that I am simply using the detection example from Quantum Mechanics to illustrate a metaphorical similarity, rather than suggesting that Quantum Mechanics directly influences our ability to pay attention and perceive things. So, rest assured, I am not trying to drag QM into the spotlight here!

Virtual Inner World is Not Linear

The third interesting aspect of biological systems is that our perception of the Virtual Inner World does not follow a straight line, but rather an 'S-curve' pattern. Picture this: as the leaves start to fall and winter creeps in, we shiver and complain about the cold. But as the temperature continues to drop, we somehow manage to adapt and get used to the chill. The same goes for our friends in scorching hot places like India, where the mercury can soar up to a blistering 120 degrees during the summer months. It's stupefying to those of us who are used to more temperate climates and how they survive without constant air conditioning. Going from 100 degrees to 120 degrees Fahrenheit does not just feel a little hotter – it is an entirely distinct experience compared to the jump from 70 to 90 degrees Fahrenheit. Our bodies are truly remarkable in their ability to adjust to extreme temperatures, don't you think?

Just like how getting hurt multiple times, in the same way, hurts less each time, eating candy one after the other becomes less sweet with each piece. This phenomenon is known as neural or sensory adaptation, and it has some interesting consequences that we walk through in Chapter 12.

In Economics, a similar concept is at play, known as the 'Law of Diminishing Return' (Note 5). If buying one shirt brings you a certain level of joy, each subsequent shirt will not bring the same amount of happiness. It's like the amusement is on a downward spiral. And if the first loaf of bread satisfies you with a certain number of units, each additional loaf will bring diminishing units of satisfaction.

Virtual Inner World is Relative, and Subjective

The fourth feature of biological systems is that our experiences of the Virtual Inner World are subjective, while our observations of the external physical world are objective. It's like comparing apples to candy - after indulging in some sweets, that apple just will not taste as sweet. Goodness, sweetness, and even pain are all relative terms. There's no single measure that works for everyone. Just like how your taste buds might change their mind about what's sweet, salty, tangy, or sour depending on the day, time, or place. It's all relative!

Have you ever gone to a concert with a friend and felt totally different about it? That is because everyone's perception is unique!

When you and your friend attend the same concert, you both experience the same external reality. However, your internal experiences of the event are subjective. This means that they are shaped by your individual preferences, past experiences, and emotional states.

Just like how your taste buds can change over time, your perception of events can also shift. This means that what you think and feel about a situation can be influenced by your mental and emotional state at that moment.

Because of these differences in perception, every experience is personal and relative. What may be exciting and exhilarating for you could be draining and frustrating for someone else. It's all about how we interpret and react to the world around us!

Virtual Inner World is Flexible and can be Modified by Virtual Beliefs and Thoughts

The fifth feature of biological systems, particularly in humans, is the power of our virtual beliefs and thoughts to shape our inner world and even influence physical changes in our bodies through the brain. In simpler terms, what we think and believe can alter our brains and bodies. It's like a mind-body makeover!

In this virtual world we create, we have the freedom to assign any meaning to objects. Pain, temperature, taste, texture, color, smell, sound - you name it, you can tweak it to your liking. There are no strict rules here, making our mental world as malleable as software. Unlike physical structures that are stubbornly resistant to change, our virtual creations can easily be modified.

These virtual changes can have real effects on our physical bodies and brains. It's a reality-shifting concept with some serious implications, which we look into in Chapter 12.

This concept is the basis of faith healing and other religious effects, such as the power of prayer and its impact on health, which act as the bedrock of many belief systems. This universal feature is what gives religion its mystical allure, as it operates on a subjective and ever-changing level, unlike the concrete laws of science. This inherent subjectivity is what sets religion apart from the objective world of scientific inquiry, making it a source of contention for many in the scientific community.

The obscure nature of religion, with its ability to influence the human body, brain, and mind, is a perplexing phenomenon that even the most skeptical of minds endeavor to understand. While some New Atheists may argue that religion and prayer offer no tangible benefits, studies presented by Koenig in his book 'Spirituality in Patient Care: Why, How, When, and Why, 2nd ed' (2008) suggest otherwise, pointing out the positive impact of prayer and religious practices on overall well-being.

Positive thinking is like an enchanted potion that brings hope and happiness to those who believe in its power. Conversely, negative thoughts are a threat to our health and well-being. So, why waste time obsessing over the idea that there's no higher power, no purpose to life and that we are all just cosmic accidents?

Studies have shown that religious people tend to live longer (Ward), probably because they have that extra dose of hope and positivity in their back pocket. It's like when you tell someone they are doing a great job - it motivates them to keep up the good work.

Now, I am not saying you need to join a cult or start praying five times a day to have a sunny outlook on life. But if religion helps some people find that inner peace and positivity, why not accept it? After all, a little faith never hurt anyone.

Many people tell me that they had a different experience when they visited Jerusalem (a religious place for Christians), or Mecca (a religious place for Muslims), or many religious temples for Hindus in India like the Badrinath Temple in Northern India or the Rameshwaram Temple in Southern India or the Jagannath Temple in Puri in Orissa state in Eastern India. People tell me that their pains were gone when they visited these religious places. How can I say that they are wrong even if I did not have any such experiences at these places when I visited?

Scores of Indian people have shared with me that their shoulder pain miraculously disappeared during their recent visits to their homes in India. Similarly, many people have attested that their physical ailments vanished after visiting sacred places like Mecca or Jerusalem. Who are we to doubt their experiences? Even more intriguing is the fact that people's stress levels, blood pressure, and heart rates decrease when they receive guidance from their religious leaders or clergy to trust in a higher power to resolve their worries.

As children, we were advised to recite a prayer to Hanuman, the God of power, when venturing down a dark and lonely road at night to ward off any fears of running into ghosts or witches. Surprisingly, it did provide a sense of comfort and peace of mind, regardless of whether it was rational or not, and whether there were any supernatural beings skulking about.

Countless individuals take the stage to express their gratitude to the Indian comedian, Kapil Sharma, for bringing joy and temporary relief from their ailments through his shows. It's truly remarkable how entertainment can provide a much-needed escape from pain. I am certain that many can relate to the feeling of finding solace in their favorite shows, games, places, or conversations with loved ones. After all, doing what brings us joy is the best medicine for the soul!

The only world that truly intrigues us is the one within ourselves, not the external physical universe. Therefore, the creator responsible for shaping our inner world is the real God in my eyes. As for the creator of the external physical world, well, they do not matter as long as the physical universe exists. Let us just assume that the external physical universe has been around forever, rendering a creator God unnecessary. No need to get into a heated debate about proving God's existence.

The external physical world is governed by physical laws that do not apply to our inner world. In our inner world, the meaning we assign to virtual objects is flexible and does not adhere to any strict rules - it's all subjective. Our virtual beliefs and thoughts have a direct impact on our inner world, which in turn can lead to physical changes in our bodies and brains. This is the foundation for many religious and spiritual experiences rooted in virtual faith.

In the next chapter, let us interpret what "virtual" means in this context and seek how virtual thoughts, faith, and beliefs shape our inner world.

Chapter 7

Virtual Inner Universe

In the previous chapter, I touched on the existence of both an external universe and an inner experiential universe that we conjure up with the help of our sense organs and brain. The external universe is all about being physical, objective, and out there for everyone to see, while the inner universe is more of a virtual, subjective, and private affair. Some even call it the mental universe.

Now, in this chapter, I interpret what this virtual inner universe is all about and how it is created. Just a heads up, this virtual universe is rooted in the physical brain. Our inner universe is like a canvas that we can paint with our virtual thoughts, beliefs, and faiths - all of which originate in the physical brain.

COVID-19 Spurred the Use of Virtual Technology

It's quite a coincidence that a concept I have been weighing in the balance for years has suddenly become all the rage since the coronavirus pandemic. The term 'virtual' has taken center stage alongside COVID-19, masks, sanitizers, and Zoom. Children were attending school virtually, colleges were operating virtually, and meetings were being held virtually. Even chemistry and physics experiments were being conducted virtually by students. Those lucky enough to work from home have been doing so virtually for almost 5 years now, since March 2020. Physicians have been seeing their patients virtually — this is known as Telemedicine.

Nowadays, people prefer video meetings and conferences virtually through platforms like Zoom, Microsoft Teams, and other similar technologies. With the help of Virtual Reality (VR) goggles, users can now get a thrill out of 3D movies and video games, taking entertainment to a whole new level. Pilots are also benefiting from flight simulators, which provide realistic training experiences without ever leaving the ground.

During the pandemic, people could virtually tour apartments and homes they were considering for lease or purchase. Who needs to physically visit a property when you can get the wall-to-wall view from the comfort of your couch?

What was considered science fiction 40 years ago is now a reality - virtual reality. People can shop virtually, but there is one major roadblock when it comes to buying clothes online: the inability to feel the fabric and gauge the quality. However, efforts are underway to develop technology that would allow you to wear a pair of gloves and experience the same tactile sensations in a virtual environment as you would in person. This same technology could potentially be applied to other sensory experiences as well.

In addition to the futuristic concepts, virtual reality has integrated into our day-to-day living. We spend more time online than we do brushing our teeth. Seriously, virtual no longer just refers to that strange cousin who lives in a different country. It is now a part of our daily routine; from the moment we wake up to the minute we hit the hay. Whether we are checking emails, attending virtual meetings, binge-watching shows, or mindlessly scrolling through social media, the digital world is our constant companion. We work, socialize, shop, learn, and unwind virtually, all in the span of a single day. It's not just a tool we use occasionally, but a vital aspect of our everyday existence.

Below, I have tried to explain the term 'Virtual' in a broader context beyond its pandemic usage.

Virtual Objects, Functions and Phenomena

When something is recreated using different materials than the original, it's known as a simulation or representation of the original object, function, or phenomenon.

And when you observe the original, it's simply called virtual. So, in other words, virtual is the high-tech way of saying "not physically there."

Anything that we observe and experience are all virtual as they are represented in the brain.

Even though the virtual world is not physically real, it can still make us feel things just like the real world does. It's like a magic trick that blurs the line between what's real and what's not. This makes the virtual world powerful because it can make us feel connected to things that are not physically there.

Stories and Movies are Virtual

Have you ever thought about the virtual nature of stories and movies? When you crack open a fiction book, you are transported to a world created by words on paper, plastic, cloth, or even an eBook. It's like a whole new world, but with fewer rabbits and more imagination. Next is a movie on a TV or a screen in a theater - they are like a fancy illusion, making us believe we are witnessing real-life events when, in reality, it's all smoke and mirrors.

I used to have a fine tooth for movies on TV, but now I see through their tricks. The actors may be giving it their all, but at the end of the day, it's all make-believe. Those fight scenes and murders. Just a bunch of talented artists pretending to be daredevils. It's like watching an intense show of pretense. So, it's all a simulation, a representation of reality.

Cartoon characters, whether they are in a book or on a TV screen, are like virtual puppets dancing on the strings of their creator's imagination. The author holds all the power to make them do the most outrageous things, like leaping across the Atlantic Ocean with a single bound. These characters are rebels against the laws of physics, free to defy gravity and logic at every turn.

By contrast, the paper book or TV screen that houses these characters is bound by the rules of the physical world. The book can be printed on any material imaginable, from paper to plastic to wood to cloth, or even exist solely in the digital domain as an eBook.

This phenomenon is known in the fields of Philosophy and Psychology as Multiple Realizability (MR). It's the frilly term for the unique ability of virtual objects, like our beloved cartoon characters, to exist in multiple forms and transcend the limitations of the physical world.

Financial Digital Transactions are Virtual

Money transactions in the tech age are as easy as a few clicks on a computer. No need to break a sweat or even touch physical cash - it's all virtual! With the power of technology, I can move millions of dollars from one account to another across the globe in seconds. Debit and credit cards have been around for ages, making way for virtual financial tools like Venmo, PayTM, Paypal, and Zelle to take the world by storm. We can transfer money among friends and relatives using apps on mobile phones.

Even good old checks have gone virtual! Just scribble down any amount you desire on a piece of paper, and bingo- it's as good as gold. Whether it's a dollar or a million bucks, the possibilities are endless in the world of virtual financial instruments.

In times past, people used to rely on the Barter system to trade goods instead of using boring old cash. Imagine swapping your wheat for someone else's rice - no money involved, just good old-fashioned exchange.

Nowadays, we have virtual currencies like Bitcoin rocking the boat. It's like Monopoly money but for real life. With Bitcoin, you can make peer-to-peer transactions online without needing a bank to hold your hand. No more Venmo, Paypal, or Zelle - just you, your computer, and some digital dough flying through cyberspace. It's like something out of a fairy tale but with more zeros and ones.

Computer Simulations are Virtual

A flight simulation is like virtual wings in the sky! This high-tech experience allows you to feel like a real pilot without ever leaving the ground. All the instruments you see are virtual, but they are so realistic you will swear you are actually flying. They observe/measure/represent some physical parameters of physical objects like wind speed, air temperature, air pressure, and so on.

Even gravity takes center stage, but it's all just a computer trick. The computer can simulate pretty much anything (virtual functions), from the force of gravity to the way your plane handles in different weather conditions. The virtual simulated gravity can pull only simulated objects and not real physical objects though.

Then Virtual Reality (VR) is like treading into a whole new space. With those electronic circuits (physical media), you can throw yourself into mesmerizing 3D virtual images that will leave you feeling like you are living in the future.

Objects in Our Inner Universe are Virtual

It's absorbing to think about how our brains create virtual representations of the world around us. Through the use of neurons as physical media, our brains can reproduce outside objects and phenomena. For example, our eyes translate outside objects into images on our retinas, while our ears convert outside sounds into air pressure on our eardrums. These representations are virtual realities too.

As I behold a delicate flower in my garden, my brain is hard at work, utilizing neurons to create a virtual representation of the physical beauty before me. These neurons and their electrochemical signals are like the brain's gardeners, cultivating a lush orchard of ideas of the outside world within the confines of my mind.

Therefore, the brain acts as a master interpreter, making sense of the external world and enabling us to react optimally for our survival. It's like a virtual reality headset, allowing us to handle the complexities of our environment with flair.

Ah, the allure of a red rose, the intoxicating scent of perfume, the indulgent taste of strawberry ice cream, the comforting touch of a fluffy cat, and the soothing sound of music - these are all examples of virtual phenomena that tickle our senses. In the world of Psychology and Philosophy, these sensory experiences are known as 'Qualia'. They are the secondary qualities that set apart the redness, fluffiness, sound, smell, and taste from the primary qualities of shapes and sizes.

Unlike primary qualities, experiences of secondary qualities cannot be neatly tucked away in our memory. Instead, we store representations of these experiences with labels like 'red' or 'fluffy'. It's easier for our brains to remember the word 'red' than the actual experience of redness. Understanding the distinction between the word 'red' and the experience of 'red' can be quite the mental workout for most people.

Our Body is Virtually Represented in the Brain

Our entire body is mirrored in the brain for sensory and motor functions. Every tiny detail of our body is thoroughly mapped out in the brain. So, when you wiggle your fingers, it's like watching a mini movie playing out in your brain. And when you stub your toe, the pain you feel is actually happening in the virtual representation of your toe in your brain - it's like a virtual reality experience gone wrong!

Virtual Time

We experience time virtually, in our unique way, while mechanical clocks measure it objectively. This 'virtual time' is independent of a clock 'physical time'. Clock time remains the same for everyone. The effects of motion and gravity of the Theory of Relativity are ignored here.

Imagine you are sitting in a long meeting, staring at the clock, waiting for the time to pass. The seconds seem to stretch endlessly, and each minute feels like an hour. Now, think about when you are having a good time with friends or immersed in a favorite activity — time flies by in the blink of an eye. This shows how our perception of time is not fixed but virtual and subjective.

Virtual Space

Just like that, when you are lost in a daydream, you can transport yourself to any corner of the universe, all while sitting at your desk or reclining on your bed. And when you are caught up in deep thoughts, you can completely lose track of where you are - your physical location becomes a distant memory. In a way, the space in your mind is just as virtual. Your real physical location can be tracked by longitude and latitude on Earth with a GPS.

The way we apprehend space is like a virtual reality game, where our subjective experiences of space do not match up with the cold, hard measurements taken by machines.

Virtual time and space are different from physically measured time and space. Both are real – one is virtually and subjectively real, and the other is physically and objectively real.

Pain is Virtual Too

Pain is also a virtual phenomenon that takes place not at the site of injury, but rather in the brain - a Central Nervous System (CNS) phenomenon. Take, for example, the case of someone who has had their leg amputated below the knee, yet still experiences pain in a leg that no longer exists. This is known as the phantom limb phenomenon, proving that pain is all in the mind (literally).

Different people can experience pain in such unique ways. One person may barely flinch at the prick of a thorn, while another may feel like they have been stabbed with a sword. There is a pain scale, for example, when it comes to getting a flu shot - one year it's a breeze, the next year it feels like a medieval torture device.

So, when you are feeling a little sore, just be aware that pain is a complex and mysterious experience that likes to play tricks on us. And at least we can blame it all on our brains, right?

Effect of Virtual Phenomena is Real

All financial transactions done through computers are virtually real. The same goes for transactions made with credit and debit cards. Then, as mentioned earlier, there is the virtual reality of using platforms like Zelle, Venmo, PayTM, and ApplePay. Money moves faster than ever in the virtual world!

I was blown away by a wise man's statement that has stuck with me ever since. He pointed out that the power of movies is so immense that they can evoke a range of emotions in people - from tears to laughter, happiness to sadness, and even anger towards a villain. It's interesting how viewers can be so deeply affected by something they know is not physically real, but merely a performance by actors (virtual phenomena) on screen. The impact of cinema is truly surprising, blurring the lines between reality and fiction for spectators. If a villain from a film were to stroll down the streets of India, my bet is that they would not exactly receive a warm welcome. In fact, they might just end up getting in a row with him- good old-fashioned street justice.

In a memorable TV interview, the renowned Indian actor Amitabh Bachchan posed a thought-provoking question: which is more real - the grief he portrayed for his acting mother in a movie or the sorrow he felt when his real mother passed away? One is tangible, the other is merely a portrayal.

Have you ever taken a moment to introspect whether the world we see is real, or just a figment of our imagination? It is an engaging concept, but the truth is, we have no choice but to trust in our virtual experiences. Our brains are the ultimate creators of our reality, shaping the world around us through our senses. So, in a way, the world as we know it exists solely within our minds.

Now, I am not suggesting that there's nothing beyond our perceptions. But without our brains to interpret the world for us, we would be nearly lost. Our brains are like the ultimate virtual reality machines, constantly constructing the world around us based on the information we receive.

Virtually Real vs. Physically Real

Simulating a physical phenomenon on a computer is virtually real. For example, you can simulate fire, gravity, and magnetism on a computer, but you will not feel the heat, weight, or pull in real life.

Physical media like books, screens, projectors, checks, debit and credit cards, Bitcoins, and neurons in the brain, as mentioned earlier, are all physical media (physically real). They exist in the tangible world. However, the stories, acting, money, and perceptions they represent are virtually real. They may not physically exist, but they have a very real impact on our lives.

Let us clear up a common misconception: the way our brains represent physical objects from the outside world is not some mystical, non-physical phenomenon. External objects are as real as it gets - they exist in a tangible, objective reality. For example, the food on your plate is real — it's a physical, tangible item that exists in the world.

However, the way our brains interpret and represent these objects is a different kettle of fish. Think of how your interpretation of that food might change depending on your mood, how hungry you are, or whether it's your favorite recipe or not. One day, it might look gut-appeasing, and the next, it could seem greasy and unappealing. This is because the brain creates its own virtual version of reality based on personal experiences, memories, and sensory inputs. So, do not be deceived - it's just our brain doing its thing. The only way for us to know the outside physical world is through virtual reality produced by the brain.

It is often said that the mind is non-physical, while the brain is physical. However, according to the laws of physics, there is no evidence of anything non-physical. Even energies such as heat, electromagnetic radiation from TV and radio antennas, microwave energy from cell phones and ovens, and sound wave energy are all tangible and measurable. These examples indicate that everything in the universe is ultimately physical, even if it may not always be visible to the naked eye.

I firmly believe that the most accurate way to describe the representation or simulation of any event or object is through the lens of **'virtual'** rather than non-physical. Therefore, it is more logical to define all mental phenomena within our inner world as **'virtual'**. Our minds are like the ultimate virtual reality simulator, constantly creating and processing information in ways that are beyond physical limitations.

Properties of Virtual Objects and Virtual Phenomena

Physical objects and phenomena are represented in virtual counterparts through simulation. Picture this: a physical book becomes a virtual story, complete with characters that come to life on your screen. These two entities may seem worlds apart, but they live in unison in physical media.

When it comes to bringing virtual objects to life on a physical medium, it takes a live agent to work wonders. That's right, a live agent (living organism) is behind the scenes, making the virtual world come alive before your very eyes.

Virtual Objects Do Not Follow Physio-Chemical Laws

Virtual objects operate in a dimension where the rules of physics take a coffee break. They do not bother with issues like conservation of mass, energy, or momentum. Laws of magnetism, gravity, and relativity? Please, those are so last season. Then there are thermodynamics and quantum mechanics - virtual objects laugh in response to such constraints.

In this virtual playground, the speed of light (3×10^{10} cm/second) is just an opinion, time and space are mere suggestions, and inertia is a foreign concept.

I can create simulations on the computer that are out of this world. From a Star Wars laser gun that shoots laser beams faster than the speed of light to a galaxy where planets defy the rules of gravity, I can bring these virtual entities to life. While these creations may not follow physical laws, they certainly make for some exciting experiments.

In addition to my cosmic creations, I can also simulate a full human digestive system using plastic model pieces. The plastic parts will adhere to all the physio-chemical rules, but the digestive system model is a whole different story. It does not have to follow any rules and can demonstrate how it digests all types of foods with ease.

Just as neurons in the brain are bound by the laws of physics, your neurons have a rebellious streak. They can dream up a sci-fi plot where a train bends the laws of physics. Imagine a train soaring through the sky at speeds surpassing the speed of light. Who needs physics when you have a barrier-defying imagination?

Virtual Objects Do Not Get Destroyed

Simulated or represented virtual objects do not get destroyed or die in the same sense as physical objects or media. Virtual objects simply cease to exist whenever physical media representing or simulating the objects gets destroyed or dies. I have explained this concept in Chapter 12, where I bring to the forefront the elusive nature of the soul.

Virtual Stocks can Take Any Value

At 3 PM on 12/21/21, a single share of Google (symbol= GOOGL) was priced at $2814 in the stock market. Meanwhile, a share of Berkshire Hathaway Inc. (Symbol = BRK. A) was valued at an enormous $433,789.38 at the same time. These shares may seem like virtual entities, but their value can fluctuate faster than you can say “stock market crash.”

Stock values are like a zigzag course - they can go up and down based on the tiniest rumor or news tidbit from the farthest corner of the globe. Some people even go as far as calling stocks and shares “fake money” because of their unpredictable nature.

Imagine having millions of shares of a company’s stock, only to see its value plummet to mere pennies in a matter of seconds due to some bad news. It’s a harsh reality of the stock market - one minute you are on top of the world, and the next, you are counting your losses.

Therefore, virtual assets, such as stocks, can fluctuate rapidly and unpredictably, depicting the fluid digital ecosystem, where values and realities can shift in the snipe of fingers.

Varied Perspectives of Objects in the Virtual Inner World

The interpretation of signals produced by neurons in the brain is subjective and varies depending on the individual’s state of mind. This adaptability is a result of the virtual nature of our inner world.

For instance, one person may find a candy to be incredibly sweet while another may not find it as appealing. Similarly, two people may react differently to the same music; one might find it relaxing while the other finds it annoying. The experience of stress is also subjective, as one person may feel weighed down by a deadline, while another remains calm under the same pressure. It's even possible for the same person to experience varying levels of pain in different situations.

Experiences also depend upon what you pay attention to. You do not feel cold if you are busy doing something else. You do not feel pain when you are watching an interesting movie.

Beauty Lies in the Eyes of Beholder

My friends used to gush about the beauty of snow when they first moved to Michigan, but now they curse it as they shovel their driveways every year. What happened to the love affair with the white stuff?

Virtual experiences are like a box of chocolates - subjective and full of surprises. Your thoughts, beliefs, faith, and attention all play a role in shaping your perception of things. Subjectivity happens due to the virtual nature of things in the inner world. I have shared plenty of examples of this in the previous chapter. Subjectivity is the reason that science cannot answer questions of religious faith and spirituality.

Components of the Virtualization Process

There are three components in a virtualization (simulation/representation) process: the subject or process being simulated, the medium in which the simulation takes place, and the active agent responsible for making it all happen. For example, an author virtually represents a story in a physical paper book where the author is an agent, the book is the medium, and characters and story are what is being virtually simulated/represented in the physical book by the agent (author).

For simulation, the agent or agency is like a living, breathing organism, while the medium of simulation or representation is a tangible object. This is like the powerhouse combo of the simulation world - one bringing life and the other bringing form.

Simulations on external physical media are always set up by us humans. We are the masterminds behind the machines and robots used for simulation. We hold the power to breathe life into virtual objects within the simulation, giving them purpose and meaning. The simulation agent, separate from the medium itself, allows anyone (public and objective) to observe and interact with the virtual world created. Just like how anyone can read a story in a book, or the amount written on a check, the external agent assigns value and power to the medium (check and book in the examples above).

However, when a representation agent is internal to a living organism, the meaning it represents can only be understood by that organism itself, internally and subjectively.

It's like an encrypted code that only the organism can decipher. For instance, a honeybee's perception of its environment is a mystery to everyone else. The meaning of chirping sounds heard by a bird that is made by another bird is only known to that bird privately and subjectively. No one else will understand it objectively.

Just before winter months in North America, birds migrate to South America to save themselves from the cold and then they come back to their hometown when summer comes. Recently, researchers have figured out that birds use Earth's magnetic field to figure out their directions.

While humans may study the patterns and try to understand how the bird perceives the world, the experience of that flight is encoded within the bird itself. It's like the bird has its secret map, much like an encrypted message only the bird can decipher. For instance, how the bird senses the magnetic fields and translates them into direction is something beyond human understanding. It is a private experience only the bird's internal processes can fully interpret subjectively.

This reminds me of another conventional example: paychecks. It's not about the type of paper or font you use - it's all about the amount, date, and signature. Just like in a story, it's not the print or paper that matters, but the characters and the story itself that make it memorable.

In the same way, the organic material of neurons and electrochemical voltages in the brain are not as central as understanding what those voltages signify. It's the living agent that gives meaning to the voltages, and that only the living agent knows.

Who is the operator behind all our virtual adventures? Who feels cold, hot, sweet, sour, tangy, happy, sad, and so on? Who savors the aroma of a brewing cup of coffee or the melody of a catchy tune? Who rejoices in the soft touch of a fluffy feline friend? It is believed that there exists a self, a mysterious 'I', that is responsible for these experiences. We will examine in more detail the concept of the self, but for now, let us just acknowledge that this self is merely a creation of our brain's neurons. I refer to this self as the 'Ego-I' or 'Empirical self' or simply 'self' with a lowercase 's', reserving the uppercase 'Self' for a different discussion in the upcoming chapter.

Chapter 8

Virtual Empirical Self (VES) Or 'self' or 'I'

Who is 'I'

I sit on my deck, which is one floor up, absorbing the sight of the lively flowers in my backyard garden. The backyard is totally private, surrounded by trees and lush greenery. In the next moment, the sweet sounds of chirping birds seize my notice. I cannot help but feel a sense of peace and tranquility. The month of July brings out the beauty of nature in my house with open space on three sides.

Slurping my morning tea, I find myself lost in thought as I type these pages on my laptop. A gentle shower catches the air and interrupts my peaceful moment, prompting me to retreat to the confines of my sunroom. But who is this 'I' experiencing all these sensory delights?

There must be someone in me, we call 'I': the observer, the seer, mover, enjoyer, feeler, listener, and thinker. There is a duality of subject and object - the seer and the greenery, the thinker and the thought, the taster and the taste of tea, the smeller and the scent of flowers, the listener and the chirping of birds.

'I' or 'self' in Western Philosophy

Various Western philosophers have diverse viewpoints on the concept of the 'self'. One notable perspective comes from French philosopher René Descartes, who famously stated "Cogito ergo sum" (I think, therefore I am), asserting that the existence of the self is undeniable. Descartes further stated, "I know that I exist", the question is, "What is this 'I' that I know?" (Note 1). This leads us to the curiosity-arousing question: where exactly is this elusive 'I' located?

Descartes brought up the point that there is a 'mind' in the brain. The concept of "I" is somehow connected to the mind, which is composed of different materials than the physical brain and body. But where exactly is this elusive 'I' or 'self' located in the brain? Hume argued that the 'I', or 'self' or 'soul' is simply a series of perceptions (1739), while James believed the 'self' is made up of unique movements in the head (1890). Bishop Berkeley saw the 'self' as a "thinking principle," (Page 185, 1975), and Dennett viewed the 'self' as nothing more than an abstraction (2007). Some, including Sam Harris, believe that the self is an illusion, as it cannot be found anywhere in the body and the brain, as he wrote in his book 'Waking UP' (Page 82, 2014).

The idea that the self is a homunculus in the brain who sees, listens, thinks, tastes, and smells was debunked quickly as it leads to an infinity absurdum meaning another homunculus will be needed to watch the first homunculus and so on up to infinity. Damasio in his 2012 book, 'Self Comes to Mind: Constructing the Conscious Brain', wrote (Page 8):

"There is indeed a Self, but it is a process, not a thing, and the process is present at all times when we are presumed to be conscious. We can consider Self from two vantage points. One is the vantage point of an observer appreciating a dynamic object- The dynamic object constituted by certain workings of minds, certain traits of behavior, and a certain history of life. The other vantage point is that of the self as knower, the process that gives a focus to our experiences and eventually lets us reflect on those experiences....... The self as knower is grounded in self as object."

Damasio claims: *"Conscious minds arise when a self-process is added on to a basic mind process."*

Harris and numerous scientists believe that the concept of 'self' is not a tangible entity, but rather a process. This is why it cannot be detected within the perimeters of the physical brain. Harris in 'End of Faith' writes below (p. 212, 2004):

*"The sense of self seems to be the product of the brain's representing its own acts of representation; its seeing of the world begets an image of one who sees. It is important to realize that this feeling – **being**, a sphere of experience- is not a necessary feature of consciousness. It is, after all,*

conceivable that a creature could form a representation of the world without forming a representation of ***itself*** *in the world. And, indeed, many spiritual practitioners claim to experience the world in just this way, perfectly shorn of self.*

A basic finding of neurophysiology lends credence to such claims. It is not so much what they ***are*** *but what they* ***do*** *that makes neurons see, hear, smell, taste, touch, think and feel. Like any other function, that emerges from the activity of the brain, the feeling of self is best thought of as a* ***process****. It is not very surprising, therefore that we can lose this feeling, because processes, by their very nature, can be interrupted."*

'I' or 'Self' in Various Religions

'Self' in Hinduism

According to Eastern religious philosophers, the 'I' is not just a mishmash of body parts like hands, feet, and stomach. No, no, they claim there is a little something extra in there - a soul! They even call this 'I' the 'Self' for good measure (Page 9, P. T. Raju, 1968). So, when you are feeling down about your liver or kidneys, just be mindful that there is more to you than meets the eye.

And let us talk about reincarnation. Hindus believe that each one of us has a Soul that takes rebirth from this life to the next until we get Moksha (Nirvana or Salvation) It is like a never-ceasing contest of tag, except instead of getting tagged, you get reborn. It is believed that our actions in this life determine our fate in the next. Some may come back as a wise and noble human, while others may find themselves reincarnated as a meek rat, a princely elephant, a peaceful cow, or even a graceful fish.

Advaita Vedanta asserts that there exists a singular ultimate reality known as Brahman, also referred to as Atman within every living being. In Vedanta, Atman is identified as the 'I', the 'Self', or the Soul with a capital 'S'.

To avoid confusion, I will use terms such as 'Ego-I', Jivatman (jiva-soul), jiva, and self to represent the empirical self (VES) with a lowercase 's', distinguishing it from the Atman or Soul. Let us keep it classy and clear, friends!

'Self' in Christianity, Judaism, and Islam

Christianity, Judaism, and Islam all share the belief in a distinct human soul separate from God. However, Islam takes it a step further by viewing the self as the sum of both soul and body. On the other hand, Christianity teaches that God is the creator of the universe and all living beings, with a special focus on humans.

In his book 'Immortal Diamond,' published in 2013, Richard Rohr has differentiated between the True Self and the False Self, drawing upon numerous references from the Bible, Genesis, and the teachings of Jesus. According to Rohr, the False Self is synonymous with the Ego, while the True Self represents the authentic essence of who you are - your soul. Rohr translates the crux of the True Self with the statement: "Your soul is who you are in God and who God is in you."

'Self' in Jainism

Mahavira, the 24th Jain saint known as a Tirthankara, made some propositions about the self. He referred to the self as a subtle body and used the term 'Jiva' to describe the soul or self, stating that it is a spiritual entity with consciousness at its core. To him, the 'Self' was more of an empirical concept. He defined the line between the true self and the empirical self, as well as between the Jiva (soul) and the 'I'. The 'I' he likened to the 'Atman' of the Upanishads, but not quite pure consciousness. Pure consciousness is more of an abstract concept in his eyes. It can get a bit confusing, though, as he believed the soul to be both eternal and non-eternal. According to Mahavira, moral progress could only occur if the soul was non-eternal and subject to change. He also believed that there are many different Jivas, each with their unique consciousness.

'Self' in Buddhism

Buddha refrained from answering this question if the 'self' exists or not. For him, removing the suffering and becoming happy were more important than knowing about the self. He declined to provide answers regarding the soul, self, 'I', or Jiva (Atta), opting instead to keep his thoughts to himself when directly asked by his disciples. Buddha made it clear that he did not wish to take a side on the matter, firmly believing in the concept of no-self (Anatta) and rejecting the notions of soul, self, or 'I'.

The concept of self for Buddha is an empirical self made of the mind, personality, intellect, and memory, all of which are constantly evolving. Similarly, the material world, body, sensation, and perception are also in a state of flux, lacking permanence. For Buddha, Nirvana stands as the only permanent entity.

On the question of 'Who experiences', Buddha would attribute this to the five senses and the mind. At times, he appears to draw parallels between the self and the Atman (Soul) of the Upanishads.

In his perspective, consciousness is like the Sunyata (Void) of self (egolessness), devoid of ego, but not devoid of content. It is filled with mental objects like perception and feeling. He believed that Atman is not everlasting and does not carry over into the next life; instead, it is consciousness that survives death. He also posited that consciousness is not eternal, but rather a continuous flow of evolving states. Upon achieving Nirvana, the cycle of rebirth is broken, putting an end to the consciousness.

We Are the Creator of Our Virtual Inner World

We learn about the external universe through the brain and sense organs – eyes, ears, mouth, nose, and skin. We create our internal world from the signals sent to the brain from sense organs, which get the signals from the external world. That is the only way for us to know the external world. I shared in Chapter 6 that we are the Creator God of our Virtual Inner World. We create our virtual reality, our virtual universe. This is subjective reality. Nothing outside matters except what we create in our brains and experience in our minds.

Imagine if all your senses decide to take a vacation - your eyes, ears, nose, tongue, and skin all clock out simultaneously. Your brain is left in the dark, deprived of any external information. In a sense, the world ceases to exist for you, leaving you in a state of eternal darkness.

Most Brain Processes Are Unconscious

According to Freud, 95% of brain processes are happening behind the scenes, unbeknownst to us. When our brain receives information from the outside world, like a visual image of an object, it goes through a whole bunch of unconscious analysis - think color, hue, edge detection, motion, contour, and more. We are oblivious to this whole process until the very end when all the info comes together to form a virtual object that we finally become aware of. If the signal is strong enough and our brain is in the right state, we pay attention to it and, hence - consciousness! The meaning behind this virtual object may also be cooked up unconsciously, without us even realizing it.

Each of us experiences these virtual objects in a unique way (subjectively), based on our past experiences and the circumstances we are in at that moment.

Phenomenal Conscious Experience – Empirical Conscious Experience

Experiences of external objects in the Virtual Inner World are called Phenomenal conscious experiences or Empirical Conscious experiences. It is widely accepted that there needs to be an experiencer (self) present for these conscious experiences to occur within us. Phenomenal conscious experience is often simply referred to as 'consciousness' in everyday language. In my research, I have labeled this consciousness as Empirical Consciousness (EC) and the self as the 'Virtual Empirical self' (VES) or 'EGO-

I'. So, in simpler terms, when we interact with the virtual world, we are actually experiencing our consciousness and sense of self.

The Virtual self (VES) and empirical consciousness (EC) are constantly transitioning. Buddha describes this consciousness as 'momentary', comparing it to the perineal flow of water in a river. Just as water never remains stagnant in one place, our consciousness is always moving from one moment to the next. Like a river, our thoughts and perceptions are fluid, never staying the same for long.

Ego-I, or VES, is a compilation of all the experiences you have accumulated since birth. It is like an onion or cabbage, with layers upon layers of experiences. Your Ego-I, or VES, expands and grows larger as you continue to gather more experiences. Buddha even alludes to this Ego-I or empirical self (VES) as a soul (with a lowercase 's'), suggesting that it persists beyond this lifetime and into the next through the process of rebirth.

'Self' (VES) is also Virtual

'Ego-I or self (VES) cannot be physically found in the brain. Homunculus is not locatable in the brain. An assumption of a homunculus leads to an infinite regress of homunculi. It is like searching for a needle in a haystack.

As I discussed in the last chapter the best way to treat objects of the Inner World is as 'Virtual'. The external world is recreated as virtual objects using neurons in the brain. 'Ego-I' or 'self' is also a virtual entity (VES) in the brain as it represents the mind, intellect, and the collection of all the past experiences of a creature. This VES is not chilling in one specific brain nook - it is spread out and connected by neurons throughout the entire brain.

There is a debate among some about whether the self (VES) is physical or non-physical. I propose that we consider mental objects, including the empirical-self (VES) or 'Ego-I', as virtual entities. This perspective allows us to sidestep the issue of non-physicality, as there is no concept of non-physicality in Physics. Let's keep it virtually real!

As we will see in the next chapters, treating objects in the inner world and 'self' as virtual will make the explanation of many spiritual phenomena more palatable.

Neurophysiological Process of Perception

When an external object is transformed into a virtual object in the brain and the self (VES) is associated (superimposed) with it, a meaning is assigned to this virtual object using past experiences (the virtual self up to that point). The self (VES) then takes on the role of the knower of the object, resulting in the creation of a fresh, updated virtual self (VES) in the process. It's like the brain's very own virtual reality makeover!

The process of association or superposition is neurologically achieved through a synchronization process. This involves all neurons scattered throughout the brain firing up simultaneously to represent the perceptible object and self (VES) with the same frequency, typically in the Gamma range of 40 Hz. This means that our sense of self (VES) is always present, but it gets a fresh update every time we perceive something new.

Think of yourself (VES) as a tree with annual growth rings. These rings tell the tale of your growth, resilience, and transformation, threading together to shape the strength and character of your being. Just as a tree's rings form its foundation; your experiences lay the groundwork for your ever-evolving identity. Peel back those rings metaphorically, and you will reveal the roots of who you are - grounded yet always reaching for the light of new understanding.

What Makes 'You' the Same Moment to Moment

What keeps a person consistent over time? Some may argue it's their physical features, like their body, face, ears, and eyes. But what truly keeps someone the same psychologically? It's the internal virtual 'self' (VES) that remains constant, even as it evolves with each new experience. The changes in this 'self' are so delicate from one moment to the next that they go unnoticed.

Despite potential physical injuries like cut ears, amputated legs, or a burned face from a fire accident, this person remains unchanged psychologically. In fact, if you were to speak with him over the phone without knowledge of his injuries, you would still recognize him from the conversation alone. I believe the most devastating affliction is when people lose their memory of self (VES), whether through minor memory loss, dementia, or Alzheimer's, rather than any physical harm to their body. Forgetting external objects or other people's names may not be as severe. After all, we all experience some memory loss as we age - it's just a part of life!

Two Selves (VESes) - Split Brain Experiment

We have two sides (hemispheres) of the brain – the left brain and the right brain. Corpus callosum connects the left and right hemispheres of the brain. The biological basis of the two selves is clear in the Callosotomy procedure in which the corpus callosum is surgically cut to prevent the spread of epileptic seizure activity to the non-affected side from the source side. This is known as the Split-brain procedure and was the first time done by Roger W. Sperry and his group, (Gazzaniga, 1965). Roger Sperry got the Nobel Prize for his work (1981). He discovered that in these patients, two parts of the brain behave differently as if there are two selves working at the same time. The left side dominantly knows language and the right side dominantly knows spatial information in right-handed subjects.

In a study by Sperry in 1968, experiments were conducted on callosotomy patients to relay the fascinating phenomenon of the two sides of the brain acting independently, almost as if there are two separate selves (Sperry, 1968). Imagine this: a word like 'Rose' is flashed on the right visual field of a patient. The left part of the brain, which is language-dominant, sees it, but the patient claims to have seen nothing at all. However, when asked to pick out the unseen object from a selection of items with his left hand (controlled by the right side of the brain), he surprisingly chooses the rose from many items on the table in front of him.

To add to the intrigue, the patient is then asked to name the object they are holding in their left hand, which they cannot see with their left brain (only the right brain can see things in the left visual field). Despite this, the patient is able to correctly name the object using their language-dominant left brain.

Imagine having two brains but only one body - that's the reality for split-brain patients. These individuals seem to have two separate selves (VESes), each operating independently. While some Neuroscientists question whether the right hemisphere is truly conscious, the evidence suggests otherwise.

After undergoing a callosotomy procedure, split-brain patients can demonstrate their unique abilities. They can draw different figures simultaneously with each hand, almost as if two different people are at work. The right side of the brain remains clueless about what the left side is up to, especially when it comes to language dominance.

This split in consciousness can lead to some pretty entertaining scenarios. Picture this: the left side of the brain saying one thing while the right side is off doing something completely different. It's like having a constant battle of wills going on inside your head. Split-brain patients are a marvel of modern neuroscience.

Multiple Selves (VESes)

When I dream, I often find myself running, engaging in activities, or interacting with others. However, it feels as though there is a separate self (VES), a 'dream self' who is witnessing the entire dream project, including my own actions. While my dream self is active, my physical body remains still and at rest in bed. It's as if I have a front-row seat to my conscious theater production!

When daydreaming, a transfixing phenomenon occurs. Picture this: you are chatting away in your daydream, and there's this other self (let's call it VES) just observing the whole scene.

It's like having a little internal debate with yourself. One VES is doing the talking, while the other VES is all ears. One VES might be like, "Dude, why would you do that?" And the other VES is just like, "I have no clue, man."

So, are we dealing with two VESes here? Or maybe a whole pack of VESes?

Even in our waking moments, we often overlook the fact that we contain multitudes within ourselves (VES). There are manifold selves coexisting within us - one self is busy running, another is indulging in a meal, yet another is behind the wheel, one more is engrossed in reading, and there's even a self observing all the other selves in action. It's like a never-ending parade of selves within us, each taking its turn in the spotlight.

It is evident that we can distinguish between the watching-self (VES) and the acting-self (VES). The self (VES) is virtually represented in the brain, with this virtual representation superimposed on external objects to perceive them. Therefore, we can separate this virtual representation of the experiencing or watching self (VES) from the acting self (VES) and virtual objects.

In a psychiatric disorder known as 'Multiple Personality Disorder', one person behaves differently at different times. One self (VES) does not know about the other self (VES). Somehow, two memories disconnect and make him behave as two different people (selves).

'Self' (VES) is the Cause of All Goodness and Evils

Self (VES) as a virtual entity being superimposed on a virtual object to perceive it is quite engaging, don't you think? It's like our personal virtual reality experience. And who does not try to claim ownership of something they see? It is human nature to want to possess things that bring us happiness or sorrow, depending on our state of self (VES) at the time.

This desire to own objects can lead to some wild behavior - for example, lying, stealing, cheating, and even kidnapping for ransom. It's like our greed takes over and we will do anything to make that object ours. Then there is ego, short-lived happiness, sorrow, and misery that come along for the ride.

Chris Hedges hits the nail on the head when he claims that evil is but the shadow cast by the light of human nature. It's an extensive inquiry into the dark side of our psyche, which I have written in detail in Chapter 5.

The Self (VES) is like the ultimate experience junkie - it's out here enjoying all the tastes, smells, sights, sounds, and feels that life has to offer. It is like the CEO of the senses, absorbing every sensation with effortless swagger.

But the Self (VES) is not all rainbows and butterflies. It has got a dark side too - it can hate, feel sorry, be selfish, be greedy, be angry, be jealous, be egoistic, be revengeful, discriminate, and even throw a tantrum or two. It's a tide of emotions, crashing and retreating, with a dash of drama thrown in for good measure.

But it is not all doom and gloom. The Self (VES) can also feel empathy, help others, love, feel happy, and even be selfless when the mood strikes. It's a complex creature, that is for sure. Therefore, the self (VES) is the puppet master pulling the strings behind the scenes.

The self (VES) craves power to dominate and manipulate others: from micromanaging their children and spouses to leading cult-like organizations, all the way up to ruling entire countries like President Putin in Russia, Xi Jinping in China, Kim Jong Un in North Korea, Benjamin Netanyahu in Israel and so on.

The trigger of all conflicts between individuals and groups, whether religious or not, can be traced back to one common denominator: the insidious nature of the self (VES). This self-centeredness has sparked wars between nations, resulting in countless lives lost due to the egotistical whims of leaders. From the devastating bombings of Hiroshima and Nagasaki to the horrific genocide of Jews by Hitler, the destructive power of the self has left a trail of devastation throughout history.

The self has been the driving force behind world wars, slavery, and the suppression of women's rights in the Middle East, as well as the restriction of freedoms in countries like Russia and China.

It's quite the paradox, is it not? The idea is that our sense of 'self' is necessary for experiencing the world around us. Also, it is the source of all good and evil. But our sense of 'self' is nothing more than a virtual entity (VES). So how can something intangible be responsible for all the evil and beauty in the world? It's not like it's a physical object concealed within us or floating around externally.

Detaching Self (VES) from the Virtual Inner World

If VES can be detached from the virtual object during the perception process, it has the power to eradicate all the evils of human nature. This revelation carries profound implications. To me, it represents the greatest enigma of human existence, merging the spheres of religion, God, mysticism, and spiritual experiences on one side. It encompasses the complexities of human nature, including greed, selfishness, love, and happiness. This eclipses mere scientific understanding. In my opinion, it poses a greater mystery than consciousness itself.

In Chapter 6, I have touched on the idea that paying attention leads to conscious experiences, while not paying attention does not. Now, let us move on to similar experiences through the filter of attachment and detachment of VES. Simply put, conscious experiences occur when VES is attached to a virtual object, and they do not happen when VES is detached. It is all about making that connection!

Detaching VES during Meditation

The primary goal of mindful meditation in Buddhism is to detach the self or Ego-I (VES) from virtual objects during the normal perception process. This entails separating one's self (VES) from the typical experience through meditation. So, instead of getting caught up in your thoughts or actions, simply sit quietly and observe. Resist the urge to react and just listen to what others are saying. Just be a seer to the ebb and flow of thoughts as they come and go.

Michael A. Singer has beautifully described about VES in his book, 'The Untethered Soul' (p. 17, 2007):

"There is a separation between you and the anger or the jealousy. You are the one who is there noticing these things. Once you take that seat of consciousness, you can get rid of these personal disturbances. You start by watching. Just be aware that you are aware of what is going on in there. It's easy. What you'll notice is that you're watching a human being's personality with all its strengths and weaknesses. It's as though there is somebody in there with you. You might actually say you have a 'roommate.'

If you would like to meet your roommate, just try to sit inside yourself for a while in complete solitude and silence."

If you take a moment to watch the sunrise and truly immerse yourself in the experience without letting your mind wander, you will find yourself completely entranced by the work of art coming to life before your eyes. At that moment, you will not experience the sense of your ego-I or self (VES) and simply exist in serenity with the sunrise.

Buddha believed that seeing objects in this way reduces suffering (Dukkha) and stress. It means just to see things as they are and not add your own biases from previous experiences through VES. That is the purpose of and that is what is done during all meditational techniques.

Pain Reduction by Detaching VES

There are two ways to detach yourself (VES) from an object. Let's say you are experiencing some shoulder or knee pain - it becomes a part of your reality, causing you agony. But, if you distract yourself by watching a captivating movie or chatting with a loved one on the phone, suddenly the pain disappears. You have successfully separated yourself from the virtual object (pain) in this scenario. However, as soon as the movie ends or the conversation wraps up, the pain comes rushing back. Why does this phenomenon occur?

Have you ever noticed that your pain disappears when you hear worse news than your pain? It's like a pain-vanishing act!

I have had people tell me that their shoulder or knee pain mysteriously goes away when they visit their families in India, only to return as soon as they set foot back in the USA. And apparently, this phenomenon is not exclusive to just one country - it happens to people from all over the globe.

But wait, it gets even more interesting! Many people swear that their pain disappears when they visit holy places like Mecca, Jerusalem, or Badrinath (a Holy place for Hindus in Uttarakhand in Northern India). A friend said to me that his ankle pain was gone permanently when he once visited Jerusalem.

When a child gets hurt, we have a little trick up our sleeves. We tell them a tall tale about a clumsy horse taking a tumble, and their pain disappears, and a smile returns to their face.

Now, these experiences may not align with scientific reasoning, but it works! Who are we to question the power of detachment of VES in pain reduction?

Pain Reduction by VES Detachment is Not Just an Illusion

Pain reduction is not merely a figment of the imagination, despite what some skeptics may suggest. When individuals report feeling pain-free while engrossed in a movie or visiting a sacred place, we often attribute this to a "psychological" effect. However, research has shown that this phenomenon is physiologically real. In fact, MRI studies have revealed a decrease in activity in the brain's pain center during such experiences (Note 7). After all, it's not the body that experiences pain, but rather the brain (or mind, if you want to get philosophical).

Living Meaningful Life by Diverting VES (Ego-I) to Purposeful Activity

I have noticed a common sentiment among retirees in India - once they hit 57-60; they feel like they are done with life. It's as if they have lost their zest for living. And unfortunately, many of them quickly see their health decline as a result. It seems that without a sense of purpose, their well-being takes a sharp fall.

In India, I have observed that elderly widows who dedicated their lives to serving their husbands often tussle to find meaning once their partners pass away. It is not uncommon for these widows to deteriorate rapidly and succumb to the grief of losing their life companions.

My wife forwarded me a reference about a man who defied all odds and lived a life that could only be described as extraordinary. Stamatis Moraitis, originally from Greece, spent the majority of his years in New York and Florida. At the age of 66, he was given a grim diagnosis of terminal lung cancer with only 6 months left to live. Instead of accepting his fate, he made a bold decision to return to his roots on the picturesque Ikeria Island in Greece to spend his final days and save on burial costs.

Once there, Moraitis immersed himself in the simple life of farming olives and grapes on his family's land. To everyone's surprise, he not only survived beyond the 6 months but lived for an additional 30 years, passing away at the ripe old age of 98 or 102. He died not from cancer, but of old age. When asked about his secret to longevity, Moraitis humorously replied, "I guess I just forgot to die." (Note 2)

My mentor, Dr. Howard Shevrin who lived an impressive 91 years, taught me a valuable lesson through his dedication to his passion for researching Unconscious Brain processing. Despite his age, he never stopped pursuing what he loved. Our weekly meetings were a sheer joy for him, so much so that he eagerly anticipated them all week long. Even on the Thursday of Dr. Shevrin's passing, he had our meeting scheduled. His wife shared with us that those meetings were the best moments of his life, and he waited eagerly for those for the whole week.

Some people believe their lives are not worth living because they struggle to walk or cook because of chronic pain. Then there are those who, despite physical limitations, have achieved remarkable feats.

Stephen Hawking was a renowned theoretical physicist and cosmologist. Diagnosed with motor neuron disease at the young age of 21, he faced the gradual paralysis of his motor functions. Despite losing his ability to speak, he used a speech-generating device controlled by a handheld switch, and later by a single cheek muscle. Hawking made cutting-edge discoveries, including the revelation that black holes emit radiation. His best-selling book, "A Brief History of Time," gripped readers from all corners of the globe. Additionally, he championed the 'many-worlds interpretation' of quantum mechanics. Hawking's intellect and resilience continue to inspire generations of scientists and thinkers (Note 3).

Morris Goodman, a college dropout turned successful insurance agent, is famously known as 'The Miracle Man' for his spectacular recovery from a devastating plane crash. After being told by doctors that he would be in a 'Vegetative' state for the rest of his life, Morris achieved the improbable and regained the ability to walk, breathe, and swallow within months. He ultimately walked out of the hospital and went on to become a renowned motivational speaker (Note 4).

Kris Carr, a multi-talented individual hailing from Pawling, New York, has worn many hats in her lifetime - dancer, actress, and photographer. However, her biggest role came when she was diagnosed with Stage IV cancer of liver and lung (epithelioid hemangioendothelioma) at the young age of 31 in 2003. Fast forward over two decades later, and Kris is still alive and kicking to this day.

In her book, 'Crazy Cancer', Kris candidly shares her experiences and inspires others to take control of their health and healing. As the founder of the 'Inner Circle Wellness' online community, Kris continues to empower individuals to become active participants in their well-being (Note 5).

Arunima Sinha made history as India's first female amputee to conquer Mount Everest and other peaks across the globe. She follows in the footsteps of Rhonda Graham from the USA, the world's first female amputee to pull off this extraordinary achievement. Arunima was thrown from a running train by robbers when she resisted them, causing many injuries on her legs and spinal cord. Despite facing adversity, she rose above it all to reach the world's highest peak (Note 6).

All these people shared a common trait: they could disconnect their negative energy source (self or Ego-I or VES) from their physical ailments and redirect it towards something they were passionate about. This shift in focus allowed them to shine and find fulfillment in their lives.

By detaching their VES (Ego-I) from their physical ailments, these individuals overcame their limitations and achieved success in various aspects of their lives. Whether it was pursuing a creative passion, helping others in need, or simply finding joy in everyday activities, they found a sense of purpose and fulfillment that catapulted them forward. This ability to disconnect from their physical ailments and focus on what truly mattered to them not only improved their mental and emotional well-being but also allowed them to live more meaningful and satisfying lives.

Another Method of Detaching VES

Another way to detach your 'self' (VES) from a virtual object is to focus much attention on the object itself (concentrate). For example, to reduce the pain in your knee is to focus full attention on your pain in the knee. Focus on the thumping sounds of the pain. Your pain will disappear. This is called the mindful meditation technique in Buddhism. In a sense, this is also a distraction (detachment) technique by paying much attention to the thumping beats of the pain.

Think of the second method as disconnecting your 'self' (VES). Your self (VES) is not something tangible - it's more like a virtual entity that you can easily move around by focusing your attention on different virtual objects within your brain/mind. By shifting your self (VES) to a specific virtual object, you can perceive it. Your self (VES) is decisive for perception because it's the one setting the agenda during the whole perception process.

The process of VES detachment is not just about reducing pain, but also about enhancing all our senses - vision, hearing, smell, touch, and taste. It's like shifting our focus away from a virtual object because attention is what matters in VES.

By detaching from VES, we can alleviate anxiety, stress, blood pressure, heart disease, and other chronic illnesses.

This virtual self (VES) believes it is the ultimate experiencer, thinker of all thoughts, and knower of all things. Could it be the mastermind behind all the objects in our Virtual Inner World? Is VES playing God? Well, in the next chapter, I break down this theory. VES is not the divine creator of our virtual domain. It simply revels in the enjoyment of all virtual objects. My question still stands: Who or what is the creator of our Virtual Inner Universe and everything within it?

Chapter 9

Consciousness

VES (self or Ego-I) acts as an agent required to perceive objects within our Virtual Inner World. VES indulges in virtual objects, expressing preferences, emotions, and engaging in various activities. These may include activities like enjoying sweets, watching movies, and experiencing a range of feelings from love to hate. Some people equate this self (VES) to 'I', using phrases like 'I like', 'I dislike', 'I love', 'I hate', 'I am happy', and so forth. However, let us not make it complex - VES is not the real deal when it comes to knowing oneself. This is more of a virtual ally, not the main character. It does not just become aware of virtual objects all on its own.

Phenomenal Consciousness

Have you ever wondered how a bowl of red strawberries can induce a cinematic experience of red strawberries in your mind? What about the taste of raspberry ice cream or the emotions evoked by a piece of music, or even the sharp sting of a needle?

When light rays bounce off those red strawberries and hit your eyes, they transform into electrochemical signals that activate the neurons in your brain. So, you are left with the joyous experience of seeing those juicy red berries. But how do these electrochemical signals create such a richly detailed experience?

Well, in the world of philosophy and psychology, we call these raw feelings 'Qualia'. The way freshly brewing coffee smells and tastes to you, the way you feel the touch of a furry cat, the way music sounds to you and the way the red color of the rising sun feels to you, are all examples of 'Qualia'. In the previous chapter, I referred to these intense conscious experiences as Empirical Consciousness (EC) or phenomenal awareness. This is what is meant by the term 'consciousness' when it is used colloquially.

Conscious experiences happen in the brain, as it is a phenomenon of the central nervous system (CNS). So, when you crush your toe, the pain is not actually in your toe - it is all happening in your brain! And that rumbling in your stomach when you are hungry? That is just your brain sending signals, not your stomach grooving to the beat. Smells, sounds, sights, touches, and tastes are all experienced in the mind, not in the specific sensory organs like the nose, ear, eyes, skin, and tongue.

There is something more needed for VES to become conscious of or experience the Virtual Inner World of color, smell, taste, touch and sound. If VES is not the true creator of virtual objects, then who or what creates these phenomenal experiences? The answer lies in Consciousness. This is a big jigsaw that has stumped scientists and philosophers alike. Consciousness is the ultimate knower, the true Self, the real 'I' behind virtual objects. I like to refer to it as the Virtual Absolute Self (VAS), the Virtual Core Self (VCS), or Pure Consciousness (PC). It's the missing piece of the virtual reality maze that we have all been searching for.

According to Harris, the biggest mystery is consciousness and the basis for spiritual experience (Page 228, 'Waking Up').

"Man is manifestly not the measure of all things. This universe is shot through with mystery. The very fact of its being, and of our own, is a mystery absolute, and the only miracle worthy of the name. The consciousness that animates us is itself central to this mystery and the ground for any experience we might wish to call "Spiritual". No myths need be embraced for us to commune with the profundity of our circumstances. No personal God need be worshipped for us to live in awe at the beauty and immensity of creation."

Vedanta posits that Consciousness reigns supreme as the ultimate reality, the absolute truth, or Brahman. It is known as Atman within each individual. Turning the coin over, Buddha rejected the notion of a permanent self. According to him, phenomenal conscious experiences or Empirical consciousness (EC) lack a self (VES), which is why he describes consciousness (EC) as Sunyata, void of a self. However, this does not mean it is all just nothingness. As Sam Harris writes in his book 'Waking Up':

"...the conventional sense of self is an illusion – and that spirituality largely consists in realizing this, moment to moment."

Let me now detail the aspects of consciousness.

Consciousness in Western Philosophy

Understanding consciousness is like trying to solve a Rubik's cube blindfolded. It's the ultimate brain teaser in the 'mind-body' debate, leaving us furrowing our brows and seeking the truth of the universe. How on earth do our brain cells conjure up the taste of raspberry ice cream or the symphony of the music note?

According to Descartes (1644), the mind, or consciousness, is composed of a substance that is distinct from the physical substance of the brain. While the brain is made up of the same stuff as the physical objects we see in our daily lives (like stones, tables, and chairs), the mind is in a league of its own.

Some people compare the brain with computer hardware and the mind with software. I suggest comparing the mind with a computer programmer or software designer.

I also suggest in my book to treat the body or brain to be physical and the mind or consciousness to be virtual.

Theories to Explain Consciousness

Throughout history, philosophers have put forth a wealth of theories to explain consciousness. From Property Dualism to reductive and non-reductive Physicalism (also known as Materialism), the field of philosophy has been a clash zone of ideas. Emergenticism, Epiphenomenalism, Panpsychism, Eliminative materialism, illusionism, Behaviorism, and Functionalism have all taken their turn on the roundtable. You may find more details in the following references:

The Rediscovery of the Mind, by Searle, J. R. (1992), *'Consciousness Explained'*, by Dennet, D., (1991), *'The character of consciousness'* by

Chalmers, D. (2010), '*Mental Reality*'' by Strawson, G. (1994), and 'Matter and Consciousness' by Churchland, Paul M., 1983.

Four Major Philosophers Claim Consciousness to be Non-Physical

Frank Jackson's knowledge argument (1982) of Mary, a color scientist learning about colors in books and experiencing colors, (Note 1), Hill's sensation argument (1991), Nagel's 1974 article 'What it is like to be a Bat', Chalmers (2010) Zombie argument (Conceivability argument) brought the non-physical nature of mental phenomena and consciousness. Many counterarguments are given against these arguments.

These philosophers have attempted to prove that even after knowing everything that is possible to know by observing the thing physically, there is still something left that can only be experienced and hence those are non-physical. You can learn all about color properties from physics books, but seeing a red rose gives a different experience and knowledge that is not possible to experience through physics books.

Chalmers gives another example that there is a possibility of a zombie who is physically just like us but without any consciousness meaning that the zombie cannot experience anything or have no feelings for anything. From this example, he claims that it means consciousness is something beyond physical properties and hence non-physical. You can learn more about these ideas from their books referenced above.

Chalmer's Challenge – Consciousness as a 'Hard Problem'

Chalmers shook things up with his assertion that consciousness is a true 'Hard problem' in comparison to the Easy problem of Consciousness. This statement sent shockwaves through the scientific and philosophical communities, challenging their beliefs and sparking intense debate.

The Easy problems of consciousness are all about cognitive functions - things like categorizing, reacting to environmental stimuli, focusing attention, remembering, reporting mental states, and controlling behavior.

These can all be neatly explained in terms of computational or neural mechanisms.

But Chalmers, much like some panpsychists, dares to look beyond the obvious. He believes that consciousness is a fundamental entity, similar to mass and charge, that simply cannot be reduced to anything else.

Consciousness Explanation as an Impasse

It seems like we are stuck trying to solve this mystery. Eliminative materialism, Illusionism, Behaviorism, and Functionalism have all been ruled out for ignoring the importance of conscious experiences and Qualia. Dualism has also been rejected for not fitting with the scientific principles of Physical science, which do not support non-physicalism. The gap between the mind and brain and how they interact is difficult to explain.

Reductive Physicalism or Identity theory suggests that the mind and brain are the same. It is promptly dismissed for failing to explain how the mental arises from the physical brain. The elusive "gap between the two" remains unaddressed. Identity theory implies the existence of two separate entities that are somehow linked. But how can these theorists then assert that the mental and physical are identical? Simply being correlated does not equate to being identical. It is like saying a mouse and a rabbit are the same because they both have four legs - correlation does not equal sameness.

Many philosophers like Searle (1992), Jackson, Sperry, McGinn, Nagel, Strawson (1994) and Davidson (1970) believe that reducing mental states to brain states is just not possible – non-reductive physicalism.

Strawson defines mental as experiential physical and brain as non-experiential physical.

In other words, mental experiences are subjective and personal, while brain phenomena are objective and observable by others.

My Theory of Virtual Physicalism

First and foremost, let us all agree that consciousness is a real phenomenon, not just some figment of our imagination as Dennett suggests in his books, 'Consciousness Explained' and 'From Bacteria to Bach and Back: The Evolution of Minds' (1991, 2017). According to him, there's no intrinsic 'redness' in there - it's all about function and explanation.

I propose 'Virtual Physicalism' (Note 2) as a theory to make sense of the mind in a more down-to-earth, physical way. Let us stay clear of all that controversy about the non-physical nature of consciousness because Physics does not define anything non-physical.

I have written in detail about what 'Virtual' really means in Chapter 7, where I explain how our brains simulate and represent the external world (that is the physical part), and then our minds interpret and make sense of it all (that is the mental part). It is done by creatures for the sole purpose of survival and reproduction.

The external world is a virtual reality show put on by our brains. This means we have the power to assign any meaning we want to the objects we perceive. It is like holding an elite pass to the ultimate mind-bending experience.

Nailing down the exact connection between our physical brains and our mental objects is like trying to catch a greased pig - slippery and elusive. Identity theorists may claim there is a correlation, but there is no simple one-to-one mapping between our brain processes and our conscious experiences. It is like sewing silk with a rope. So, the reduction from experiences to brain processes is not possible.

Take a mango, for instance. It is not just a simple fruit - it is a whole metaverse of possibilities! From its size and weight to its ripeness, color, taste, touch, smell, sound when it falls on the ground, price, availability, suitability for pickling, and more, there is a whole universe of virtual aspects to consider for the same physical mango.

You might focus on just a few of these aspects, while someone else might hone in on different ones. And even if you both direct attention to the same aspect, your experiences could be totally different. It just goes to show that there is more to a mango than meets the eye - or the taste buds!

Neuroscientific Explanation of Consciousness

Many attempts have been made by Neuroscientists to find how the brain produces consciousness. What are the necessary and sufficient conditions to produce consciousness in the brain? Singer has suggested that synchronization of several parts of the brain using Gamma frequency (40-80 Hz) is involved in the production of consciousness (Engel and Singer, 2001); Llinas et al., 1998).

Quantum Mechanics Explanation of Production of Consciousness

Roger Penrose, a physicist, and Stuart Hameroff, an anesthesiologist, have made attempts to utilize Quantum Mechanics (QM) to explain the nature of consciousness within the brain (1994, 2004, 2014). Alas, their efforts have not yielded the desired results. While Quantum Mechanics undeniably is the anchor of our understanding of the physical world, it appears that its application may not be necessary when it comes to elaborating the mysteries of neurons and cells at the macro level. After all, sometimes the simplest explanations are the most reasonable.

Global Work-Space Theory (GWS)

Baars's Global Workspace (GWS) theory (1988, 2005, 2003) suggests that for sensory information to become conscious, it must be shared among various regions of the brain. Unconscious processing, on the other hand, is confined to a small portion of the brain, such as during a coma, vegetative state (VS), minimally conscious state (MCS), sleep, or anesthesia.

Dehaene, Naccache, and Changeux (2001, 2004, 2005, 2006) argue that the GWS theory pertains to the content of sensory information rather than the state of consciousness itself. They propose that consciousness is linked to widespread Gamma frequency synchronization throughout the entire brain, a concept also supported by Linas, Singer, and others. However, there are conflicting instances where consciousness is lost during generalized epileptic seizures, despite increased metabolism and higher frequency synchronization.

In simpler terms, it is like a busy marketplace of thoughts, where ideas exchange and collaborate to build consciousness. But sometimes, even with all the fancy footwork, consciousness decides to take a break during a seizure. It is a brainy mystery that keeps researchers on their toes!

Number and Quantity Alone Can Not Produce Consciousness

It is not just about hitting the golden number of neurons to produce consciousness - the cerebellum has more neurons than the rest of the brain combined, yet it is not the mastermind behind our awareness. Even during anesthesia and sleep, sensory stimulation causes increased cerebral activity in the whole brain (Alkire 2008, Kakigi et al 2003, Kroeger and Amzica 2007). Ketamine anesthesia produces dreams as reported by patients afterward even though they are not conscious at that time (Sarasso et al., Nov. 2015). Our brains are just as busy, if not busier, during dreamland as they are when we are wide awake. So, even if you are snoozing away, your brain is working overtime to entertain you with some flights of fancy.

Subliminal Stimulation Does Not Produce Consciousness

From experiments done in our lab and by other researchers (Shevrin et al., 2013, Bernat et al. 2001; Maksimow et al., 2006; Itoh et al., 2005; and Langsjo et al., 2005), it is found that subliminal stimulation causes no conscious experience of the stimulus, even though there is widespread brain activity in the gamma band. Stimuli are presented for 1 msec on a Tachistoscope or on a monitor using a masking technique so that subjects do not become conscious of the stimuli (Shevrin et al., 2013, Bernat et al. 2001) and Luo et al., 2009; Diaz & McCarthy, 2007) (Note 3).

Neuronal Synchrony Does Not Cause Consciousness

Boly et al. (2009) concludes: "(e.g., that synchrony is good but too much synchrony as in seizures, is bad)". Tononi and Edelman (1998) define consciousness as: "what disappears when we fall into a dreamless sleep."

This means that during unconsciousness, we do not perceive anything internally or externally about ourselves.

Integrated Information Theory (IIT)

Tononi claims that consciousness is integrated information (IIT) (Tononi, 2004; Tononi 2008a) because consciousness is highly informative and highly integrated or unified. He defines a term (symbol **ϕ** pronounced as Greek letter PHI) which is an intrinsic property of a system when different elements of the system interact causally. PHI (**ϕ**) must be above a certain threshold for the system to become conscious.

According to IIT (Integrated Information Theory, a theoretical framework developed by neuroscientist Giulio Tononi, which aims to explain the nature of consciousness), low levels of **ϕ** can be observed during deep sleep, coma, and anesthesia. Excessive firing by all components of the system can also lead to low **ϕ**, such as during seizures. Loss of consciousness typically occurs during sleep, characterized by high-amplitude slow waves in the Theta band (0.5 - 4 Hz). This phenomenon is attributed to Bistable dynamics, where the system responds in an 'All or None' manner, particularly evident in the corticothalamic system during sleep. This impairs the system's ability to integrate information effectively (Tononi 2008b). Interestingly, lesions in the Thalamocortical system (Note 4) can result in loss of consciousness, whereas lesions in other brain regions do not have the same effect (Tononi and Laureys, 2008).

Causal IIT Needed for Consciousness

Merely having integrated information is not enough to spark consciousness, according to Koch in his latest masterpiece, 'The Feeling of Life Itself' (2019). He states that a system must be 'causal' to truly give rise to consciousness. What does that mean? Well, it denotes the system can impact itself internally and be influenced by the external environment, while also being able to affect both itself and said environment. In plain words, a computer cannot just fake it till it makes it when it comes to consciousness. Sure, it can simulate all sorts of things - gravity, magnetism, digestion - but it lacks that central causal power.

So, while a computer might be able to mimic the effects of gravity, it cannot pull you towards it. Sure, it can simulate magnetism, but it cannot attract any iron particles. As Searle so aptly put it in 'Rediscovery of Mind' (1992), a computer can simulate digestion, but it is not the same as the real deal happening in your stomach. Koch drives the point home in his book (Page 149, 2019) - you just cannot fake that causal power:

"The difference between the real and the simulated is their respective causal powers. That is why it doesn't get wet inside a computer simulating a rainstorm. The software can be functionally identical to some aspect of reality, but it won't have the same causal powers as the real thing."

Causal IIT is Not Good Enough to Produce Consciousness

Renowned Canadian researcher, Paul Thagard, has taken a critical stance on Koch's Integrated Information Theory (IIT). In his review of Koch's latest book, 'The Feeling of Life Itself', Thagard points out that according to Koch's theory, even the toilet tank should be considered conscious due to its cause-effect feedback loop. However, the toilet tank is about as conscious as a rock (Note 5).

Thagard goes on to point out the illogicality of Koch's theory by suggesting that everyday devices like cell phones and computers could also be considered conscious based on their feedback and cause-effect mechanisms. But just because your phone can predict your next Google search does not mean it understands the meaning of life.

Let me share another example that completely disproves this idea. The development of self-driving cars is nearing perfection. Once perfected, these vehicles will be able to autonomously drive from point A to point B and back again without a single accident. However, despite having fail-proof feedback systems and cause-effect relationships, these cars lack any semblance of consciousness. They are completely unaware of the purpose behind their trips. Only the owner of the car holds that knowledge. So, while self-driving cars may be on the brink of perfection, they still have a long way to go before they can truly understand the meaning behind their automated drives.

I wholeheartedly agree that information integration and cause-effect feedback are decisive components of producing consciousness. However, they alone cannot create the perfect flavor.

While information integration and cause-effect relationships in the brain are like the super team of consciousness creation, they need a touch of glam to truly bring it to life. Conscious experience is like a perfectly synchronized routine - it is all about unity and meaning.

Consciousness is not just about throwing a bunch of information together and hoping for the best. It is about curating a masterpiece that is not only integrated but also meaningful, useful, and intentional or subjective to the system itself (living creature, in this case).

'State Consciousness' is the Fundamental Property of Life and a Prerequisite for Phenomenal Consciousness

Living Creatures are Sentient

In my opinion, understanding phenomenal consciousness is the ability to internally assign meaning to external stimuli, a unique capability possessed only by living creatures. This innate capacity allows living beings to interpret and respond to their surroundings in a way that non-living systems, such as robots or cell phones, simply cannot replicate.

The act of giving meaning is a survival mechanism, ingrained within living organisms to ensure their continued existence for reproduction. This function is not dependent on any external force or deity; it is a self-contained process that only sentient beings can carry out (Note 6).

In light of this remarkable ability, I propose that we refer to living creatures as 'Sentient'.

Robots are not Sentients

Even if we manage to create robots that can imitate the functions of living creatures, such as moving and speaking, they will never truly understand the purpose or meaning behind their actions. It's like memorizing a physics formula without understanding its meaning - robots just do not have the capacity to read between the lines.

We can teach a computer all the mathematical formulas on this planet, but it will never understand the essence of what those formulas represent. Robots simply lack the prerequisite qualifications for understanding the complexities of life and consciousness that humans and other living creatures have.

While complex robots may be able to process information systematically, they lack the prime element of 'State Consciousness' necessary to develop a virtual self (VES). Hence, robots are not capable of having conscious experiences like living beings because they are not sentients like living beings.

The ability to experience consciousness is given or built-in living creatures, a quality that robots will never be able to replicate. Life is defined by the innate drive to reproduce and survive, with reproduction serving as the ultimate purpose for existence. Living creatures process external stimuli with the singular goal of ensuring their survival and passing on their genetic material.

Therefore, living creatures have a hidden (virtual) agenda - to survive and reproduce. Survival is for the virtual self (VES). They assign internal meaning to external stimuli to fulfill this primal urge. So, while robots may be able to parrot certain aspects of life, they will never have the inherent drive for survival and reproduction that defines the essence of living beings.

Living Creatures are Always in 'State Consciousness'

For a creature to be 'sentient' means to have the capacity to give internal meaning to external stimuli that requires the creature to be in a particular state. I like to call it 'state consciousness'. It is not your run-of-the-mill experience of jamming out to music or admiring red flowers or catching a whiff of perfume. Nope, this is next-level stuff.

Living beings are always rocking that 'state consciousness' vibe, whether they are phenomenally conscious or not.

However, being phenomenally conscious or unconscious of the environment and being in a conscious state are two different things. A complex brain and 'state-consciousness' are required to produce phenomenal consciousness. So, what about those creatures with less evolved brains? They are not exactly living their best conscious lives, even if they are still in 'state consciousness'.

Efforts are being made by scientists and researchers to find how the brain produces phenomenal or empirical consciousness (EC). What are the necessary and sufficient conditions for the brain to produce empirical consciousness and what part of the brain is involved in the production of empirical consciousness? Deep sleep, coma, VS, MCS, and under anesthesia are said to be empirically unconscious and efforts are being made to find out how the brain produces these "empirically unconscious" states vs. empirically conscious experiences during awake and dream states. I want to emphasize that 'state consciousness' is the most necessary underlying condition but not sufficient for the production of empirically conscious experiences in the brain.

'State Consciousness' is Needed even for Unconscious Information Processing

Did you know that most of the information processing that goes on in our brains happens without us even realizing it (in an awareness sense) even in an awake state? We only become consciously aware of the stimulus after our brains have already processed them.

When we do not pay attention to a particular external object, we do not become phenomenally conscious of it even though we are in 'state consciousness' during all that time.

For example, have you ever driven to work and back home without paying attention to the road? You are in state consciousness, but you are not actively aware of everything around you. It is like your brain is on cruise control while you are listening to NPR radio, music station, or lost in thought. We are not in a non-conscious state (like that of a stone or a robot) while driving. We are not empirically or phenomenally conscious of certain external environments. An expert typist can type without being empirically conscious of each word or each letter on the keyboard.

'State Consciousness' is Present During Anesthetic Procedure

A vast number of experiments, including one by our group, have shown that the brain is capable of processing auditory stimuli and forming memories even while under anesthesia during surgery (Bunce et al., 2001). Research has shown that music played during surgery can lead to improved and speedier recovery (Note 7).

According to a study by Stefano Sarasso in November 2015 (Consciousness and Complexity During Unresponsiveness Induced by Propofol, Xenon, and Ketamine), subjects who underwent Ketamine anesthesia reported having dream experiences during surgery. Interestingly, Auditory and Somatosensory Evoked brain responses (BAEP and SSEP) (Note 8) from external sound and electric current under anesthesia and during deep sleep are strikingly similar to those during the awake state, but with reduced amplitude. It shows that we are always in 'state consciousness', whether we are phenomenally conscious or not.

'State Consciousness' is Present During Subliminal Stimulation

In the Odd-ball experiments, conducted and replicated by the esteemed group (Bernat et al. 2001, Silverstein et al. 2013), we have discovered some attention-grabbing findings. It turns out that brain responses called Event Related Potentials (ERPs) for odd stimuli during subliminal stimuli presentation (when subjects are unaware of the stimuli) and supraliminal stimuli presentation (when subjects are conscious of the stimuli) exhibiting strikingly similar shapes, with the only difference being that ERPs for subliminal stimuli have smaller amplitudes compared to those for supraliminal stimuli.

In these Odd-ball experiments, a single stimulus stands out among a vast array of similar stimuli - similar to finding a red apple among a bunch of green ones presented in random order on a T-scope or LCD screen. The subjects are in 'state consciousness' during both subliminal and supraliminal presentations of all stimuli. All living beings are always in a state of consciousness, regardless of their level of awareness. While we process information unconsciously in terms of our experiences, we are always in a state of consciousness. This unconscious information processing is still meaningful to the individual (Shevrin et al., 2013 and Bazan et al., 2019).

'Sentience' Means Presence of 'State Consciousness'

In my view, the definition of 'Sentience' should be being in 'state consciousness'. Living beings are only in a non-conscious state (insentient) when they are deceased. I prefer to use a 'non-conscious state' to differentiate from empirically unconscious phenomena (brain processes). Objects like stones, chairs, robots, and computers are always in a non-conscious state. 'State Consciousness' is obligatory for empirical conscious experiences. Therefore, stones, chairs, and computers can never have empirical conscious experiences because they are always in a non-conscious state (insentient) and never in 'state consciousness'. Living beings are always in 'state consciousness' (Sentient).

Deep Sleep, coma, VS, MCS, and under anesthesia states are very similar in that these patients may not have empirical conscious experiences, but subjects are in 'state consciousness'. They are not in a non-conscious (dead) state. These states have lots of high amplitude Slow Waves (Theta waves of 0.5-4 Hz) in the corticothalamic system, which is due to Bistable Dynamics (excessive low and excessive high firing of neurons) (Achermann and Borbely, 1997; Amzica and Steriade, 1997).

During sleep, sensory information reaches the cortex. Many experiments have been performed to show that even sleeping brain can detect and process stimuli in a similar way as it is done during awake state (Langford et al. 974; Oswald et al. 1960; Portas et al. 2000). All autonomic functions of living creatures like breathing, heart function, digestion, kidney function continue to work all the time (in awake, sleep, VS, Coma, MCS, etc.) as long as they are living.

Recent research has revealed that patients can maintain consciousness even while in a coma (Note 9). Additionally, a study on locked-in patients has shown brain activity in unconscious individuals, offering a fresh perspective on awareness (Note 10).

Loss of conscious awareness during sleep is not caused by the brain completely shutting down. The metabolic rate remains high in certain areas of the brain during sleep, similar to when we are awake (Steriade et al., 2001). Sensory information continues to reach the brain and is processed unconsciously, similar to when we are awake (Kakigi et al., 2003, Portas et al., 2000). In deep sleep, high-frequency brain waves (gamma waves) are low, similar to when we are dreaming and still conscious (Cantero et al., 2004).

Basic Rhythm of the Brain Required for 'State Consciousness'

My hypothesis is that slow-wave oscillations during deep sleep (NREM sleep) act as a sweeping wave throughout the entire brain. These oscillations are the fundamental rhythm of the brain, much like other biological rhythms such as the biological clock, lung breathing cycle, and the functions of the liver, kidney, and heart. This underlying rhythm is imperative for achieving 'state consciousness' and is responsible for generating all other brain states. Massimini et al. (2004, pg. 6868) have even compared the Slow-Wave to the PQRST waves of the heart cycle or Electrocardiogram (ECG or EKG).

I wish to caption that living beings are constantly in 'state consciousness' until they breathe their last. The brain is continuously processing information in living beings, even in the absence of empirical conscious experiences. This concept of 'state consciousness' persists in living beings, whether they are in a vegetative state, coma, minimally conscious state, locked-in syndrome, or under anesthesia, regardless of their level of empirical consciousness.

All Living Creatures are Conscious

If we redefine the everyday term 'Consciousness' to 'State Consciousness', all living beings can be considered 'Conscious'(sentient). Now, whether an animal has an empirical phenomenal conscious experience (EC) or not is a different matter. Phenomenal consciousness happens only in creatures with more evolved brains, especially Cortex, to be able to causally integrate information and when all other necessary and sufficient conditions for phenomenal consciousness are met. Conditions for phenomenal consciousness include proper strength of the stimulus, duration of its presentation, attention, being in an awake or dream state, and a few more factors yet to be found.

A Complex Brain is Required for VES and Phenomenal Conscious Experiences

To create a unified virtual object, a complex brain with causal connections to integrate information is needed. The evolution of a complex brain, particularly the cortex, leads to the development of a complex 'virtual self' (VES), as discussed in the previous chapter. This is most prominent in mammals, especially in humans, and is a central factor in producing phenomenal conscious experiences.

The VES is the entity that assigns meaning (intentionality and subjectivity) to stimuli for its survival. It is the defining force that takes pleasure in virtual objects. The more advanced the brain, the more sophisticated the VES becomes, resulting in a heightened awareness of the environment.

Animals with simple or less evolved brains and hence less evolved 'virtual self' (VES) may not have as vivid empirical phenomenal conscious (EC) experiences. However, they are in 'state consciousness' (Sentient). More recently, scientists are learning more and more about other creatures showing signs of consciousness such as in fish, octopus, bacteria, and plants.

Woodruff (2017) has presented his thesis that ray-finned fishes of the teleost subclass (Actinopterygian) are sentient. In his book 'Other Minds: The Octopus, the Sea, and the Deep Origins of Consciousness' (2017), marine biologist Peter Godfrey-Smith writes about marine life. He describes the intelligent behaviors exhibited by creatures such as octopuses, fish, insects, cuttlefish, and even E-Coli bacteria. These remarkable beings adapt their actions based on their surroundings, almost as if they have a sense of awareness. It's simply stunning to witness the complex ways in which these creatures handle their environments. Godfrey-Smith's work scuba-dives into the depths of the ocean and the wondrous creatures that inhabit it.

Plants are also Conscious

In recent years, there has been a growing belief that plants are not just mindless greenery, but rather conscious, sentient beings with intelligence. It has been suggested that plants have the ability to distinguish between themselves and others, depicting a level of complexity in their information processing. Plants engage in complicated communication not only within their species but also with other organisms such as fungi, bacteria, viruses, and insects. This calls into question our traditional view of plants as passive entities and opens up a new frontier of possibilities in understanding the intelligence of the flora around us.

Plants are more than just pretty decorations - they have feelings and can feel pain. For example, sundew and mimosa are so sensitive that even a touch of 1 microgram can set them off, while raindrops do not even register on their radar. Some people even think that playing music can help plants grow. Some experts believe that a plant's roots are like their little brain or nervous system. It is unbelievable to think that plants can respond to anesthetics and chloroform, suggesting they might have some level of intelligence.

Some suggest that plants lack the necessary nervous system and brain required for consciousness and mental capabilities. However, others believe that plants exhibit signs of consciousness through classical conditioning, perception, memory, and learning - all vital pieces of animal consciousness. In fact, plants communicate with each other and with animals, defend their health, and even make decisions.

Researchers at the University of Murcia in Spain and the Rotman Institute of Philosophy in London, Ontario, Canada, have found that plants may have a sense of self. In an experiment with French bean plants, they observed that the plants would opt for a different route to reach a cane if one was present in the pot, even if it was a foot away. They claim that plants could sense the cane in their vicinity and choose a path in a predictable way (Note 11).

As previously mentioned, redefining the colloquial term 'consciousness' to refer to 'state consciousness' could potentially allow us to consider plants as sentient beings. While plants may not have the same level of phenomenal consciousness as humans, they still exhibit signs of awareness and responsiveness to their environment.

Pure Consciousness (PC)

'State Consciousness' is the defining quality that sets living organisms apart as 'sentient' beings. It is a necessary component for generating tangible conscious experiences. The creation of a 'Virtual-Self' (VES) within a complex brain adds depth, meaning, intentionality, and subjectivity to these experiences. VES, in turn, produces phenomenal conscious experiences by getting attached to a virtual object when present. To put it simply, the VES is like a series of nested boxes, with each compartment representing a different experience. In this metaphorical nested box, VCS, VAS, or PC is the innermost compartment, devoid of any experiences.

The Pure Consciousness state (PC) is an enwrapping phenomenon in the domain of 'State Consciousness'. It occurs when phenomenal awareness arises without the presence of any external stimulus. In this state, the same consciousness functions as both subject and object, leading to its classification as a virtual experiencer. I like to refer to this state as the Virtual Core Self (VCS) or Virtual Absolute Self (VAS). In my opinion, this is the True Self and True Soul of all living beings. Stay tuned for a detailed explanation of VAS in the upcoming chapter.

Deep sleep is a state where there is no empirical experience whatsoever. When mystics, Eastern practitioners, and Buddhist meditators achieve a similar experience of nothingness while awake, they refer to it as Pure Consciousness (PC).

When meditating in a wakeful state, one may experience a sense of 'nothingness' or void. However, during deep sleep, there is a lack of any conscious experience. In meditation, all sensory information from the external environment and internal memory is intentionally halted, allowing for a sense of self-control and inner peace.

In the next chapter, I provide an in-depth look at how various religious philosophies also describe that Consciousness is fundamental, the basis of spirituality, and mystical experiences.

Chapter 10

Pure Consciousness (PC) in Various Religions

In the previous chapter, I shared the concept of 'Pure Consciousness' (PC), also known as the Virtual Absolute Self (VAS) or Virtual Core Self (VCS). This special case of 'State Consciousness' is the mainstay of all living creatures. It is the foundation for every conscious experience we go through. Essentially, it is (the basis of) what makes us sentient beings, providing us with a constant awareness of our existence. PC gives meaning to the external world for our survival and reproduction. In simpler terms, it's the driving force behind our capability to pilot through life's phases with purpose and understanding.

VCS is like the invisible operator of consciousness - you cannot see it, but you know it is there. It is not something you can observe, like a tree or jam out to your favorite song. Nope, VCS is more like a gut feeling, an intuition (instincts) that all living beings are empowered with.

This can be likened to the cousin of deep sleep (NREM- Non-Rapid Eye Movement Sleep) - you cannot quite put your finger on it, but you know it's hanging around somewhere. It is a virtual entity like virtual particles or dark matter which are not detected by any device but are needed to explain all the visible physical phenomena of the physical universe.

While machines may be clueless when it comes to detecting VCS or Pure Consciousness (PC), we humans are the prime audience for this spectacle. We can experience PC in all its glory, unlike those virtual particles and dark matter that remain forever out of reach.

I want to clarify that when I compare virtual particles and VCS, it's purely metaphorical. I do not want to confuse you by equating VCS to virtual particles or dark matter.

Religious philosophies worldwide have their names for Pure Consciousness (PC or VCS). Mystics from various faiths allege experiencing this Pure Consciousness. It is like everyone is trying to describe this as an omniscient, omnipotent, and omnipresent God from their unique perspective. In

Vedanta, it's called Brahman which is the same as Atman for every living being.

Spiritual Experiences in Different Religions

The process of personal devotional and prophetic experiences differs from mystical experiences. In Buddhism, Nirvana is a personal experience with a personal Being. In Hinduism, Moksha is a personal experience with a personal Being or with an Ultimate Reality, Brahman. At the same time, Sufism in Islam, Meister Eckhart's experience in Christianity, and Kabbalism in Judaism are mystical experiences with God. Muhammad experienced God's direct intervention in his life. Christians' Promised Land and the Pure Land of Mahayana Buddhism are quite similar, but you will not find them in any other religion. Older religions were chock-full of mythology and mysteries.

The next era of religions was all about getting social and getting your ritual on. We are talking Vedic religion and the big three Abrahamic religions of the West - Islam, Christianity, and Judaism. Then came the devotional, surrender, and Bhakti era, where mystical experiences were all the rage. This comprises Kabbalah for the Jews, Sufism for the Muslims, and some experiences from the Christian Saints. Many Hindu mystics can also be included in this group.

After that, the knowledge-era came strutting in and it's still going strong. Buddhism, Jainism, and Vedanta or Upanishadic philosophy have played major roles. Knowledge of the mind, brain, consciousness, self, and soul through science has also emerged and evolved.

Kabbalah of Judaism

Moses ben Maimonides penned the 'Commentary on the Mishnah,' condensing the core beliefs of Judaism into 13 articles. These articles entail the existence of the Creator, his unity, his immateriality, his eternity, the omniscience of God, the truth about prophets, the superiority of Moses among prophets, the Revelation of the Law to Moses at Saini, the immutability of the Laws, personal worship of God, coming of Messiah, and Resurrection of the dead.

Moving on to the mystical beliefs of Judaism - Kabbalah. This mystical teaching is all about the Zohar, also known as the 'Splendor.' It was supposedly written by Moses De Leon in Spain and analyzes deeply the notion of God as "En Sof," infinite and mysterious. From this infinite source come ten qualities, or "Sefiroth," like wisdom, intelligence, justice, and mercy, that shape the world.

One of the Kabbalah's biggest followers was Isaac Luria from a Jewish family, who hightailed it out of Spain and settled in Palestine in 1492 A.D. Luria was all about reincarnation, believing that souls were created when the world was born and would eventually reunite with the divine at the time of salvation (Note 1).

There was a movement known as 'Enlightenment' led by Moses Mendelssohn (1728-1786) who interpreted Judaism based on the ideas of Leibnitz and believed in God, in his Providence, and the immortality of the soul. East Prussian philosopher, Immanuel Kant was also an important figure to modernize Judaism based on logic and simplified rituals.

Sufism of Islam

Sufism, also known as Tasawwuf, is the ascetic and mystic aspect of Islam that focuses on purifying the inner self (Tazkiya) and spirituality. Those who practice Sufism are called Sufis, and their goal is to connect with God by returning to their original pure state, known as 'Fitra' through intuitive and emotional faculties. While Sufism is primarily associated with Sunni Islam, it has also influenced Shia Islam to some extent. Sufis strive for perfection in worshiping Allah (ihsan) as outlined in the Hadith. They view Muhammad as a spiritual guide, the perfect human who symbolizes Absolute Reality, and they follow his teachings and practices, known as Sunnah.

Sufism is the branch of Islam that picks apart the science of the soul. Followers of Orthodox Islam believe that they will be reunited with Allah in paradise after the last judgment. However, Sufis take a more proactive approach, seeking to achieve closeness to Allah in this lifetime.

Contrary to popular belief, Sufism is not a mere academic pursuit. It is a path of devotion aimed at attaining union with God, as proposed by Imam Al-Ghazali. This involves taking up hardships, seeking solitude, maintaining silence, enduring hunger, and sacrificing sleep. It's like the intense meditation practices found in Buddhism and Hinduism, but with a unique Sufi curve.

Practices in Sufism

In Sufism, one must pay homage to the saints by visiting their tombs and Dargah (shrine). Some most famous Dargahs include Dhahbaz Qalandar in Sindh, Ali Hujwari in Lahore, Pakistan, Bahauddin Zakariya in Multan, Pakistan, Moinuddin Chishti in Ajmer, India, Nizamuddin Auliya in Delhi, India, Shah Jalal in Sylhet, Bangladesh, and Afaq Khoja near Kashgar, China.

Other practices include Dhikr, meaning remembering or being aware of Allah by worshipping through ceremonies and rituals known as Sema which may include singing and recitation (also known in the Indian subcontinent as Qawwali music), instrumental music, dance, Sufi whirling, incense, meditation, ecstasy, and trance. Sufi whirling, also known as Sufi spinning, is a form of physically active meditation where practitioners let go of their desires and ego (VES) to focus on connecting with Allah. It's like planets orbiting around the Sun, aiming to reach the source of perfection.

Another practice by Sufis is known as Muraqaba which is like intense meditation by withdrawing all his attention from the outside world, concentrating inwardly, and turning his full consciousness towards God (Allah). Sufi Saint Amir Khusrau originally started Qawwali in the 13th century by infusing Persian, Arabic, Turkish, and Indian classical music, which is now performed at all Dargahs. Pakistani singer, Nusrat Fateh Ali Khan, has made Qawwali popular in the modern world. The most famous

Sufi poets and philosophers include Rumi, Khoja Akhmet Yassawi, and Attar of Nishapur, Rudaki, Nizami and so on (Note 2).

Jainism

Mahavira of Jainism summarizes his theory in nine categories – Jiva, Ajiva, Bandha, Paap, Punya, Asrava, Samvara, Nirjara, and Moksha. Jiva is the soul characterized by consciousness. Ajiva is anything other than soul, i.e. non-living matter or body. Asrava means the inflow of Karma (both good and bad) affecting the soul. Bandha (bondage) is the attachment of Karma to the soul. Samvara means stoppage of Karma to the soul. Nirjara means shedding or detachment of Karma from the soul. Moksha means liberation or salvation or Nirvana when there is no Karma attached to the soul. Knowledge of these nine principles is important for the liberation of the soul. Not only good Karma but withdrawal from Karma is the only way to liberation (P. T. Raju, 1968).

In certain passages of his writings, Mahavira distinguishes between the true self, known as Atman, and the empirical self, referred to as 'I'. Mahavira identifies the soul, or Jiva, as the empirical self - the vessel through which one gains knowledge. When discussing liberation, he appears to liken the soul to the Atman of the Upanishads - pure and unchanging. According to Jainism, there are numerous Jivas, each possessing consciousness (Note 3).

Buddhism

Buddha speaks of a consciousness that endures beyond the physical body. However, consciousness is a worldly phenomenon that is constantly evolving. So how can it possibly outlast the body? Buddhists have provided an answer: consciousness is in a state of constant flux, a continuous process that carries on even after the death of this body to the body in the next life. The self is simply a series of individual moments of consciousness (Note 4).

In the context of Nirvana, Buddha made it clear that it is not the removal of worldly problems and miseries rather it is changing attitude towards suffering and that frees man from suffering. Nirvana is the extinction of flame or fire of desire, greed, anger, ignorance, etc. These need to be extinguished to achieve Nirvana.

Consciousness is the cause of birth and rebirth because the body, sensations, and perceptions cease at death. However, Consciousness continues and if Consciousness is sunk to rest, then rebirth stops for him. Nirvana is like an expiring flame that has no more fuel to burn (P. T. Raju, 1968).

Many meditational techniques have been developed by Buddhists to experience and achieve the Nirvana state such as Zen, Dxogchen, Vipasana and others (Note 5).

Hinduism – Upanishad or Vedanta

In Hinduism, the most philosophical aspect lies within the Upanishads, which translates to "a closed session." The word 'Upa' means 'near' and 'sad' means 'to sit,' punctuating the necessity of close, intimate learning. Upanishads are considered to contain secret knowledge, with only a select few granted access to their teachings. There are 112 (or some argue 108) Upanishads in total, with 13 standing out as the main ones:

Chandogya, Brhadaranyaka, Taittiriya, Kena, Katha, Isa, Svetasvatara, Mundaka, Taittiriya, Aitareya, Kausitaki and so on. The Upanishads, also known as Vedanta, are considered the 'Anta' (end) of Vedic literature. They were created around 700 BC and were not the work of just one person, but rather a collaborative effort over a long period of time.

Upanishad contains the idea of only one God or one supreme reality. These ancient texts contain knowledge of Atman (Soul) and Brahman and liberation from rebirths. Brahman is nothing but universal Consciousness and Atman is individual Soul or Consciousness, and Atman and Brahman are not different.

Many authors have commentary and explanation about it: Chakravarty (1992), Alston (1971), Krishnananda (eBook: Lessons on the Upanishads: 1990), Forman (1990), Mehta (1970), Gangolli (1986), Raina (1995), Islam (1988), Verma (1992), Bahadur (1977), Houde (1960), Ram (1995), RadhaKrishnana (1995), Parrinder (1973), Gupta (1991), Indich (1980), Rao (1984), Hanson (2009), Woods (1977), Elenjimittam (1977), Sureshananda (1999), Tedlock (1992), Mikhailov (1981) and so on.

Sankara, a South Indian Brahmin (788 – 820 A.D.) and devout follower of Shiva, plumbed the depths of Upanishadic writings. He proclaimed that Brahman, the Absolute, and Atman within a person are one and the same. According to Sankara, one does not transform into Brahman upon liberation. Rather, liberation is attained by shedding ignorance and recognizing that one has always been a Brahman at heart.

Sankara describes Brahman as the epitome of non-dual, transcendental, and purely spiritual reality. Each Jiva, or soul, recognizes this divine essence as Atman or the Self with a capital 'S'. This concept is beyond definition, as the Upanishads convey through the cryptic phrase *'Neti, Neti'* - meaning 'not this, not that'. The true nature of Brahman remains elusive, yet its essence can be understood through the wisdom of various Upanishads. Here are the teachings summarized in four key sayings from these ancient texts (Indich), and (Note 6- Ref. 149-152):

1. Brahman is Consciousness - *Prajnanm Brahma* (*Aitareya* Upanishad): This Mahavakya identifies Brahman, the ultimate reality, as pure consciousness. It suggests that the essence of existence and the universe is not material but rooted in an all-pervading, infinite consciousness. Consciousness is not a byproduct of matter; it is the foundational reality.
2. I am Brahman – *Aham Brahmasmi* (*Brihadaranyaka* Upanishad): This statement signifies the unity between the individual self and Brahman. It declares that the essence of one's own self is the same as the ultimate reality.

3. Thou Art That – *Tat Tvam Asi* (Everything is Brahman) (Chandogya Upanishad): It accentuates that everything in existence shares the same divine essence.

4. This Atman is Brahman - *Ayam Atma Brahma* (Mandukya Upanishad): This Mahavakya further elaborates on the identity between Atman (individual soul) and Brahman (universal soul). It suggests that the self we perceive within is not distinct from the ultimate reality but is a manifestation of it.

These *Mahavakyas* (key sayings) collectively teach that the separation between the self and the universe is illusory. The realization of non-duality (Advaita)—that everything is Brahman—is the ultimate goal of spiritual practice.

Properties of Brahman (PC or VCS)

Brahman is Non-Dual (Advait), eternally existing, original, all-pervading, Permanent, *Akshara* (cannot be destroyed), transcendental, Omniscient, Omnipresent, Omnipotent, Independent, pure, homogenous, infinite, self-caused, self-luminous, self-revealing, Absolute and Ultimate reality.

Non-Dual means that Brahman is self-luminous, self-revealing and self-knowing and does not require any other support or instrument of knowledge, such as a sense organ or mind. For knowing anything else, sense organs and the mind are needed, and subject-object or knower-known duality is there. Brahman is existence, knowledge, and infinity or Bliss (SatChitAnand).

Brahman is the same as the Virtual Absolute Self (VAS) or Pure Consciousness (PC) or Virtual Core Self VCS) as defined in the previous chapter. Brahman is characterized by many negative terms: *Acintya* (unthinkable), *Anirvacaniya* (indescribable), Immutable (unchangeable), Imperishable (undecaying), Immortal, unborn, uncaused, Ineffable, without qualification, without any activity, passive, beginningless, formless, deathless and birthless. It can neither be produced, nor destroyed. One cannot kill Soul or Atman. All these definitions make

Brahman a puzzling thing. It's quite perplexing to see so many negative terms used to describe a positive Brahman.

It cannot be known in a traditional process of knowing as an object by subject – knower, knowledge, and known. It is neither cause nor effect. It can only be experienced with subject and object at the same time. Brahman or Atman is knowing the subject and reality itself as one thing, not two. Knower and known (subject and object) are the same for Brahman/Atman. Knowing the subject (VCS or Brahman) and the objective world are identical. This means virtual objects are experienced with the help of Brahman/Atman (VCS). The basis of knowing all virtual objects is Atman or Brahman or VCS or PC. When Brahman or Atman is known, all perceived objects are already known.

Vedanta's 'World' is the Same as the 'Virtual Inner World'

In my opinion, the 'world' that Vedanta refers to is not the physical outside world, but rather to what I described in the previous chapter as the Virtual Inner World that we perceive. We can only perceive the physical external world through the Virtual Inner World we create in our brains. Everything we experience, including our selves (VES), must have Atman (PC, VCS, or VAS) as its foundation. The only way to truly know Atman (PC or VCS) is through intuitive experience, which does not rely on our senses, mind, or intellect, which are insentient and subject to change. Mind, senses, intellect, memory, and ego-I (VES or self) are all objects to Atman (VCS or PC), so Atman or VCS, PC, or VAS cannot be objects to our mind, senses, Ego-I, self, soul, or intellect.

Virtual Inner World as *'Maya'* or Illusion

Adi Shankaracharya teaches us that the world is merely an illusion (*'Maya'*), or as he puts it, "Brahman Satyam, Jagat Mithya" (Brahman is the only truth, everything else in the world is false or illusion). In simpler terms, he is saying that everything we see and experience is not as real as we think.

To break it down further, think of it like this: the Virtual Inner World we conjure up in our minds may be like an illusion (*'Maya'*). It's there one moment, and poof, it's gone the next. Unlike physical objects in the real world, our mental creations are constantly shifting and changing as we shift our focus from one object to the next.

Sure, the external physical world is out there somewhere, but who's to say we are perceiving it accurately? As also stated in the previous chapter, our minds are like master illusionists, creating a virtual reality that may not always align with what's going on outside our heads.

I want to emphasize that illusion *('Maya')* here does not mean that objects in the Virtual Inner world are unreal or imaginary. They are virtually real objects. Examples of virtually unreal objects can be the murder of a villain in a film or book (novel), the fake smile of a woman in a Coke advertisement or a mirage.

Atman (PC) as Witnessing Principle

In Vedanta, Brahman is referred to as Saakshi, the witnessing entity or principle. It is the knowing principle that enables phenomenal consciousness in living beings. Brahman is ever-present in living creatures during wakefulness, dreaming, and deep sleep states, as well as in the fourth state known as *'Turiya'* where only Brahman exists. It's like the ultimate cosmic spectator, always watching over us, even when we are deep in dreamland or lost in the depths of sleep.

Our understanding of Atman is limited, as we can only perceive it through the filter of other objects during the perception process. As we transition from wakefulness to dreaming, deep sleep, and the Turiya state, our ignorance gradually diminishes, allowing us to experience Brahman. It is like the Sun being obscured by clouds on a gloomy day - even though we cannot see it, it's there. And when the clouds finally part, the brilliance of the Sun becomes unmistakably clear.

In our virtual world, Atman is the all-knowing principle that reigns supreme. Once you understand this concept, there's nothing else you need to know. Even negative thoughts rely on Atman for their existence - it's like they are crashing at Atman's place rent-free!

Think of it this way: if you know clay, you do not need to memorize every clay pot out there. And if you are familiar with gold, you have got a PhD in all things bling. Atman is like that rope mistaken for a snake in the dark - once you flick on the light switch of knowledge, you realize it was just a rope all along.

Atman (aka VCS, PC, or VAS) is the chill, laid-back observer in this cosmic show, while Ego-I (VES) is the drama queen stealing the spotlight. It's like Atman is sipping a margarita on the sidelines, while Ego-I is doing a dramatic monologue center stage.

Phenomenal Consciousness is Bondage

As mentioned in previous chapters, when we experience an external object, it is called phenomenal consciousness. It is also called 'modified consciousness' because 'Pure Consciousness' (PC or VCS or Atman) is modified by a virtual object. 'Modified consciousness' is also called 'Bondage' because Atman (PC or VCS) is bound to a virtual object.

Realization of Atman (PC or VCS) is done by getting rid of Bondage. This is done by detaching VES (Ego-I) from the virtual object. This is all about shifting attention or focus away from the virtual object.

According to Sankara, this is the road to experiencing the ultimate *'Turiya'* state (*'Samadhi'* or Spiritual experience) and achieving Nirvana or moksha (salvation) in this life.

Deep Sleep and Spiritual Experiences are Different

Some people mistakenly believe that deep sleep is some sort of spiritual experience that Sankara denies. Sankara clarifies that while deep sleep may be free of suffering and duality, it's not quite the same as a spiritual experience. In deep sleep, your self (VES) is basically on vacation - no virtual objects (internal and external) to distract you, no attention being paid by your Virtual Entertainment System (VES). In contrast, a spiritual experience requires an intense focus on an object of devotion, leading to a sense of unity with reality.

Deep sleep is like a blackout in terms of awareness, while spiritual experiences are all about being present and in the moment. Spiritual experience is a "duality in unity" kind of deal. When you wake up from a deep sleep, all you know is that you had a good snooze. But after a spiritual experience, you are fully aware of the blissful ride you just took. It's like waking up from a dream and realizing you were the star of the show.

Religious Experiences in Christianity

In the Christian religion, saints claim to have experienced a mystical union where the soul and God become one, and the individual ego is surrendered in a divine ecstasy. Figures like St. John of the Cross, Richard of St. Victor, Meister Eckhart, and St. Francois de Sales have all spoken of these experiences of divine love. Love here implies the union of two entities – God and the soul when one completely surrenders to the other. It's kind of like the devotional practice of Bhakti Yoga in Hinduism. However, Sankara is all about knowledge and getting rid of ignorance (*'Avidya'*).

All religions speak of an Ultimate Reality and Absolute Truth, which may go by different names depending on the faith. Saints, Sufis, and mystics all strive to seek and experience this higher power through various methods. This Ultimate Reality is like the top-tier section of consciousness - we are talking Pure Consciousness (PC or VAS or VCS). In Vedanta, they call it Atman or Brahman. I like to think of it as the virtual creator God within each of us. The ultimate purpose of engaging with this Reality (PC, VCS, or virtual God) is achieving a state of 'Pure Consciousness' - a permanent state of happiness or bliss. In the coming chapter, I address what ties together all these different methods for experiencing Pure Consciousness or the Ultimate Reality in various religions.

Chapter 11

Experiencing Pure Consciousness

In the previous chapters, I discussed the concept of Pure Consciousness (PC or VCS) being the driving force behind every experience, making it the essence of all living beings. It is like having a little virtual creator (God) inside each of us, allowing us to interact with the world through our senses.

This is the ultimate power-up that enables us to see, hear, touch, taste, smell, and fully experience the physical universe. Everything we experience is virtual, including our very own Ego-I (VES). This Ego-I is a compilation of all our past experiences, with the current one sitting on top like the cream of the crop.

In a way, VES is like a spiral staircase, with each step adding to the foundation of past experiences, shaping our perception of reality.

These experiences define how we see the virtual objects in front of us. Virtual Empirical Self (VES) gives meaning to these objects, becoming the ultimate virtual expert. We live to please VES, as it craves more virtual goodies and becomes attached to them. This attachment leads us to do both good and evil deeds, all in the name of VES.

But hidden beneath the virtual frenzy is the Pure Consciousness (PC), Virtuous Core Self (VCS), Virtual Absolute Self (VAS), or the Brahman. VCS is the subtle observer, the silent watcher, the passive knower of all things. It is like getting to the seed of a fruit—you only reach the core once you peel back the coats of virtual experiences.

PC or VCS is the be-all and end-all of existence for all living beings. Once you pick up this concept, experiencing PC becomes a stroll in the park. PC or VCS is not something you can touch or see with your naked eye. It is like trying to catch the sky with your hands - impossible!

When you let go of your Ego-I (VES), that is when you can tap into the wonders of PC. It is like shedding layers of virtual reality and stepping into a world of Pure Consciousness. When Ego-I (VES) is negated (removed or detached), PC is experienced. If we can remove virtual objects and VES from experience, whatever is left in the experience will be Pure Consciousness (PC or VCS).

Just like the Sun hidden behind clouds, Pure Consciousness (PC) is always there, waiting to shine through. It is like trying to see the bottom of a pond through muddy water - once the mud settles, clarity emerges.

If we can quiet our minds and stop getting caught up in virtual distractions, we can tap into that deep well of PC or VCS. It is like experiencing deep sleep - except we are not aware of it in the same way we are of being awake or dreaming, because our virtual experiencer is missing during those peaceful slumbers.

While most creatures without complex brains may experience a state similar to deep sleep. Humans would like to experience PC state actively with the experiencer VES, minus the virtual objects. This is what mystics do, and it is the basis for all types of meditation. Various religions teach many techniques to experience this state. In the following discourse, I analyze the common underlying principle that unites all these methods.

Principle of Realizing Pure Consciousness

Various religions offer different techniques for achieving spiritual enlightenment or experiencing God. Despite their differences, all these methods share a common goal: to eliminate virtual objects from spiritual experience.

Now, you might be wondering, why bother with all that? Well, if you are seeking Ultimate Reality, Absolute Truth, God, Brahman, Atman, VAS, PC, or VCS, then this is the way to go. By removing these distractions of virtual objects, you can soak in the serenity of happiness, or as Vedanta puts it, the 'experience of Bliss'.

You will be able to distance yourself from all the worldly affairs of greed, desire, and action, and relish eternal happiness. After all, this is the purpose of everyone's life. Happiness, happiness, and more happiness!

It is believed that Buddha's main aim was also to eliminate sorrow (Dukkham) and find happiness in life. This is why he chose to leave his lavish palace after witnessing the suffering of a sick person, an elderly individual, and a deceased body being prepared for cremation. The essence of Buddhist meditational practices is centered around alleviating sorrow and finding inner peace.

All religions guide us toward the ultimate goal of experiencing a state of divine connection - the experience of God. In Vedanta, that is known as Brahman or Atman.

When you (your VES) are experiencing a virtual object, you are indirectly experiencing Virtual God. In normal phenomenal conscious experience, PC is superimposed on the virtual object, and you do not experience PC (Virtual God) directly. Once you detach VES from the virtual object, you will not experience the virtual object, rather you will experience the ultimate reality or VAS or VCS or Brahman, or Atman, or Pure Consciousness (PC) or Virtual God.

This principle also applies to feelings of pain and sorrow. By shifting focus from the source of discomfort to something more engaging and beneficial, one can alleviate those negative emotions. Another effective approach is to detach the Ego-I or VES from the pain. This gives peace, happiness or bliss.

Now, let us take a closer look at the art of detachment of VES and interpret how it is the fundamental principle behind all religious practices aimed at realizing a higher power (PC or VCS or God).

First Method – Detaching VES by Keeping Attention Away

Like Buddha, the definitive goal of all theistic religions is to cast away grief and open up to happiness. The principle for achieving this blissful state and connecting with the divine (VCS or PC) is to refrain from VES and all those virtual distractions. Instead, engage in something that truly captivates you - whether it is strumming a guitar, tickling the ivories, painting a masterpiece, getting lost in a good book, hitting the field for a game, battling it out in a computer game, molding clay, pondering life's mysteries, penning a novel, belting out a tune, chatting with your close friend (bosom buddy), or binge-watching an interesting show or movie.

All of these require concentration on the task you are doing at that time and not thinking of your self (VES) at that time. When this concentration is so much that you are not aware of even the task you are doing, your physical location, and time, you are close to realizing the ultimate truth: VAS, VCS, PC or Virtual God, or Atman or Brahman.

Remember when I mentioned how your knee or shoulder pain vanishes when you divert your attention elsewhere? It is like a disappearing act! By disconnecting from VES, you can achieve the same pain-free state.

One might wonder if resorting to violence, such as killing non-believers, suicide bombing, forced conversions, or destroying religious shrines, can achieve the same goal of diverting attention from VES. However, true enlightenment comes from understanding and tolerance, not from fear and destruction.

In my opinion, these actions arise from jealousy, greed, and lust, which are all indicators of VES involvement. Therefore, pursuing such destructive behaviors will not lead to the concentration needed to attain peace of mind or connect with a higher power. These actions are typically driven by personal, social, or political motives, rather than a genuine desire for spiritual growth. While the question of whether you will end up in heaven remains uncertain, one thing is for sure - indulging in these negative behaviors will not bring you true happiness or bliss in this lifetime. So, why not opt for a more fulfilling and virtuous path instead?

Second Method – Concentrating on One Object

Another method is to focus solely on a single object. Take, for instance, watching a sunrise or sunset. By fixating your attention solely on the sun, you will eventually only see its radiant red hue. If you continue to concentrate even more intently, you will find yourself completely immersed in the pure experience. Before you know it, the red color will fade away, leaving you in a state of blissful oblivion.

In meditation, the core principle is to focus solely on one object, typically a dot in the center of your vision. By being engrossed in this dot, you can achieve a state of Pure Consciousness (PC). However, the mind likes to wander off to other distractions, like Ego-I or VES and other virtual worldly temptations, which can disrupt your focus.

As stated in a previous chapter, directing your focus on pain can help alleviate it. This concept is reminiscent of the mindful meditation practices found in Buddhism. By consciously paying attention to each part of your body, from your toes to your head, while breathing in and out, you can shift your focus away from virtual objects and distractions. Instead of fixating on the pain itself, you are observing the process of pain and not the end result which is a feeling of pain without getting caught up in the associated VES.

I had read that in the past, Tibetan monks had to ace a meditation test before they could officially become monks. They had to sit on an ice slab and melt it without even flinching from the cold. It is all about keeping their focus elsewhere or detaching VES.

The same principle is used by fire walkers. By diverting their attention away from the fire and detaching VES, they can walk on hot coals without getting burned. It is a phenomenon even physicists cannot fully explain. They have been trying to make sense of this paradox since it was first observed around 100 years ago.

Religious Rituals Achieve the Same Goal (Bliss)

Engaging in religious rituals, offering prayers to God, and reading Holy Books such as the Bible, Quran, Gita, or Ramayana, all operate on a common principle: shifting your focus away from yourself (VES or EGO-I). It is not about what you are reading. The actual content of the Holy Book may not matter. You do not even have to understand it or pay attention to its message. The idea is to keep away from your 'self' (VES or Ego-I) and virtual objects during the time of prayer.

I am drawn to the melodic tempo of the Ramayana, a revered Hindu scripture. The rhythmic recitation intrigues me, even if I may not fully grasp its meaning. It is like a symphonic composition for my ears, soothing and enchanting.

Some devotees chant their deity's name 108 times, carefully counting each bead on their pearl or Rudraksha garland. It is a ritual that exceeds religious boundaries, whether in temples, mosques, churches, synagogues, or Gurudwaras. The common thread? A temporary escape from our EGO-I (VES) while engaging in prayer.

Going on a pilgrimage does the same magic. Visiting a new place does the same trick. The best meter is that time must fly during the time you are doing these things as you are having a good time- a happy and blissful experience.

Compare these with when you are informed about some bad news, e.g. an accident of a close family member, and how it makes you (your Ego-I or VES) worry and time moves so slowly as if time has stopped for you.

Three Methods for Spiritual Experience

Hinduism has systematically devised three paths for spiritual enlightenment - experiencing Pure Consciousness (PC), also known as VCS, VAS, Brahman, Atman, or God.

Bhakti Yoga (Devotional Method)

Bhakti Yoga, also known as the devotion path, involves activities such as visiting temples, engaging in prayers and rituals, and reading Holy books. This spiritual practice is often referred to as Savikalpa Samadhi, where individuals experience a determinate spiritual connection. However, true non-duality, meaning complete unity with Brahman (VCS or VAS or PC), is achieved through Nirvikalpa Samadhi, an indeterminate spiritual experience.

Savikalpa meditation involves directing your attention to a specific deity, such as Lord Rama, Lord Krishna, or Lord Jesus, often represented by an idol or image. Nirvikalpa meditation takes it a step further by detaching your attention even from these divine figures. To put it simply, to transcend means to shift your focus away from all objects and your 'self' (VES of Ego-I) altogether.

Karma Yoga (Action Method)

Karma Yoga, also known as the action or work method, is like the cool cousin of traditional yoga. It is all about doing something you love with laser focus, without letting your Ego-I (VES) get in the way. Imagine you are jamming on your guitar, not stressing about winning a competition or making a bank. Or maybe you are playing a game, just for the sheer joy of it, not caring if you win or lose. It is all about the process, not the result. You experience peaceful, enjoyable and happy times without any worries during the action.

In the Bhagavad Gita, Krishna shares some wisdom with Arjuna, telling him to go into battle without getting hung up on the outcome. Arjuna was all like, "But they are my cousins!" And Krishna was like, "Just do your thing and let the chips fall where they may."

The engaging verse "**Karmanye Vadhikaraste Ma Phaleshu Kadachana**" is the most popular shloka from Bhagavad Gita Chapter-2 verse-47.

This translates into: *"You have a right to perform your prescribed duties, but you are not entitled to the fruits of your actions. Never consider yourself to be the cause of the results of your activities, nor be attached to inaction."*

Jnana Yoga (Knowledge Method)

Jnana Yoga (knowledge path) is the third method through which one seeks to learn and realize the Ultimate Truth. I am currently walking this enlightening path. According to Sankara, the knowledge path reigns supreme among the three paths. Once you attain a deep understanding of the Ultimate Truth, liberation awaits you.

The way it works is that you detach your 'self' (VES or Ego-I) knowingly and deliberately at each step of your life. Just sit back and observe what is going on around you. Take note of all those thoughts flashing in your mind, but do not let them ruffle your feathers. That is how you detach from your 'self' (VES).

In the above three methods, the common principle at work is detachment of VES. You transcend VES. Once VES is detached, you are connected to PC or VCS or 'Brahman' or 'the Bliss', which is the main purpose of everyone in this life.

Ecstatic Love in Christianity and Islam

In Christian tradition, the love of God takes center stage. The bliss of Bhakti yoga mirrors the ecstatic experience of love felt when a seeker unites with God. Sufis, the mystics of Islam, also describe a similar experience of ecstatic love when united with Allah. Love represents the merging of two distinct entities - the individual soul and God becoming one. This union can only be achieved when a seeker fully surrenders to God, letting go of their Ego-I (VES). These are some seriously emotional states we are talking about here.

Both Christianity and Islam press on the need to help those in need through donations. This may be similar to the Karma Yoga of Hinduism.

Ecstatic Experiences in Normal Situations

Extreme emotions like ecstatic joy, extreme sorrow, and intense anger are said to be so overwhelming that they make you lose your 'self' (Ego-I or VES) in the moment. In these states, your Ego-I takes a backseat, leaving you feeling completely out of control. If you have ever been so happy that you found yourself in tears, you know exactly what I am talking about. It is like your emotions are driving the car and you are just along for the ride.

When you are in the depths of despair after losing a loved one, you may put on a brave face in public. But as soon as you see someone you are close to, all bets are off. You cry rivers of emotions and sob uncontrollably as you cling to them for dear life. Your 'self' (VES or Ego-I) is completely out of your control at that moment. There is no perception of anything else to you in your surroundings at that moment. It is like a tornado of emotions has taken over, leaving you powerless in its wake.

Imagine this: you are out there in the world, being a total hero. You save a stranger from drowning, perform CPR on someone having a heart attack, or just lend a helping hand without expecting anything in return. And guess what? The gratitude and joy you feel in those moments are off the charts. It is like a warm hug for your soul.

But then there is the whole "helping a friend or relative with the expectation of getting something in return" deal. Sure, it is nice to have a favor in your back pocket for a rainy day, but it does not quite hit the same level of satisfaction. It is like trying to scratch an itch with a glove on - just not as fulfilling.

Now, forgiveness? That is a completely different scenario. Letting go of grudges and moving on from someone's mistakes can bring you that same level of happiness. It is like a weight lifted off your shoulders, leaving you feeling lighter and freer.

Pure Consciousness (Brahman or Atman) in Advaita Vedanta

In Advaita, there is no duality, so there is no need to talk of love between two entities or surrendering one to the other. Only VCS (Self or PC) is there. Removal of Avidya (ignorance) is what is needed with knowledge. Ignorance causes wrong identification of Self (VCS or VAS or PC) to virtual objects (illusion or 'Maya'). That is why it is said that liberation or Moksha is not to be attained, rather VCS or PC is always there like the Sun behind the cloud of ignorance. You only need to remove the cloud of ignorance to see the Sun or to experience VCS or PC. That is why Sankara says that Jnana Yoga (knowledge path) is superior to the three paths mentioned above.

Bondage and Liberation in Eastern Religions

According to Eastern religious philosophies, ignorance leads to selfish actions and bondage. During a phenomenal conscious experience, the virtual object is 'bound' to PC or VCS (Atman) and because of ignorance, it is called Bondage. Bondage to virtual objects is through greed and desire of VES. Liberation from bondage occurs when one detaches VES from virtual objects leading to the realization of PC or true enlightenment.

Atman, or PC or VCS or VAS perceives a virtual object as 'This', while VES or Ego-I sees it as 'mine' out of sheer ignorance. Just like how space is liberated when a pot is shattered, the liberation of Atman or VAS or PC or VCS occurs when VES or Ego-I is detached. Vedanta teaches us that virtual objects and Ego-I (VES) are mere illusions or Maya, and once this realization dawns upon us, true freedom is attained.

Harris, in his book, 'Waking Up', writes a similar thought (Page 82, Harris):

"My goal in this chapter and the next is to convince you that the conventional sense of self is an illusion – and that spirituality largely consists in realizing this, moment to moment. There are logical and scientific reasons to accept this claim but recognizing it to be true is not a matter of understanding these reasons. Like many illusions, the sense of self disappears when closely examined, and this is done through the practice of meditation."

Meditational Methods in Buddhism

Non-religious philosophies such as Buddhism have developed a wealth of meditative techniques, including Zen, Ch'an, Dzogchen, Vipassana, and mindful meditation, all aimed at alleviating sorrow (Dukkha) and attaining happiness (Bliss, Nirvana, Moksha, salvation, and so on).

Buddha also pressed on the relevance of recognizing desire, greed, and attachment as the root causes of suffering, advocating for detachment as the path to liberation from such afflictions.

Conclusively, all religions point to God as the Ultimate reality, the Absolute Truth. Vedanta refers to it as Brahman (Atman for each individual). This Ultimate reality is Pure Consciousness (PC or VAS or VCS), a state or principle of knowing rather than a tangible thing or person. While it cannot be perceived as an object or a person, it is present in all experiences. To experience it, one must detach their EGO-I (VES) and other virtual objects from the experience, a task that Mystics and Sufis excel at.

Different religions offer various methods to achieve this enlightenment. Western religions advocate for a path of love and devotion, while Hinduism suggests both a devotional and meditational approach. Nevertheless, non-religious philosophies like Buddhism and Jainism focus on meditational techniques to reach this ultimate goal. So, whether you are a devout believer or a philosophical wanderer, there is a path for everyone to find their way to Pure Consciousness.

The universal principle that underpins all these methods is shifting your focus away from virtual objects. This is also achieved by detaching Ego-I or VES from virtual objects during the perception process.

When we start to see through the illusion that virtual objects have any real importance, we are taking a big step towards freeing ourselves from their hold on us. This means that our sense of self, or our Ego-I, is no longer tied up in how we perceive these virtual objects. Instead, we can start to see that our experiences are fleeting and temporary.

Once we are able to separate ourselves from the influence of virtual objects, we can start to see the world more clearly and objectively. This means that we are not clouded by our own biases or ego-driven desires. Our awareness expands, giving us a better understanding of reality that goes beyond the distractions of the Virtual Inner world.

Chapter 12

Puzzling Questions of Life

Religious believers often argue that science does not measure up when it comes to answering life's big questions. Questions like: What's the rationale for the universe? Why are we here? Who are we, really? Are we the only ones out here in this vast universe? It is like a staircase of questions but with way higher stakes.

We think about the purpose of our existence, the meaning of life, and whether there is a big plan or if we are all just floating around aimlessly. Are we special creations of a higher power, or just a cosmic accident? And what is the deal with heaven and hell - are they real places, or just metaphors for the human experience?

Then there is another pressing mystery: the afterlife - is there a soul, and what happens to it when we perish? Are we destined for eternal bliss or eternal damnation? And speaking of damnation, is Jesus the lone bridge to heaven, or are there other ways to land a spot in the exclusive lounge?

What about reincarnation - is there life after death(reincarnation) as believed in Eastern religions like Hinduism, Buddhism and Jainism? Can God perform miracles, and if so, do they actually work? Are ghosts real, and why does God sometimes seem to have a penchant for natural disasters? Do humans have free will?

So many questions, so few answers. But at least we are all in this existential crisis together, right?

Sam Harris, in his book, 'Waking Up', wrote that life's questions are great but false (Page 202):

"What is the meaning of life? What is our purpose on earth? These are some of the great, false questions of religion. We need not answer them, for they are badly posed, but we can live our answers all the same. At a minimum, we can create the conditions for human flourishing in this life – the only life of which any of us can be certain."

Some authors believe that science and religion are compatible, and both are needed. Others proclaim that science and religion are very similar, and both can answer life's important questions.

Science is impartial and unable to clear up the complexities of human emotions and experiences such as love, hate, beauty, happiness, sorrow, hope, forgiveness, courage, evil, suffering, pain, sadness, loneliness, desire, greed, lust, anger, and the list goes on. It is like asking a calculator to compose a symphony – it is just not designed for the task. So, while science can provide valuable visions into the physical world, it leaves much to be desired when it comes to understanding the nuances of the human heart and soul.

In previous chapters, I have tried to suggest that science and religion do not mix well, as they each address different fields of inquiry. However, the majority of individuals rely on both to steer their lives. By "most people," I am referring to the average person, not the die-hard extremists from one extreme to the other - the fervent believers or the staunch atheists. These extremists insist that only one of the two - science or religion - holds the answer to truth. Science centers solely on the physical aspects of the universe, while religion believes in the non-physical nature of God.

I attempt to answer some of these questions in this chapter from my perspective of the virtual nature of God, which I have sought to defend in previous chapters.

Does God Exist?

When deliberating the existence of God, I find myself asking a more curious question: 'What is the nature of God?' Different religions offer varying perspectives on this matter. Christianity, Islam, and Judaism envision a creator God who is personal and loving, always looking out for you. Alternatively, Buddhism and Jainism do not believe in the whole creator God idea. Hinduism, conversely, holds different schools of thought. The Vedas believe in a creator God, while Vedanta sees Brahman as the ultimate reality or God, the all-knowing principle.

The concept of a creator is often used by religious believers to justify the existence of a God who created the universe. However, in previous chapters, I have argued that if we consider the physical universe to be constantly changing and eternal, then a creator God may not be necessary.

If we do not need a creator God to create and manage the universe, then the answers to the following questions are obviously 'no':

- Did God create the universe and control it?

- Does God control every event in our lives?

- Did God create humans as a special species?

- Why does God allow natural disasters to harm His people?

True Nature of God

The defining question for humans is: How do we become aware or conscious of the world around us? How do we experience the sights, sounds, tastes, touches, and smells that make up our reality?

In the previous chapters, I have argued that the true creator (God) is the mastermind behind the virtual universe that exists within each of us. This virtual universe is constantly being created and recreated every second, providing us with the awareness and consciousness we need to navigate our surroundings. It is the only universe we can truly know, as there is no other way for us to connect with the external physical universe.

However, this virtual universe within us is not a permanent fixture. It is ever-changing, with each passing moment.

I call this virtual creator in us as Virtual Absolute Self (VAS) or Virtual Core Self (VCS) or Soul. Religious philosophies refer to it as Pure Consciousness (PC, Self or Soul with capital 'S'). Vedanta calls it Brahman (or Atman for each individual).

Is God Real? – God is Virtually Real

Ok so, there is no physical God who created this universe and runs it whom you will be able to meet in heaven. If there is no such God, then there is no heaven or hell where you are going to meet God when you die and get rewarded or punished.

However, if believing in a virtual God gives someone hope, courage, strength, love, purpose, and happiness so that he or she can live happily every day of his or her life, what is wrong with that? This virtual God can be Jesus, Rama, Krishna, Hanuman, Shiva, Allah, Yahweh, or Buddha.

I recently caught wind on NPR about a woman who attempted suicide four times and stunningly survived each time. On her final try, she experienced a vision and heard voices telling her that she had a purpose in life and should not give up. This sense of hope, courage, and purpose gave her the strength to carry on. What is the harm in that? Whether or not there is a physical God is beside the point - it is all about the power of positive thinking. There are innumerable similar stories out there of people being saved by a glimmer of hope or a newly gained purpose. It does not matter what religion she followed or which deity she saw in her vision - what matters is that she found a reason to keep going (Note 1).

Purpose of the Universe

It is easy to answer the related question: 'What is the purpose of the universe?'. A purpose implies a beginning and an end, which means something has to be created. If the universe has been around forever, then it does not need a purpose other than just existing and changing for eternity.

When we think about the purpose of the universe, things can get pretty complicated. Especially when we consider how the universe is always changing and evolving. It's not just sitting still, it's growing, transforming, and expanding all the time. So maybe the universe's purpose (final state) is not predetermined. Maybe it's not about where it started or where it's going, but about what it's doing right now.

This idea suggests that the universe doesn't have just one single purpose (one final state). Instead, it has endless possibilities that reveal as time goes on. It's like the universe is always trying out new things, seeking different paths, and expressing itself in unique ways. It's not just a boring old thing that stays the same—it's always changing and evolving.

Purpose of Life

In the first paragraph, all the questions mentioned relate to God, or as religious believers like to call it, 'Teleological'. However, if we entertain the idea that the physical universe has existed eternally and does not require a God to create or run it, then these questions do not necessarily need a 'Teleological' connection. They can be answered on a more local level.

For instance, when weighing the 'purpose of life', on a universal scale, it is simply to live and procreate, as evidenced by observing other creatures in nature. On an individual level, you are free to choose whatever purpose you want for your life. It does not alter the universal purpose of nature, nor does it interfere with anyone else's personal purpose in life.

Meaning of Life

When ruminating over the question of the 'meaning of life', one must understand that it is us, the living creatures, who bring purpose and virtue to everything around us. Unlike lifeless objects such as stones and robots, we have the unique ability to impart meaning to the world. This vast contrast between sentient beings and non-sentient entities is what sets us apart.

Take, for instance, the Hindus who skillfully carve a stone into an idol of Lord Shiva, known as a Shivling, and then proceed to worship it with reverence. To them, this piece of stone holds a special meaning.

As stated in previous chapters, the act of attributing meaning to an object is what gives rise to subjectivity and intentionality, qualities that are exclusive to living beings and cannot be replicated by inanimate objects like stones or robots.

Subjectivity and intentionality emerge from the meaning that we, as living creatures, assign to external objects. For example, the idol of Lord Shiva holds great importance for Hindus, but may not have the same or any meaning for a tribe in the depths of the Amazon jungle if they found it. It is all about the outlook through which we view the world around us.

Why are We Here (on Earth)

The answers to the questions of "Why are we here on earth?" and "Where are we going?" should be plain as day by now. We are here to procreate and eventually lay to rest - it is the circle of life! It is the one thing that is guaranteed for all living beings.

But beyond just nature's purpose of procreation and death, we can learn, grow, and make a positive impact on the world around us. We can experience love, joy, and connection with others. We can learn from our mistakes, triumph over setbacks, and evolve into our best selves. As for where we are going, that remains a mystery. Some believe in an afterlife, while others believe in reincarnation. Whatever the destination may be, we must live each day with purpose, gratitude, and kindness towards others.

Is there Life on Another Planet?

The question of whether we are the only ones in this vast universe has scientists scrambling for answers. They are out there, peering through telescopes and crunching numbers, hoping to chance upon some extraterrestrial neighbors. So far, no dice. But they are not giving up hope just yet.

Despite the lack of concrete evidence, scientists are optimistic that somewhere out there, in a galaxy far, far away, there is some form of life chilling on a distant planet. Sure, we might never get to shoot the breeze with these cosmic buddies due to the whole physical distance thing, but that does not mean we are God's favorite children or anything.

With billions of galaxies, stars, and planets out there, the odds are definitely in favor of life existing elsewhere in the universe. It is like an immense universal game of hide and seek, and we are just waiting for someone to surface from behind a nebula and yell, "Found you!" (Note 2).

But even if we never get to swap stories with our alien pals, we have one thing going for us - our super-evolved brains. We are not just wandering around randomly like a bunch of space zombies. Nope, we are considering the big questions, like the meaning of life, the existence of God, and whether or not we are merely avatars in a cosmic simulation.

And if you are feeling particularly adventurous, you can even tap into the Ultimate Reality of life, also known as Pure Consciousness. We have the capability to experience the Ultimate Reality of life (Pure Consciousness, VAS or VCS) if we desire so. It is like the deluxe section of the universe, where you can kick back, relax, and contemplate the mysteries of the cosmos. So, who needs aliens when you have got all that going on, right?

Rebirth or Reincarnation

When deliberating the question of what lies beyond this life, various belief systems offer different perspectives. Hinduism, Jainism, and Buddhism suggest the possibility of rebirth and reincarnation, while Christianity, Judaism, and Islam contemplate the concepts of heaven and hell. Christianity also holds the belief in the resurrection of Jesus, compounding the afterlife discussion.

According to science, the physical body of living beings is composed of matter subject to the law of conservation of matter and energy. This means that when living creatures pass away, their physical bodies undergo a transformation, converting into different forms of matter. Whether through cremation or burial, the body ultimately becomes ashes and gases, returning to the earth and the atmosphere.

In a sense, the physical body experiences a form of rebirth or reincarnation as its matter is recycled and indirectly used for the creation of new life.

All religions have their own take on what happens to our souls after we die. Christianity, Judaism, and Islam believe in a one-way ticket to either heaven or hell. Meanwhile, Eastern religions like Hinduism, Buddhism, and Jainism are all about rebirth or reincarnation.

Vedanta is all about Brahman or Atman (Soul) as the principle of knowledge. They are saying that if you think of the soul as Pure Consciousness (PC), then the whole reincarnation thing starts to make a lot more sense.

According to Vedanta, Pure Consciousness (PC) is like the basis of knowing stuff. It is always hanging out in all living organisms as a virtual entity. So, every living creature has this Virtual Absolute Self (VAS) or Virtual Core Self (VCS) or Soul (PC) that is witnessing everything.

Vedanta calls this whole shebang Brahman (or Atman in each living creature) and they think it is the Ultimate truth and Absolute reality.

Virtual entities do not follow the same rules as physical things. They simply appear or disappear based on the existence or non-existence of corresponding physical things.

Just like the principle of gravity, Atman (or VAS, PC, Soul - whatever you want to call it) is a principle of knowing. Just like gravity is there in all physical bodies, Atman (PC or Soul) is there in all living creatures. The Atman (PC or Soul), like gravity, is not subject to birth or death.

If Atman or (Brahman or VAS or PC) is understood as the virtual principle of knowing then it will not be difficult to understand Vedanta's claims that Brahman (or Atman or PC or VAS) is birthless, deathless, eternal, immutable, passive, ineffable, uncaused, beginningless, formless, immortal and so on. Hence, Atman (Brahman or VAS or PC or Soul) cannot die and get born again. It can neither be produced nor destroyed. One cannot kill Soul (Atman). With these qualities, its birth and death (reincarnation) are meaningless.

As mentioned in the previous chapter, virtual entities such as PC, Soul, Atman, VAS, and VCS do not adhere to the physical laws of conservation of matter and energy. This is because it is a principle of knowledge like the law of gravity.

Unlike physical matter and energy, which are finite, virtual entities have no bounds ('Anant'). This unique characteristic allows for the continuous creation of new Souls, even as the world's population grows. So, to answer my curious question as a young boy about where all these new Souls come from - it is simply a matter of channeling the infinite potential of the virtual world.

A newly born living creature is not produced from scratch from matter but is procreated from an existing living creature. Pure Consciousness is always there in all living creatures. A newly born creature gets PC or VAS when a new living creature is born from its parents.

For example, a new physical body automatically has gravity which is created from the division of a bigger physical body, e.g. moon got gravity when it was split from the earth.

Atman or Brahman, Soul or VCS or VAS or PC can never exist out of living creatures if it is considered as a principle of knowledge in the same way that gravity never exists outside a physical body because gravity is a principle.

Pure Consciousness (PC), also known as Atman/Soul or the principle of knowing, ceases to exist in a person when that person shuffles off this mortal coil. However, Atman or Soul, as a principle of knowledge, is eternal and does not perish. Life and PC are inherently connected.

For instance, gravity disappears if a body breaks down into energy or particles.

Similar to gravity, the PC or Soul (Atman) is a principle rather than a tangible entity that can be quantified like one, two, and three. It is not a case of 'Soul number one is mine, Soul number two is yours, and so forth.'

The Soul is a timeless principle of knowledge that is immortal, eternal, and indestructible. It is not something that can be born or die or killed because it exists as a virtual principle. Rebirth of something has no meaning if it did not even die (destroyed) in the first place. The soul as a principle of knowledge ceases to exist for a creature when that creature dies, and the soul comes to exist when a new creature takes birth. Life and PC (Soul) are inherently connected.

Virtual Soul

As referenced above, the Soul, or Atman, is a principle of knowledge and Pure Consciousness (PC) that exists as a virtual entity within all living creatures. It is eternal, never experiencing birth or death. When a living creature disintegrates, the Soul as a principle ceases to exist in that living creature much like how the principle of Gravity is constant and unchanging, only ceasing to exist if the physical body disintegrates.

Soul or PC or VCS or VAS or Atman or whatever name we give it to this principle of knowledge, it connects us to the universe and to each other. It is the source of our wisdom and intuition. Through the soul, we come to know the true meaning of purpose, courage, love, happiness, empathy, wisdom, happiness, hope, forgiveness, and through that, we can understand and eliminate sorrow, hate, suffering, pain, sadness, loneliness, greed, lust, anger and so on.

Heaven and Hell

When it comes to the debate of heaven and hell, it is like chasing a solution with no evidence. No one has taken a trip to the afterlife and returned with a detailed Yelp review, so we are left to speculate. Some believe, some do not - it is a multi-path scenario.

As for the whole meeting God in heaven or hell and getting rewarded or punished deal, well, let us just say I am not convinced. In my humble opinion, the universe does not need a higher power to keep things in check. If heaven and hell exist, they are just part of the cosmic furniture - no divine creator is required to create and operate it.

So, why wait around for some heavenly judgment day? Our actions in this life are what count. Good deeds bring good vibes, bad deeds bring bad juju - it is as simple as that. Let us focus on making the most of the here and now and leave the afterlife mysteries for another day.

If we view PC or Soul (VAS) as a principle of knowledge, then the question of whether the Soul goes to heaven or hell becomes irrelevant. The idea of the Soul being rewarded or punished in the afterlife is a non-issue. Therefore, prophets like Jesus are not necessary to show us the way to heaven's door.

The confusion arises when PC, VAS, or Soul is seen as a tangible entity – person or thing. If we see it as a virtual principle, it becomes evident that it is immortal (deathless), always present as a principle (eternal and birthless). However, the soul does not exist beyond the bodies of living beings and does not travel to heaven or hell. So, let us not get caught up in the semantics and focus on the bigger picture - the Soul is eternal!

Virtual Ghost

The explanation above should make it abundantly clear that ghosts cannot exist as physical beings, as the Soul, Atman, or PC cannot exist independently outside of a living creature. Ghosts are merely a creation of the human mind, existing as an illusory virtual entity within our brains.

While the idea of ghosts may provide comfort or excitement for some, we must remember that they are not tangible beings that can interact with the physical world. Belief in ghosts often derives from a desire to connect with the supernatural or to find meaning in the unknown. However, we must approach these beliefs with a critical mindset and recognize that the human mind is capable of creating elaborate illusions. By understanding the nature of ghosts as products of our imagination, we can appreciate the power of the mind while also acknowledging the limitations of our perception.

Consciousness in Buddhism

Soul or PC is different from Buddha's empirical self (Ego-I) which I argue that the Ego-I is nothing more than a virtual entity (VES) that exists in our brains during our awake and dream states but takes a snooze during deep sleep. Ego-I is the enjoyer of all experiences and is made up of a collection of all past experiences, personalities and memories.

According to Buddha, this Ego-I is just a temporary entity. It takes birth and dies, only to come back as a brand-new entity every single moment during our awake and dream states. It is like an unceasing cycle of appearance, disappearance, and reappearance - a constant reincarnation of the Ego-I. Each moment brings a fresh new Ego-I into the mix, making it impossible to tell one from the other in our day-to-day lives. It is like A bout of Ego-I, constantly changing with every passing moment in the same life.

For Buddha, Consciousness is void (Sunyata) of self (Ego-I) but has mental objects as content. He does not believe that the Soul or Atman of Vedanta transcends death and takes rebirth. For him, it is Consciousness that takes rebirth. For him, Consciousness is not permanent (eternal) but changes each moment. Rebirth of Consciousness, for him, is within this life. Nirvana stops the rebirth of Consciousness. Death causes Consciousness to end as well.

My belief is that this 'consciousness' that Buddha refers to here is the 'Phenomenal Consciousness' that I have mentioned in previous chapters while Atman is 'Pure Consciousness' (VAS).

Buddha did not believe in God, heaven, and hell. His main concern was to reduce suffering (Dukkha) in this life by changing our attitude towards suffering. Various meditation methods are developed in Buddhism, e.g. Vipasana or Mindful Meditation, to achieve Nirvana. Buddha suggested many rules of life to follow to live and to reduce suffering in this life. All religions have developed similar philosophies to live a good life.

Science Cannot Explain Virtual Aspects of Life

Physics, Chemistry and Mathematics cannot study and explain moral aspects of life such as good, bad, like, dislike, love, hate, hope, help, forgiveness, beauty, happiness, sorrow, courage, evil, suffering, death, pain, sadness, loneliness, desire, greed, lust, anger and so on. These are virtual and subjective, like taste, touch, smell, vision, and audition. Such aspects cannot be objectively quantized and studied like physical objects. There is no meter or tool to record these entities and therefore, out of the bounds of science.

Everyone cannot have the same experience of love, hate, like, dislike, pain, happiness, sorrow, suffering and so on for the same stimulus (object or person). Even the same person does not have the same experience of taste, touch, love, like, dislike, and smell at different times even for the same object.

The perception of pain can vary greatly from person to person, even when faced with the same physical sensation, like a thorn prick. Factors such as past experiences and current state of mind have a major impact on how we experience pain. These variables, being virtual, can easily be influenced by other virtual elements within the brain.

As suffering is a subjective experience, it brings up a complication for the justice system when it comes to punishing criminals fairly and objectively. For example, how should someone be punished for the extreme act of amputating another person's legs? On the other extreme, I read the news that a woman sued McDonald's for hundreds of thousands of dollars after just spilling hot coffee on her thigh and getting burned (Note 3).

There is a fine line between seeking justice and seeking compensation for personal injury.

Throughout history, various societies, religious groups, and countries have upheld unique moral values and laws for their people. What may be deemed unacceptable in one society could be perfectly normal in another.

Virtual Free-Will

In Chapter 6, I discussed how your 'self' (VES or Ego-I) has the power to assign meaning to virtual objects in your Virtual Inner World. This meaning is as flexible as a yoga instructor doing the splits. You can feel a range of sensations - from heat to cold, sweetness to bitterness, love to hate, and everything in between - all for the same physical object. It is like a series of emotional highs and lows, with no strict rules to follow. The ultimate goal? Survival.

This flexibility is what gives humans their subjectivity and Intentionality. For example, one person may shrug off a paper cut like it's no big deal, while another acts like it is the end of the world. It is all about perspective, my friends. Did you know that you can control your anxiety and stress by various breathing techniques in Yoga?

Some people just seem to feel more glee than others, even despite the same success. It seems like they have got a happiness superpower or something. You might be starving, but you can choose to hold off on dinner until your friend arrives so you can chow down together.

It is because of the virtual nature of these experiences that allows us to choose their meaning freely, which ultimately gives rise to free will. So, acknowledge the freedom and flexibility that comes with being human. This is what makes life interesting, after all.

Miracles and Miracle Healing

I do not buy into the whole 'pulling a rabbit out of a hat' type of miracle, where someone can supposedly conjure up physical objects out of thin air. I mean, come on, we are not living in a fairy tale here. For example, an Indian spiritual leader used to produce diamond rings, bananas, and apples in front of his followers in India. To me, that is just smoke and mirrors.

Every miracle that relates to the physical world must have an explanation in Physics. For example, feet of Jesus oozing water in Bombay (Chapter 2, Note 10), Ganesh idol drinking milk (Chapter 2, Note 11), ashes showing up on Photographs of Sai Baba at homes of his followers (Chapter 2, Note 9), and bread and wine becoming skin and blood during Eucharist (Chapter 2, Note 12). I have never witnessed any such miracles with my own eyes.

I am more inclined to believe in miracles that relate to our physical body and life, like miracle healing. I have laid out the reasoning behind this in previous chapters, so trust me on this one. Each person has the capacity to do this miracle healing on his or her own body. Only that person and no one else can do this miracle healing on his or her own body because his or her VES is the one that triggers the healing. They may be influenced by someone or their God, or Jesus or Allah, or Mohammad, or temples or churches or mosques, and so on, which may affect their virtual belief and thoughts and that then indirectly may affect their bodies. The influence does not necessarily have to come from religion or God. It can be anyone else like a political leader, motivational speaker, religious Guru, a movie or a book, whom someone trusts and believes.

The concept of 'Self' (VES or Ego-I) is necessary for all experiences to occur. When attention is shifted away from the virtual object, these experiences vanish into thin air.

People have reported their pain magically disappearing after visiting shrines, reciting Holy Books, attending sermons, or simply praying to their higher power. It is like a spiritual band-aid that works wonders. This is the secret to achieving happiness, a formula that even saints and mystics swear by.

Even followers of Buddhism and Jainism, who do not believe in a traditional God, can achieve the same results. Buddhism, for example, relies on meditation techniques like mindful meditation (Vipasana) and Zen meditation to work like a charm. It is like a mental spa day but without the cucumber slices. I have shared the underlying principle for these techniques in detail in the previous chapter.

It is not important to know whether God exists or not - what matters is that someone out there believes in God's existence. It makes no difference which religion you follow or which deity you worship. What truly counts is the power of belief itself. Belief is like an extraordinary power that can shape our flexible Virtual Inner World, molding it according to our thoughts and beliefs.

Like a sleight-of-hand artist working their wonder, belief works by shifting our attention away from the negative and toward the positive. It is all about focusing our attention on what brings us cheer and fulfillment while letting go of anything that brings us down.

Contrary to the beliefs of New Atheists, prayer has some sweet benefits. In his book, "Spirituality in Patient Care: Why, How, When, and Why, 2nd Ed (2008)," Koenig delivers enlightening information with examples of how prayer and other religious practices can have a positive impact. Like, did you know that people swear their knee and shoulder pain disappear when they get a hug from 'Hugging Amma' in Kerala, South India? That is some next-level healing power right there (Chapter2, Note 8).

The source of hope, courage, and purpose is not important. Whether you are finding these in Rama, Krishna, Hanuman, Durga, Jesus, Allah, Buddha, Mahaveer, or some other source, it does not matter. What counts is that hope, courage, and purpose give you the power to plow through life's tough times. So, stay the course with whatever floats your spiritual boat, because at the end of the day, it is all about finding that inner strength to own life.

Throughout history, there have been countless stories of people defying the odds and emerging victorious when confronted with obstacles. From surviving being buried under rubble after an earthquake to winning against terminal illnesses, the power of hope, prayer, courage, and purpose cannot be underestimated.

It has been proven time and time again that positive thinking can have a great impact on our health and well-being. While negative thoughts can lead to detrimental effects, an optimistic mindset can bring about hope, happiness, and courage.

In his book, Ward boldly asserts that religious individuals tend to live longer due to their enduring sense of hope, purpose, and positive outlook on life.

Positive thoughts and beliefs give rise to virtual entities such as hope, courage, and purpose, which have a deep impact on the mind and brain, ultimately influencing all bodily functions and physical well-being. This phenomenon is subjective, meaning it differs from person to person, making it difficult for science to study as it is not objective.

Despite the limitations of the aftermath of positive thoughts and beliefs on our well-being, many individuals have experienced the transformative power of a positive mindset. Whether through practices like meditation, affirmations, or simply choosing to focus on the good in life, people have found that breeding positivity can lead to increased resilience, improved mental health, and even faster recovery from illness. While science may struggle to quantify and measure these subjective experiences, the evidence of their benefits is clear in the lives of those who choose to adopt positivity.

Chapter 13

Conclusion

Sentient Being and Non-Sentient Matter

In the expansive dimensions of life, there are two distinct categories: the sentient beings and the non-sentient matter. Sentients refer to living creatures empowered with the ability to perceive and interpret the world through their senses and cognitive faculties. This intelligence, which I refer to as "State Consciousness," is formative for their survival and propagation. It is this unique capacity that sets them apart from the non-living entities that lack such awareness.

Humans have more evolved brains which make them conscious of perception and to ask deeper questions such as the purpose and creator of life and the universe. They seek better survival and happiness not only in this life (world) but wish to survive beyond this life after their death.

The Power of Belief and Happiness

As a young boy, my pursuit of God began with bowing down to idols in a temple. I was filled with curiosity, passion, and eventually, obsession to know the truth about God. After years of research, I arrived at the conclusion that the existence of God is not the most pressing question. Instead, what truly matters is 'understanding the nature of God' and 'how that belief shapes an individual's life'. Whether or not God exists is irrelevant compared to the impact of one's belief in God. It is the belief itself that holds the power to transform a person, regardless of the reality of God's existence.

Think about it - our life of approximately 100 years is a drop in the ocean of multi-billion years of the universe. For all practical purposes, the universe can be safely assumed to exist for our life. What matters more, if not the most, is how to live 100 years of a happy and peaceful life without any worries. In Buddha's book, whether the universe was a divine creation or an eternal fixture was not exactly a page-turner. For him, the more pressing question was to end sorrow (Dukkham) in this life and to get (liberation) from the endless cycle of birth and rebirth (Nirvana). He was focused on finding peace and enlightenment right here, right now.

Human Nature, Not Religion is the Cause of Conflicts

It is a common misconception that religion is the underlying catalyst for all conflicts. In reality, the true culprit is often the insatiable human nature driven by greed and desire. Wars and fights are typically inflamed by factors such as politics, social issues, historical grievances, economic disparities, and personal egos. Not all conflicts originate from religious differences. In fact, there have been numerous wars and fights throughout history that were completely unrelated to religion.

In a twist of irony, both theists and atheists are deemed incorrect in their interpretations of scriptures, as the former follow them wholeheartedly while the latter vehemently oppose them.

My Proposition for a New Dawn

I suggest that if we view the physical universe as constantly changing dynamically and cyclically but existing eternally, then the concept of God as its creator becomes unnecessary. No intelligent designer and fine tuner will be needed to create it.

My claim is that science and religion are not compatible at all. One cannot expect answers from one domain to satisfy the inquiries of the other. Science, with its cold, hard facts, is as objective as a robot, while human nature is as subjective as a teenager's mood swings. Science simply cannot identify the complexities of human emotions like love, hate, greed, desire, hope, courage and all the other bits that make life interesting.

We need a new branch of psychology and philosophy to step up to the plate and examine the finer points of human nature. Sure, there have been some feeble attempts in this direction, but we need to turn it up a gear.

Creation of Virtual Inner World

I propose the existence of two distinct spheres: the physical world and the Virtual Inner World. We create the Virtual Inner World within ourselves, using our sense organs and brain. We use our eyes, ears, tongue, skin, and nose to sense the Physical world around us, and the Virtual Inner World is born! The Virtual Inner World is the only world that living creatures can know exists. The Physical external world always exists.

What's super intriguing is that each of us has our unique Virtual Inner World. We have the power and smarts to develop this reality however we please. I assert that we are all mini-Gods, creating our little universes inside our heads.

Two Realities – Physical Objective and Virtual Subjective

The External Physical world is objective and out there for everyone to see. In contrast, the Virtual Inner World is like your diary - subjective and just for you to know about.

For instance, if you weigh an object on a scale and it says 10 pounds, that's a fact that everyone can agree on. But if you ask a bunch of people how heavy they think it is, you will get a range of answers - from "light as a feather" to "heavy as a brick." And you know what? They are all right! People's feelings and perceptions are valid, even if they differ.

In this sense, I say that there is a duality. It's like the yin and yang of life - science and religion. Science is all about facts and figures, while religion is more about personal beliefs and experiences.

So, let's not pit them against each other like two rival sports teams. Instead, let us appreciate the beauty of their differences and how they both contribute to our understanding of the world.

Our Virtual Inner World is created by the sense organs and the brain. For example, sound is sensed in the ear and sensed data is sent to the brain. Most of the processing (95%) in the brain is done unconsciously which we are not aware of. It is only when the dust settles that we finally become aware of it. This awareness or phenomenal consciousness is colloquially referred to as 'consciousness'.

Everything we experience is virtual. Some examples of virtual are computer simulations, financial transactions, Bitcoins, checks, novels and movies. Gravity and magnetism can be simulated on a computer, but they cannot pull physical objects towards them. Only simulated virtual objects can be affected by simulated gravity. Millions of dollars can be transferred between accounts with just a few clicks on a computer - talk about virtual wealth! Stories can be told in books, on paper, eBooks, or even plastic pages - the medium does not matter. Time and space, as we perceive them, are also virtual. Virtual time seems to fly by when we are having fun, but it drags on when we are going through the motions - even though the real-time on a clock remains the same.

Every millimeter of our body is mapped virtually in our brain. Pain, believe it or not, is all in our heads. Literally. When we feel pain, it's not actually at the source of the problem, but rather a virtual sensation created by our brains. It is beautifully illustrated by a person with an amputated leg feeling the pain in his toes which are not even there.

Just as a computer can simulate any scenario, our brains can interpret signals from our senses in any way they please. The ultimate goal? Survival in the physical environment. It does not matter if our neurons are made of gold or our voltages are off the charts. What matters is the meaning we assign to those signals.

I want to punctuate again that the Virtual Inner World is subjective and unique to each individual. It can vary even within the same person, depending on different times, places, and circumstances.

I have debated the application of laws of Physics, such as Quantum Mechanics, EPR Theory, String Theory, and Theory of Relativity, to the

Virtual Inner World, as some theology authors attempt to do. While Quantum Mechanics is undoubtedly an underlying theory in explaining physical phenomena, it falls short when it comes to the complexities of the Virtual Inner World. Courage, hope, beauty, goodness, gratitude, purpose, compassion, love, grace, and the like are simply beyond the reach of QM.

The Shifting Sands of 'I'

One eye-catching aspect of the Virtual Inner World is that we only experience what we choose to focus on. It is like having a selective vision - if we are not paying attention to something, it might as well not exist at that moment. Attention is the gateway to our conscious experience. If we ignore something, it is like it is dispersed like dust in the breeze (even though it's still physically there). Pain is not felt if you move your attention away from the pain.

Experiencing sensations like cold, hot, sweet, sour, pain, different smells, and touch is not linear. Doubling the temperature will not make you feel twice as hot, and doubling your salary will not make you twice as happy. It is like our senses have a mind of their own, playing by their own rules.

The Virtual Inner World is flexible, and hence can be shaped by virtual beliefs and thoughts. This is the basis of miracles or faith healing and the power of prayer on people's physical and mental health.

The Virtual Inner World is subjective and personal; therefore, science cannot explain and accept it. I have given many examples of this phenomenon.

There is an experiencer to experience the virtual objects in the Virtual Inner World. It is 'I'. I call it the Virtual Empirical Self (VES) or 'Ego-I'. When VES is attached to the virtual objects in the Virtual Inner World, VES experiences the virtual object.

The VES (Ego-I or 'I') is the one who experiences phenomenal consciousness such as 'I like', 'I see', 'I love', 'I dislike', 'I have a pain', and so on. It is like our own personal virtual reality character, claiming all the experiences as its own. But when it comes to how this 'I' actually becomes aware of things like the smell of fresh coffee, well, that is still a riddle for scientists. A complex brain is required for it. How brain takes input data and converts it to experience? There are tons of theories out there, but no one has cracked the code just yet.

Virtual Physicalism

I suggest that we treat experiences as virtual rather than non-physical - Virtual Physicalism. This concept is not only easily acceptable in the field of science, but it also opens up a whole new world of possibilities for finding solutions to various problems.

Now, you might be thinking, "Is Virtual Physicalism not just another form of Dualism?" Well, not quite! While it may seem like it at first glance, the virtual aspect of Virtual Physicalism has its basis in the physical world. So, rest assured, we are not violating any Physicalism rules here.

For example: Emotions may not be something you can hold in your hand, but do not underestimate their power! They may not be physical objects, but they sure know how to make our hearts race and our palms sweat. Think of them as virtual influencers, pulling the strings behind the scenes of our physical state.

By recognizing that emotions can exist within us without being fully measurable, we can better understand their impact on our well-being and actions. It's all about finding that sweet spot of acknowledging their presence without letting them take the wheel.

To put it simply, Virtual Physicalism allows for a more flexible interpretation of non-reduction. In our Virtual Inner World, the meanings we assign to virtual objects can vary, leading to a lack of a one-to-one mapping between physical signals and virtual meanings. Someone can be happy with several different objects at different times. The same object can make you happy at one time and sad at another time.

Virtual Empirical Self (VES) or 'I' or 'self' or 'Ego-I'

In Western science and various religions, the concept of 'I' is defined and debated in countless ways. Buddhism, for example, rejects the idea of a 'self', while Sam Harris boldly declares it to be nothing more than a mirage. As for me, I view the self as a virtual entity - a complex concoction of past experiences, memories, and personality traits that shape who we are. It is like a cabbage with layers upon layers of unique experiences, each contributing to our sense of self.

I like to think of these different aspects of our 'self' as multiple selves (VESes) - each one taking on a different role at any given moment. But if we treat the self as a virtual entity, then its illusory nature can be understood easily.

Some people mistakenly confuse the 'I' with the concept of a 'Soul', which is believed in some religions to undergo rebirth or reincarnation.

The concept of Self, or 'VES' (Ego-I), is the key instigator behind both the good and evil within us. VES is constantly seeking to acquire more of the virtual objects it perceives, leading to desires and greed that can push us towards both lawful and unlawful actions such as cheating, stealing, and lying. However, VES is not all bad - it can also inspire acts of selfless help, empathy, and love. On a larger scale, VES has the potential to spark conflicts and even wars.

Attachment, Detachment, and the Mystery of Experience

It is a paradox that the self (VES), which is necessary to experience the external world, is also the source of goodness and evil. By disconnecting our Ego-I or self from virtual objects, we can rid ourselves of the darker aspects of human nature. Science is at a loss to explain this enigma, leaving us to ponder its implications on mysticism, spirituality, and human nature of love, greed, hope, and happiness. To me, it is a knotty question even more perplexing than the concept of consciousness itself.

The VES (self) must shift its focus either towards (attachment) or away (detachment) from the virtual object to perceive or not perceive it. This can be achieved by connecting or disconnecting the VES from the virtual object. Just as the VES must be linked to the virtual object to experience it, it can also be detached to avoid experiencing unpleasant sensations, like pain.

So, VES is your virtual reality remote-control-pumping experience, a detachment for a peaceful escape!

People tell their experiences that their knee pain or shoulder pains were gone when they visited temples or churches or did activities of their liking like painting or watching a movie or visiting places that they liked. This is not just a placebo effect - scientific MRI studies have confirmed the reality of this pain reduction.

I have quoted a few among thousands of examples of people who have defied their physical limitations and even overcome terminal illnesses by leading purposeful lives and engaging in activities that bring them joy. It is inspiring to see the power of mind over matter in action.

Pure Consciousness, Spirituality, and the Nature of Reality

I propose that all living beings have what I like to call 'State Consciousness' - a form of intelligence honed over millions of years of evolution that allows them to adapt to their environment to survive. This unique trait is what sets living creatures apart from non-living entities, making them 'sentient' as opposed to 'non-sentient'. It is a central aspect of life and a prerequisite for a creature with a complex brain to develop phenomenal consciousness. 'State Consciousness' is the ability to derive meaning from external stimuli. By this definition, even plants can be considered 'sentient' or have 'state consciousness'.

In humans, I call 'state consciousness' to be 'Pure Consciousness' (PC) which is when phenomenal consciousness emerges without any virtual objects in the Virtual Inner World. PC is a virtual experience where the subject and object become one. I also like to think of this as the Virtual Core Self or Virtual Absolute Self (VCS or VAS), which I believe represents the True Self or True Soul in humans. PC is the ultimate knower of virtual objects and the VES (self).

Numerous religious philosophies assert that Pure Consciousness is the basis of spiritual and mystical experiences, distinct from personal devotional or prophetic experiences. In Buddhism, Nirvana is a personal connection with a divine being. Hinduism's Moksha involves a personal experience with the Ultimate reality, Brahman. Sufism in Islam, Meister Eckhart's Christian experiences, and Kabbalism in Judaism, all involve mystical connections with the divine.

In Vedanta, Brahman is depicted as a non-dual and purely spiritual reality. This means that living creatures perceive only one reality, which is Brahman - the principle of knowledge. The Virtual Inner World is only accessible through Brahman (Atman in each creature), while the Physical Universe remains unknowable to us. From a universal standpoint, there exist two worlds - the Physical Universe and the Virtual Inner World.

Atman, the self (also known as 'I' or VES), and all other virtual objects are Brahman, and Brahman is Pure Consciousness (PC) that is in the driver's seat. Simply put, everything is just Pure Consciousness (PC) in the Virtual Inner World.

Sankara, the mastermind behind Vedanta, preaches that the world is nothing but a grand illusion. His 'world' is the Virtual Inner World that we experience every second, not the physical world that remains unknown to us.

Now, do not get it twisted - illusion does not mean that the virtual objects in the Virtual Inner World are make-believe. They are virtually real compared to physically real. The illusion here means that virtual objects in the virtual inner world change quickly when we bounce our attention from one virtual object to the next.

Experiencing Pure Consciousness (PC) and Bliss

In normal perception, PC is there except that we have VES also attached to a virtual object. When VES, or the Ego-I, disconnects from the virtual object, the PC takes center stage. It is like the Sun shining behind a cloud of ignorance - once the cloud dissipates, the Sun's brilliance is revealed.

This phenomenon is what mystics experience during meditation. A similar experience occurs during deep sleep, but it goes unnoticed because VES is not around to witness it. During meditation, external sensory input and internal memory are deliberately put on pause, creating a feeling of emptiness and tranquility - like a peaceful void.

Many creatures without complex brains experience a state similar to deep sleep. However, humans have the unique ability to enter a state of Pure Consciousness (PC) with the Experiencer (VES) without the presence of virtual objects. This is what mystics do, and it is the foundation for all forms of meditation.

Various religions provide a vast array of methods for achieving enlightenment. Non-religious philosophies such as Jainism and Buddhism offer meditative techniques to reach this ultimate goal. Hinduism suggests a combination of devotional practices and meditation. Christianity and Islam suggest the path of love and devotion. Despite the differences in approach, all these methods are united by a common underlying principle.

One might question, why bother with all this spiritual methodology? Well, if you are on the quest for Ultimate Reality, Absolute Truth, God, Brahman, Atman, VAS, PC or VCS, then this is the way to go. By booting desire and greed away, you can soak in pure happiness and experience 'Bliss'. Buddha's essence was to release grief and open the heart to eternal bliss.

The objective here is to eliminate the distractions of the virtual object and focus on the spiritual. Once you cut ties with the virtual object, you will be liberated from its hold and able to tap into the ultimate reality - whether you call it VAS, VCS, Brahman, Atman, Pure Consciousness, or even Virtual God.

Many religions, both theistic and non-theistic, offer a variety of meditative techniques to help individuals achieve spiritual enlightenment. Take Buddhism, for example, where the main goal of mindful meditation is to detach oneself from the ego-I, known as VES. This principle extends to all emotions, even the unpleasant ones like pain and sorrow. By redirecting your focus away from the source of your suffering and towards something more positive, you can effectively eliminate pain and negative feelings. The same can be achieved by separating your ego-I, or VES, from the pain itself. This simple act can bring you peace, happiness, and a sense of bliss. So, why not give it a try and see for yourself the transformative power of detachment?

Engaging in religious rituals, offering prayers to a higher power, reading holy texts, and visiting sacred places all share a common goal: shifting focus away from the 'self' (VES or Ego-I). It does not matter which deity you worship, which temple you frequent, which prayer you recite, or which scripture you peruse - the idea is to distance yourself from that virtual object and VES. The beauty of it all? You do not even have to fully understand the meaning of the Holy book you are reading! The purpose is to delight in the current moment and let time slip away effortlessly.

Hinduism has developed three systematic paths – Bhakti Yoga (Devotional method), Karma Yoga (Action method), and Yoga Jnana Yoga (Knowledge Method). Action method means you take action without worrying about its result.

Christianity and Islam follow the Bhakti method. Ecstatic love is felt when a seeker unites with God. Sufis experience the same love when they unite with Allah. This love is between two entities – the individual soul and God becoming one. This is only achieved when the seeker fully surrenders his 'self' (VES).

Volunteer help and donation in Christianity and Islam are like the action path (Karma Yoga) of Hinduism.

The same universal principle applies to all these methods – detaching your 'self' (VES) from whatever you are doing or shifting focus away from a virtual object.

Believe it or not, belief is a powerful force that can impact our reality. Our virtual beliefs have the ability to influence not only our minds but also our bodies. When we wholeheartedly accept something as true, it becomes a part of our Virtual Existence System (VES). It's not about whether the belief is right or wrong, but rather the upshot it has on our physical well-being. These beliefs have the power to direct our experiences and mold our future.

Let's say: you receive some bad news, and suddenly your stress levels shoot through the roof. It does not matter if the news is true or false - your body reacts the same way. But if you can distract yourself from that bad news, whether it's by doing something logical or not, you will see a decrease in your blood pressure, anxiety, pain, and stress.

Here's another example: you are told that wearing a ring with a Ruby stone will bring you good health. If you trust the source (like your favorite astrologer), your body will actually respond by lowering your blood pressure, anxiety, pain, and stress. It is all about what we choose to believe. Knowledge is power.

Faith is all about believing without needing a logical explanation. So, if prayer is your thing, you will be happy to know that it can help reduce your blood pressure, anxiety, pain, and stress.

This principle, I discovered, also works on beliefs. Shifting your attention away from the source of pain, stress, blood pressure, and anxiety can lead to a surge of joy, happiness, and bliss (VAS). It's about finding that sweet zone where you can shun the negativity and revel in the positive energy.

Religion and Faith in Personal Growth

Religion, spirituality, and faith can be the superhighways to personal growth and fulfillment, as long as they are used for positive and constructive purposes (for yourself only). However, when these beliefs are weaponized for group agendas, it's just politics in disguise - and we all know how messy that can get.

I do not get carried away by the whole 'apple or gold ring magically appearing out of thin air' kind of miracles. But I do believe in the wonder of self-healing. The power to heal yourself lies within you and only you. No one else can do it for you. Sure, you may be inspired by someone you trust and have faith in. It may not have to be a higher power like God. It could be anyone - a charismatic political leader, a wise religious guru, a supportive friend, a knowledgeable teacher, a guiding mentor, an inspiring motivational speaker, or even an absorbing actor in a movie or novel.

If we consider Atman, Brahman, VCS, VAS, PC, or whatever you want to call it, as a knowledge principle similar to the force of Gravity, then we are talking about a virtual entity that does not die or take birth. So, the whole idea of reincarnation or rebirth becomes a tough nut to crack. If something does not die, how can it be reborn?

Now, if we throw the eternal universe into the mix, all those arguments about God being a cosmic creator, destroyer, or heavenly rewarder start to lose their luster. The question of whether God is a male or female and why are there multiple Gods, will not be relevant.

AI is all the rage these days, with enthusiasts believing that one day we will have conscious robots roaming around. However, the missing ingredient in robots and computers is what we call 'State Consciousness' or PC. This means that AI will never be able to create truly conscious robots. After all, only living creatures can truly give meaning to things. Computers and robots simply follow the instructions they are given through programming. They may be able to analyze data and perform complex tasks, but they cannot assign meaning to anything on their own. It is like memorizing a Physics formula without actually understanding it - robots can do impressive things, but they are just following orders. So, while AI may be impressive, true consciousness is still a space reserved for us humans.

The concept of separating state and church has its limitations. Take Europe, for example - countries like Sweden, Norway, and Denmark still pay church tax, yet they are less religious and happier. It's a paradox, really.

One cannot just wipe out the majority of the population to eradicate religion, because most people are religious. So, is one religion superior to the others? Personally, I believe that all religions, along with science, should be taught in schools. Let students learn and decide the truth for themselves. After all, knowledge is power, and a little enlightenment never hurt anyone.

Bliss Beyond Boundaries

The principle I have innovated for achieving happiness is universal - it does not discriminate based on religion. It is like the ultimate happiness hack that works for everyone, regardless of their religious beliefs. That is why I am all for people being free to practice any religion they choose. Even atheists can get in on the happiness action using the method I have suggested.

If you are a seeker looking to find your way, my advice is to cast off all your current beliefs and religious affiliations.

When you step foot in a sacred space, do not just approach it as a mere transactional moment, as if ticking off a list of desires—asking for health, wealth, or blessings. Take a moment to go in-depth into your thoughts. Ask yourself the big questions about life's purpose, the nature of the divine, and what it means to feel connected. Real spiritual growth does not come from materialistic wish lists but from a quest for truth, wisdom, and inner peace. Stop viewing spirituality as a quick fix and start researching the enlightening revelations waiting to be discovered within.

Keep in mind that it's not about getting quick fixes but about being all ears to the questions that surface along the way. It's like an infinite pursuit of self-discovery, where each step brings you closer to exposing the untold stories of your existence and the universe. The essence of spirituality lies in the art of looking within, staying present, and being humble enough to realize that personal growth is a lifelong adventure.

I have poured my heart and soul into this book, hoping it clarifies the truth about God's existence for those who are seekers.

I am currently penning about the relationship between attachment and detachment of VES ('I'), a common principle that yields various effects in the pursuit of happiness, regardless of religious beliefs. This phenomenon will be further elaborated in my upcoming book, 'Physical Body – Virtual Soul'.

Acknowledgments

I would like to extend a heartfelt thank you to my wonderful family, especially my wife, who not only encouraged me to write this book but also designed the cover page. She is even more excited about this book than I am - if that's even possible!

A well-deserved praise to my circle of friends who listened to my book idea passages, with a special mention to my friend, retired Physics Professor N. L. Sharma. Our discussions on Physics and religious Philosophy have been thought-provoking, and I have learned a great deal of Physics from him outside of the classroom.

I am grateful to my colleague, Dr. Linda Brakel, who has been a dedicated reader of my work, providing candid feedback and constructive criticism. Her input has been invaluable, and her suggestion to add sub-headings helped me organize the content.

Nitin Dutta, the editor of my book, did a marvelous job. He suggested ideas and changed sentences where needed. I appreciate his efforts. Nitin decorated my perspectives into sentences and paragraphs. I cannot thank him enough for what he has done to my book.

Notes

Chapter 1

Note 1: Soul has weight

https://en.wikipedia.org/wiki/21_grams_experiment

Note 2: Experiment on Reincarnation by Ian Stevenson

https://en.wikipedia.org/wiki/Ian_Stevenson

Note 3: Center for OBE in the brain

https://www.npr.org/sections/health-shots/2023/07/05/1185868647/brain-out-of-body-experience

Note 4: Religious 'Nones' are now the largest single group in the U.S. as per NPR news

https://nam02.safelinks.protection.outlook.com/?url=https%3A%2F%2Fwww.npr.org%2F2024%2F01%2F24%2F1226371734%2Freligious-nones-are-now-the-largest-single-group-in-the-u-s&data=05%7C02%7Cramesh%40med.umich.edu%7C528615d0e89a46389a4008dc3ff0baa3%7C1f41d613d3a14ead918d2a25b10de330%7C0%7C0%7C638455550384151015%7CUnknown%7CTWFpbGZsb3d8eyJWIjoiMC4wLjAwMDAiLCJQIjoiV2luMzIiLCJBTiI6Ik1haWwiLCJXVCI6Mn0%3D%7C0%7C%7C%7C&sdata=8asAgL2504pi777KU%2Fp9xwZWmTSFToM2NTxiHetr6HE%3D&reserved=0

Note 5: Religious Groups by Percent of Population in 2022

https://www.pewresearch.org/religion/2022/12/21/key-findings-from-the-global-religious-futures-project/

Note 6: Visa Temples in India

https://www.travelandleisureasia.com/in/destinations/india/visa-temples-in-india/

Note 7: Cyclical Model of the Universe

https://en.wikipedia.org/wiki/Cyclic_model

https://www.quantamagazine.org/physicists-debate-hawkings-idea-that-the-universe-had-no-beginning-20190606/#comments

Chapter 2

Note 1: Need for Spirit as explained by Bronisław Malinowski

https://en.wikipedia.org/wiki/Bronis%C5%82aw_Malinowski

Note 2: Oldest Indian religious scriptures - Vedas

https://en.wikipedia.org/wiki/Vedas

https://www.learnreligions.com/what-are-vedas-1769572

Note 3: 45000 Christian denominations as per World Christian Encyclopedia

https://www.ggcn.org/wp-content/uploads/tokyo2010/resources/2020_updated_papers/World_Christian_Encyclopedia_Tokyo2020_Update.pdf

Note 4: The capital of Israel was moved to Jerusalem under the Trump Administration on Dec 6th, 2017

https://en.wikipedia.org/wiki/United_States_recognition_of_Jerusalem_as_capital_of_Israel

Note 5: Big Bang Theory

https://en.wikipedia.org/wiki/History_of_the_Big_Bang_theory

The history of the Big Bang theory began with the Big Bang's development from observations and theoretical considerations. Much of the theoretical work in cosmology now involves extensions and refinements to the basic Big Bang model. The theory itself was originally formalized by Father Georges Lemaître in 1927. Hubble's Law of the Expansion of the Universe provided foundational support for the theory.

Note 6: The evolution concept was finally accepted by the Catholic church (Vatican)

https://www.smithsonianmag.com/smart-news/pope-would-you-accept-evolution-and-big-bang-180953166/

Note 7: Scope Trial, also known as 'Monkey trial', for teaching evolution in school in Tennessee

https://www.britannica.com/event/Scopes-Trial

Note 8: 'Hugging Amma' cures pain just by hugging

https://en.wikipedia.org/wiki/Mata_Amritanandamayi

Note 9: Sai Baba – People claim that ashes appear on his photographs at their homes

https://www.britannica.com/biography/Shirdi-Sai-Baba

Note 10: A Jesus statue oozing water in Mumbai

https://www.google.com/search?q=Jesus+sfeet+was+oozing+water+in+Mumbai&sca_esv=71b2db2a9157258c&sca_upv=1&sxsrf=ADLYWILOsWFh_zK8HPYPLCn2H-o4zmFNng%3A1717602632150&ei=SIlgZv_nCOOKptQPiviVqAQ&ved=0ahUKEwj_q4S26MSGAxVjhYkEHQp8BUUQ4dUDCBA&uact=5&oq=Jesus+sfeet+was+oozing+water+in+Mumbai&gs_lp=Egxnd3Mtd2l6LXNlcnAiJkplc3VzIHNmZWV0IHdhcyBvb3ppbmcgd2F0ZXIgaW4gTXVtYmFpMgcQIRigARgKMgcQIRigARgKMgcQIRigARgKMgcQIRigARgKSLhCUABY9j9wAHgBkAEAmAH2AaABuSOqAQcxNy4xOS4yuAEDyAEA-AEBmAImoAKwJcICCxAAGIAEGJECGIoFwgIREC4YgAQYsQMY0QMYgwEYxwHCAg4QLhiABBixAxiDARiKBcICCxAAGIAEGLEDGIMBwgILEC4YgAQY0QMYxwHCAgsQLhiABBixAxiDAcICDhAAGIAEGLEDGIMBGIoFwgIFEAAYgATCAggQLhiABBixA8ICCBAAGIAEGLEDwgIFEC4YgATCAgQQABgDwgIIEC4YgAQY1ALCAgsQLhiABBjHARivAcICBhAAGBYYHsICBRAhGKABwgIHEAAYgAQYDcICCxAAGIAEGIYDGIoFwgIIEAAYgAQYogTCAgUQIRirAsICBxAhGAoYqwKYAwCSBwcxMS4yNS4yoAeYpAI&sclient=gws-wiz-serp

In 2012, a statue of Jesus Christ in a Catholic church in Mumbai, India, began to drip water from its feet, attracting widespread attention. Some local Catholic Christians believed the incident was a miracle, but rationalist and atheist author Sanal Edamaruku found that the water was actually coming from clogged drainage pipes behind the wall where the statue stood. Edamaruku said that the water was sewage water seeping through the wall due to capillary action, and posed a health risk to people who believed it was a miracle.

Note 11: Ganesha statue drinking milk

https://en.wikipedia.org/wiki/Ganesha_drinking_milk_miracle#:~:text=With%20this%20result%2C%20the%20scientists,the%20front%20of%20the%20statue.

Note 12: Bread and wine converted to skin and blood during Eucharist

https://en.wikipedia.org/wiki/Eucharist

Note 13: Earthquake in Afghanistan, Turkey and Syria

https://www.aljazeera.com/news/2023/10/8/powerful-earthquakes-kill-2053-people-in-afghanistan-here-is-what-to-know

https://www.worldvision.org/disaster-relief-news-stories/2023-turkey-and-syria-earthquake-faqs

Note 14: Hurricane Katrina

https://www.history.com/topics/natural-disasters-and-environment/hurricane-katrina

Note 15: Kedarnath temple Flooding in 2013 Uttarakhand in India

https://indianexpress.com/article/research/here-is-what-happened-in-kedarnath-and-rest-of-uttarakhand-in-2013-5482050/

Note 16: Sunami in 2004 in Indian Ocean

https://www.rand.org/hsrd/hsoac/projects/puerto-rico-recovery/hurricanes-irma-and-maria.html

Note 17: Pureto Rico Hurricane Mariain 2017

https://www.rand.org/hsrd/hsoac/projects/puerto-rico-recovery/hurricanes-irma-and-maria.html

Note 18: The Russia-Ukraine war started in 2022 and still going on

https://www.bbc.com/news/world-europe-60506682

Note 19: Isiaiah:45-7

https://www.biblestudytools.com/rsv/isaiah/45-7.html

Chapter 3

Note 1A: A saying by Blaise Pascal

https://www.goodreads.com/author/quotes/10994.Blaise_Pascal

Note 1: Mumbai 11/26, 2008 terrorist attack

https://www.britannica.com/event/Mumbai-terrorist-attacks-of-2008

Note 2: Israel and Hamas war broke out on Oct 7, 2023

https://www.nytimes.com/news-event/israel-hamas-gaza

Note 3: Golden Temple attack in 1984 by then Indian Prime Minister, Indira Gandhi

https://en.wikipedia.org/wiki/Operation_Blue_Star

Note 4: Air India flight 182 from Canada to India was bombed by Sikh terrorists on 23 June 1985

https://en.wikipedia.org/wiki/Air_India_Flight_182#:~:text=Air%20India%20Flight%20182%20was,%2D237B%20registered%20VT%2DEFO.

Note 5: Assassination of Rajeev Gandhi in 1991

https://en.wikipedia.org/wiki/Assassination_of_Rajiv_Gandhi#:~:text=The%20assassination%20of%20Rajiv%20Gandhi,India%20on%2021%20May%201991.

Note 6: Buddhists killing Muslims in Burma

https://www.bbc.com/news/magazine-22356306

Note 7: 9/11, 2001 Attack on the U.S. soil

https://en.wikipedia.org/wiki/September_11_attacks

Note 8: Attack on Rafah, Gaza Strip

https://en.wikipedia.org/wiki/12_February_2024_Rafah_strikes#:~:text=On%2012%20February%202024%2C%20Israel,coincided%20with%20Super%20Bowl%20LVIII.

Note 9: Article 370 about ownership of property in Kashmir, India

https://www.hinduamerican.org/issues/kashmir-struggle/faq-article-370?gad_source=1&gclid=CjwKCAjwmrqzBhAoEiwAXVpgohmEGbXNj5ockpQURsAmVOpdKV3FF27f3VsWlx-H11DGEE3FA52lhxoC4jUQAvD_BwE

Note 10: The Most Terrifying Cults in History (CBS News)

https://www.cbsnews.com/pictures/cults-dangerous-deadly-history/19/

Note 11: Dera Sacha Sauda run by Gurmeet Ram Rahim Singh

https://en.wikipedia.org/wiki/Gurmeet_Ram_Rahim_Singh

Note 12: Mother Teresa's Noble Prize lecture

https://www.nobelprize.org/prizes/peace/1979/teresa/lecture/

Note 13: CNN documentary showing Jesus in Kashmir, India during the age of 13 and 29.

https://www.youtube.com/watch?v=9DXCZFRsyl8

Suzzane, Olsson, 'Jesus in Kashmir: The Lost Tomb', Book surge, Jan 1, 2005.

Note 14: Increased Mass Shootings in the USA

https://www.bbc.com/news/world-us-canada-41488081

https://www.gunviolencearchive.org/reports/mass-shooting

Note 15: The Human Health Bill was signed in Michigan on 11/21/23 by Governor Gretchen Whitmer so that abortion can never be challenged

https://www.michigan.gov/whitmer/news/press-releases/2023/11/21/governor-whitmer-signs-reproductive-health-act

Note 16: Demonstration in Texas about abortion drug ruling in court

https://www.npr.org/2023/04/15/1170268300/planned-parenthood-rally-abortion-pill-mifepristone-supreme-court

Note 17: Renovated Kashi Vishwanath Temple

https://en.wikipedia.org/wiki/Kashi_Vishwanath_Temple

Note 18: Ayodhya temple inauguration on Jan 22, 2024

https://religionunplugged.com/news/2024/1/30/e32kma08t8kh7jp88ip6unzwsrflhs?gad_source=1&gclid=Cj0KCQjwvb-zBhCmARIsAAfUI2sSqpCobcFveec2yQ5XMdqD9xCZoNrHxaSBe_JZp4aRrPqY4VdzB0AaAiaHEALw_wcB

Note 19: BJP could not win with a majority vote in the 2024 Indian general election despite the construction of 2 major temples of Lord Shiva and Rama

https://en.wikipedia.org/wiki/2024_Indian_general_election

https://www.google.com/search?q=Indian+2024+election&sca_esv=f07dd38fdcfe8355&sca_upv=1&sxsrf=ADLYWIIY0yEAJ6BI9KR7UdrVmgwjSVfIMQ%3A1718631019522&ei=azpwZry_H4aaptQPrZq80AI&ved=0ahUKEwj8oKy73-KGAxUGjYkEHS0NDyoQ4dUDCBA&uact=5&oq=Indian+2024+election&gs_lp=Egxnd3Mtd2l6LXNlcnAiFEluZGlhbiAyMDI0IGVsZWN0aW9uMgUQABiABDIFEAAYgAQyBRAAGIAEMgUQABiABDIFEAAYgAQyBxAAGIAEGAoyBRAA

GIAEMgUQABiABDIHEAAYgAQYCjIHEAAYgAQYCki1HlAAWM0ccAB4AJABA
JgBpAGgAbwOqgEEMTMuN7gBA8gBAPgBAZgCFKAC7A_CAgoQIxiABBgnGI
oFwgIKEAAYgAQYQxiKBcICDhAuGIAEGLEDGIMBGIoFwgIIEAAYgAQYsQPC
AgsQABiABBixAxiDAcICCxAuGIAEGLEDGIMBwgIQEC4YgAQY0QMYQxjHARi
KBcICChAuGIAEGEMYigXCAhAQABiABBixAxhDGIMBGIoFwgINEC4YgAQYs
QMYQxiKBcICDRAAGIAEGEMYyQMYigXCAgsQABiABBiSAxiKBcICEBAuGIAE
GLEDGEMYgwEYigXCAgsQABiABBiRAhiKBcICCxAAGIAEGLEDGMkDwgImEC
4YgAQYsQMYgwEYlwUY3AQY3gQY4AQY9AMY8QMY9QMY9gPYAQHCAgU
QLhiABJgDALoGBggBEAEYFJIHBDEyLjigB9ipAQ&sclient=gws-wiz-serp

Chapter 4

Note 1: Impacts of the COVID-19 Pandemic on Incidents of Mass Violence in the USA

https://scholarworks.utrgv.edu/cgi/viewcontent.cgi?article=1076&context=cj_fac

https://www.bbc.com/news/world-us-canada-64377360

https://www.ncbi.nlm.nih.gov/pmc/articles/PMC10149110/

https://www.cnn.com/2021/09/16/us/mass-shootings-increased-in-pandemic/index.html

Note 2: The evolving attitudes of Gen-X towards evolution published in 'University Record' of the University of Michigan on April 10, 2024

https://news.umich.edu/the-evolving-attitudes-of-gen-x-toward-evolution/

Note 3: "Why I am not a Christian?" By Bertrand Russel

https://docs.google.com/file/d/0B6099bbYlhJneElDWUMxd0RPbEU/edit?pli=1&resourcekey=0-SEyflBRRQ1EF6N1tFz4QMQ

Note 4: Boston Bombing on April 15, 2013

https://en.wikipedia.org/wiki/Boston_Marathon_bombing

Note 5: Oklahoma Federal Building Bombing on April 19, 1995

https://en.wikipedia.org/wiki/Oklahoma_City_bombing

Note 6: Blaise Pascal's Wager Theory

https://en.wikipedia.org/wiki/Blaise_Pascal

https://www.britannica.com/biography/Blaise-Pascal

https://www.worldhistory.org/Blaise_Pascal/

https://plato.stanford.edu/entries/pascal-wager/

Chapter 5

Note1: Harris, Sam, 'An Atheist Manifest', TruthDig, December 7th, 2005

http://www.truthdig.com/dig/item/200512_an_atheist_manifesto

Note2: Nasbandi – The forced sterilization program in India in 1975 by Sanjay Gandhi, son of the then prime minister of India

https://search.yahoo.com/yhs/search?hspart=mnet&hsimp=yhs-001&type=type9097303-spa-4056-84481&param1=4056&param2=84481&p=when+was+emergency+in+Inida

Chapter 6

Note 1: 2022 Noble Prize of Physics for EPR explanation

https://www.scientificamerican.com/article/the-universe-is-not-locally-real-and-the-physics-nobel-prize-winners-proved-it/

Note 2: Theory of Relativity

https://www.livescience.com/does-gravity-make-you-age-slower

Note 3: Double Slit experiment-placement of detector causes detection https://en.wikipedia.org/wiki/Double-slit_experiment

Note 4: Ambiguous images

https://en.wikipedia.org/wiki/Ambiguous_image

Note 5: Law of Diminishing Returns in Economics

https://www.investopedia.com/terms/l/lawofdiminishingmarginalreturn.asp

Chapter 8

Note 1: Descartes – Dualist theory of mind and consciousness

https://plato.stanford.edu/entries/descartes/

Note 2: Pain and MRI showing pain reduction is real physiological and not just psychological

https://www.ncbi.nlm.nih.gov/pmc/articles/PMC5953782/

Note 3: The Person who forgot to die from Ikeria, Greece

https://www.businessinsider.com/ikaria-greece-blue-zone-terminal-cancer-diagnosis-live-longer-2023-8

Note 4: Stephan Hawking

https://en.wikipedia.org/wiki/Stephen_Hawking

Note 5: Morris Goodman – A high-school dropout became a successful insurance agent and survived a plane crash, recovered from a vegetative state, and became a motivational speaker

https://en.wikipedia.org/wiki/Morris_E._Goodman

Note 6: Kris Carr, a multi-talented woman, survived stage IV liver and lung cancer, and became a motivational speaker

https://en.wikipedia.org/wiki/Kris_Carr

Note 7: Arunima Sinha, the first Indian woman and second world woman to climb all major mountains in all continents even with amputated legs caused during train travel when she fought bravely with robbers who threw her from a running train.

https://en.wikipedia.org/wiki/Arunima_Sinha

Chapter 9

Note 1: Frank Jackson's knowledge argument

https://en.wikipedia.org/wiki/Knowledge_argument

Note 2: 'Virtual Physicalism' by Kushwaha, Ramesh in 'Academia Discussion' July 2023

https://www.academia.edu/83303420/Virtual_Physicalism?sm=b

Note 3: Subliminal Stimulation

A word (e.g., "happy") or an image (e.g., a smiling face) is flashed on the screen for 1 millisecond.

This brief duration ensures that the subject cannot consciously recognize the stimulus.

Masking Technique:

Immediately after the stimulus, a masking pattern (e.g., random letters or symbols, or a neutral image) is displayed. This "mask" disrupts the brain's processing of the original stimulus, preventing it from reaching conscious awareness.

Experiment Outcome:

Subjects are unaware of what they see, but their behavior or responses may still be influenced. For instance, they might feel slightly happier after seeing the word "happy" or respond more positively to stimuli associated with it.

The effect can be seen in the signals that the brain produces in response to the subliminal stimulus.

This technique is employed in cognitive psychology and neuroscience to study implicit processing in the brain.

Note 4: The Thalamocortical System

The thalamocortical system is a network of neural connections between the thalamus (a deep brain structure) and the cerebral cortex. It facilitates the processing and relaying of sensory, motor, and cognitive information, as well as maintaining states of consciousness and attention.

Note 5: Critique of Koch's idea of Consciousness
https://www.psychologytoday.com/us/blog/hot-thought/202006/critique-christof-kochs-account-consciousness

Note 6: Meaning and examples of Sentients

For example: Why Dogs Are Sentient:

Awareness: Dogs are aware of their surroundings and can perceive stimuli such as sounds, smells, and sights.

Feelings: They exhibit emotions like happiness when wagging their tails, fear when cowering, or sadness when whining.

Response to Pain: Dogs react to physical pain by yelping or withdrawing, showing their ability to experience and respond to discomfort.

Learning and Memory: They can learn commands, recognize their owners, and remember specific routines or events.

This capacity to perceive, feel, and respond emotionally demonstrates sentience, which refers to the ability to have subjective experiences. Dogs, like many other animals, clearly exhibit this quality.

Why Human Beings Are Sentient:

When a person watches a heartfelt movie:

Awareness: They perceive the visuals, dialogue, and music through their senses.

Feelings: They may feel joy, sadness, or empathy for the characters.

Reflection: They might contemplate the themes of the story, relating it to their own experiences.

Response: Tears may flow during emotional scenes, or laughter might burst out during humorous moments.

This combination of conscious perception, emotional response, and subjective experience illustrates human sentience, which is the ability to experience feelings and sensations.

Note 7: Music for faster recovery from surgery

https://www.thelancet.com/journals/lancet/article/PIIS0140-6736(15)60169-6/abstract

https://scienceblog.com/548714/listening-to-music-may-speed-up-recovery-from-surgery/

https://www.thelancet.com/journals/lancet/article/PIIS0140-6736(15)60169-6/fulltext, *The Lancet*, Oct. 24, 2015

Note 8: BAEP and SSEP

BAEP: Brainstem Auditory Evoked Potential:

Refers to electrical responses recorded from the brainstem following an auditory stimulus, often used to evaluate hearing and neurological function.

SSEP: Somatosensory Evoked Potential:

Refers to electrical responses recorded from the brain following a sensory stimulus, commonly used to assess the integrity of sensory pathways.

Both are diagnostic tools used in neurophysiology to monitor nervous system function.

Note 9: People in Coma may be conscious

https://www.sciencefocus.com/the-human-body/comas-conscious-communicate

https://www.neurology.columbia.edu/news/some-people-who-appear-be-coma-may-actually-be-conscious

Note 10: Unconscious patients

Brain activity in unconscious patients offers new views of awareness (sciencenews.org), July 28, 2015.

Note 11: Plant consciousness

http://www.esalq.usp.br/lepse/imgs/conteudo_thumb/Plant-Consciousness---The-Fascinating-Evidence-Showing-Plants-Have-Human-Level-Intelligence--Feelings--Pain-and-More.pdf

https://qz.com/1294941/a-debate-over-plant-consciousness-is-forcing-us-to-confront-the-limitations-of-the-human-mind/

Chapter 10

Note 1: One of the Kabbalah's biggest followers was Issac Luria from a Jewish family settled in Palestine in 1492 A.D. who believed in soul and reincarnation.

https://plato.stanford.edu/entries/mysticism/

Note 2: Sufism and Dargahs

https://en.wikipedia.org/wiki/Sufism#Devotional_practices

Note 3: Jainism

https://en.wikipedia.org/wiki/Jainism

https://www.worldhistory.org/jainism/

Note 4: Buddhism

https://www.kadampanewyork.org/dharma?gad_source=1&gclid=Cj0KCQjwvb-zBhCmARIsAAfUI2sF4EEMV_zKZKfL5qauCRxTQOMoX9_nmw9k7dletJsVGJXsQsTYm1MaAhQHEALw_wcB

Note 5: Zen and Vipasana

https://www.meditationlb.org/method-to-let-go?gad_source=1&gclid=Cj0KCQjwvb-zBhCmARIsAAfUI2t3sQd-TXsCG0FmJgFAym7lBXW8B7KwueMWs3IBeYzT2-lvX_HNJV0aAplFEALw_wcB

https://www.longchenfoundation.org/longchen-training/the-lions-roar/?gad_source=1

Note 6: https://en.wikipedia.org/wiki/Upanishads

Chapter 12

Note 1: Found reason to live after 4 suicide attempts

https://www.npr.org/2023/05/12/1175711869/woman-who-had-post-partum-depression-says-she-attempted-suicide-4-times

Note2: Life on other planets

https://science.nasa.gov/universe/exoplanets/life-in-the-universe-what-are-the-odds/

Note3: McDonald was sued for the spill of coffee on a lady's thigh

https://www.lawinsider.org/post/the-2-9-million-coffee-spill-liebeck-v-mcdonalds-restaurants

Chapter 13

Note 1: AI needs massive amounts of electricity.

From NPR radio on 5/22/24 on the 'Things Explained' program.

https://www.scientificamerican.com/article/the-ai-boom-could-use-a-shocking-amount-of-electricity/

References

Achermann P and Borbely AA. 'Low-Frequency (1 Hz) Oscillations in the Human Sleep EEG'. *Neuroscience* 81: 213–222, 1997.

Alkire, M. T. (2008). 'General Anesthesia and Consciousness'. In S. Laureys & G. Tononi (Eds.), *Neurology of Consciousness: Cognitive Neuroscience and Neuropathology* (Vol. 1, p. 424). London: Academic Press — Elsevier.

Alston, A. J. (Translator), 'The Realization of the Absolute- The Naiskarmya Siddhi of Sri Suresvara', Shanti Sadan, London, 1971.

American Psychiatric Association. 'Diagnostic and Statistical Manual of Mental Disorders', 5th Ed., Text Revision (DSM-5-TR); Washington DC, 2022.

Amzica F and Steriade M. 'The K-Complex: its Slow (1 Hz) Rhythmicity and Relation to Delta Waves'. *Neurology* 49: 952–959, 1997.

Baar, Stephen M., 'Modern Physics and Ancient Faith', The University of Notre Dame Press, Indiana, 2003.

Baars, B. J. (1988). *A Cognitive Theory of Consciousness*. Cambridge: Cambridge University Press.

Baars, B. J. (2005). 'Global Workspace Theory of Consciousness: Toward a Cognitive Neuroscience of Human Experience'. *Progress in Brain Research*, 15045–15053.

Baars, B. J., Ramsoy, T. Z., & Laureys, S. (2003). 'Brain, Conscious Experience and the Observing Self'. *Trends in Neuroscience,* 26(12), 671–675.

Bahadur, Krishna P., 'The Wisdom of Yoga – A Study of Patanjali Yoga Sutra', Sterling Publishers Pvt. Ltd. AB/9 Safdarjang Enclave, New Delhi, India, 110016, 1977.

Barret, David, B., Kurian, George, T., and Johnson, Todd, M., (Editors), 'World Christian Encyclopedia: A comparative Survey of Churches ad Religions in the Modern World', Vol. 1, 'The World by Countries: Religionists, Churches, Ministries'; Vol.2: 'The World by Segments:

Religions, Peoples, Languages, Cities, Topics. 2nd ed., Oxford University Press, New York, 2001.

Bazan, A., Kushwaha, R., Winer, E. S., Snodgrass, J. M., Brake, L. A. W., Shevrin, H., 'Phonological Ambiguity Detection Outside of Consciousness and Its Defensive Avoidance', *Frontiers in Human Neuroscience,* Vol=13, 2019, pp.77.

Bechtel, Stefan, and Stains, Laurence, Roy, 'Through A Glass, Darkly', St. Martin's Press, N.Y., 2017.

Berkeley, G., 'Philosophical Works', edited by M. R. Ayers, Dent, London, 1975.

Bernat, E., Shevrin, H., & Snodgrass, M. (2001), 'Subliminal Visual Oddball Stimuli Evoke a P300 Component', *Clinical Neurophysiology*, 112, 159e171.

Blackmore, Susan, J., 'Beyond the Body - An investigation of out-of-body experiences with a new postscript by the author, published on behalf of the Society for Psychical Research (SPR)', Academy Chicago Publishers, 1992.

Boly, M., Massimini, M., & Tononi, G., (2009), 'Theoretical Approaches to the Diagnosis of Altered States of Consciousness', In S. Laureys & G Tononi (Eds.), *Progress in Brain Research,* (Vol. 277, p.383-398), Elsevier.

Bowker, John, 'Licensed Insanities: Religions and Belief in God in the Contemporary world', Darton, Longman and Todd, London, 1987.

Bunce, S., Kleinsorge, S., Villa, K., Kushwaha, R., Szocik, J., Hendricks, C., Brakel, L., Shevrin, H., 'Neurophysiological Evidence for Implicit Learning and Memory under Adequate General Anesthesia', presented at *the 5th International Conference on Memory, Awareness, and Consciousness in Anesthesia*, June 2001, New York.

Campbell, Joseph and Kudler David, 'Myths of Light: Eastern Metaphors of the Eternal (The Collected Works of Joseph Campbell)', New World Library, April 17, 2012.

Capra, Fritjof, 'The Tao of Physics: An Exploration of the Parallels Between Modern Physics and Eastern Mysticism', Shambhala Publication, September 14, 2010.

Chakravarty, Alston, Krishnananda, Forman, Mehta, Gangolli, Raina, Islam, Verma, Bahadur, Houde, Ram, Parrinder, Gupta, Indich, Rao, Hanson, woods, Elenjimittam, Sureshananda, Indich, Tedlock, Hanson, Mikhailov

Chakravarty, Nilima, 'Indian Philosophy- The Pathfinders and The System Builders (700 B.C. to 100 A.D.)', Allied Publishers Ltd., New Delhi, India 1992.

Chalmers, D. (2010), *The Character of Consciousness*, Oxford University Press.

Chaney, Daniel K., 'Religion Refuted – Debunking the case for God', C. H. Press, 2014.

Chopra, Deepak, 'The Future of God- A Practical Approach to Spirituality for Our Times', Harmony Books, New York, 2014.

Chopra, Deepak, 'The Souls Journey into the Mystery of Mysteries – How to Know God', Harmony Press, February 2000.

Churchland, Paul M., 'Matter and Consciousness', A Bradford Book, The MIT Press, London, England, 1983.

Comte-Sponville, Andre', 'The Little Book of Atheist Spirituality', Viking published by the Penguin Group, New York, N.Y., Translated by Nancy Houston, 2007.

Connor, James A. 'Pascal's Wager: The Man Who Played Dice with God'. *San Francisco: Harper San Francisco. pp.* 180–1, *2006.*

Coyne Jerry A., 'Faith vs. Fact: Why Science and Religion Are Incompatible', Viking, Penguin Publishing Group, Penguin Random House, LLC, New York, N.Y., 2015.

Coyne, Jerry A., 'Why Evolution is True', Viking Adult, January 22, 2009.

Damasio, Antonio, 'Self Comes to Mind: Constructing the Conscious Brain', Vintage, March 6, 2012.

Darwin, Charles, 'The Origin of Species by Means of Natural Selection', John Murray, London,1859.

Davidson, D. (1970/1980), 'Mental Events. *In Actions and Events',* Oxford University Press.

Dawkins, Richard, 'The Blind Watchmaker: Why the Evidence of Evolution Reveals a Universe without Design', W. W. Norton & Company, January 1, 1986.

Dawkins, Richard, 'Selfish Genes', The Oxford University Press, Oxford, 1976.

Dawkins, Richard, 'The God Delusion', Bantam Press, New York, 2006.

Dawkins, Richard, 'Outgrowing God: A Beginner's Guide', Random House, New York, N.Y., October 2019.

Dawkins, Richard, 'Science and God: A Warming Trend', Science, Vol. 277, Issue 5328(15th August 1997, p. 890-893) https://www.science.org/doi/10.1126/science.277.5328.890

Dehaene, S., & Changeux, J. P. (2004). 'Neural Mechanisms for Access to Consciousness'. In M. Gazanniga (Ed.), *The cognitive neurosciences* (3rd ed., pp. 1145–1157). New York: Norton.

Descartes, R., 'Discourse' and 'Method and Meditations', Translated by L. J. Lafleur, Indianapolis: Library of Liberal Arts, 1960

Dehaene, S., & Changeux, J. P. (2005). 'Ongoing Spontaneous Activity Controls Access to Consciousness: A Neuronal Model for Inattentional Blindness'. *PLoS Biology*, 3(5), e141.

Dehaene, S., Changeux, J. P., Naccache, L., Sackur, J., & Sergent, C. (2006). 'Conscious, Preconscious, and Subliminal Processing: A testable taxonomy'. *Trends in Cognitive Sciences,* 10(5), 204–211.

Dehaene, S., & Naccache, L. (2001). 'Towards a Cognitive Neuroscience of Consciousness: Basic Evidence and a Workspace Framework'. Cognition, 79(1–2), 1–37.

Dennet, D. C., *From Bacteria to Bach and Back: The Evolution of Minds*. New York: W. W. Norton, 2017.

Dennet, D., 'Consciousness Explained', Little Brown, Boston, MA, 1991.

Dennet, Daniel, 'Breaking the Spell: Religion as a Natural Phenomenon', Penguins Books, February 6, 2007.

Descartes, R., 'The Philosophical Writings of Descartes', Volume 1 and 2, translated by J. Cottingham et. al., Cambridge University Press, Cambridge, 1985.

Diaz, M. T., & McCarthy, G. (2007). Unconscious word processing engages a distributed network of brain regions. *Journal of Cognitive Neuroscience,* 19(11), 1768–1775.

Ecklund, Elaine Howard, and Scheitle, Chrisopher P., 'Religion vs. Science – What Religious People Really Think', Oxford University Press, 2018.

Ehrman, Bart, 'Armageddon: What the Bible Really Says about the End', Simon and Schuster, March 21, 2023.

Elenjimittam, Anthony, 'The Upanishads', Aquinas Publications, Institute for Inter-Religious Understanding, Sadhna Hall, Mount Mary, Bandra, Bombay-400050, India, 1977.

El Fadl Khaled M. Abou, 'The Great Theft: Wrestling Islam from the Extremists', Harper One, October 4, 2005.

Engel, A. K., & Singer, W. (2001), 'Temporal Binding and the Neural Correlates of Sensory Awareness', *Trends in Cognitive Sciences*, 5(1), 16-25.

Forman, Robert, K. C., 'The Problem of Pure Consciousness – Mysticism and Philosophy', Oxford University Press, New York, 1990.

Frazer, Sir James George, 'The Golden Bough: a Study in Magic and Religion', 1st edition (1890).

Gangolli, D. B., 'The Essential Adi Shankara', Adhyatma Prakasha Karyalaya, Banglore, 1991.

Gangolli, D. B., 'The Magic Jewel of Intuition – The Tri-Basic Method of Cognizing the Self', Adhyatma Prakasha Karyalaya, Holenarasipur, India, 1986.

Gazzaniga, M. S., Bogen, J. E., Sperry, R. W., 'Observations on Visual Perception After Disconnection of the Cerebral Hemispheres in Man', Brain, 88(2), 1965.

Gilbert, Elizabeth Gilbert, 'Eat, Pray, Love: One Woman's Search for Everything Across Italy, India, and Indonesia', Riverhead Books, January 30, 2007.

Gould, Stephen, J., 'Rocks of Ages: Science and Religion in the Fullness of Life', Random House Publishing Group, 1999.

Guillen, Michael, 'Amazing Truths – How Science and Bible Agree', Zondervan, 2015.

Gupta, Bina, 'Perceiving in Advaita Vedanta – Epistemological Analysis and Interpretation', Lewisburg-Bucknell University Press, London, 1991.

Gutting, Gary, 'Talking God – Philosophers on Belief', W.W. Norton and Company Inc. New York, N.Y., 2017. First appeared in 'The Stones' column of 'New York Times'

Hameroff, S. & Penrose, R. (2014), 'Consciousness in the Universe: A Review of the "ORCH OR" theory', 'Physics Life Reviews', 11, 39-78.

Hanson, Rick with Mendius, Richard, 'The Practical Neuroscience of Buddha's Brain - Happiness, Love and Wisdom', New Harbinger Publications, Inc., 2009.

Harris, Sam, 'The End of Faith- Religion, Terror and the Future of Reason', W. W. Norton & Company, 2004.

Harris, Sam, 'Waking UP – A guide to spirituality without Religion', Simon and Schuster, New York, N.Y., 2014.

Harris, Sam, 'Letter to a Christian Nation, Vintage Books, January 8, 2008.

Harris, Sam, 'Making Sense: Conversation on Consciousness, Morality, and the Future of Humanity', Harper Collins Publisher, New York, N.Y., 2020.

Harris, Sam, (Ph.D. Thesis, 2009, Uni of CA), published in 2010, 'The Moral Landscape: How Science can Determine Human Values', Ph. D. Thesis at University of California, 2009, Published in 2010.

Hedges, Chris, 'I Do Not Believe in Atheists', Free Press, A division of Simon and Schuster Inc., New York, N.Y.. 2008.

Hedges, Chris, 'American Fascists: The Christian Right and the War on America', Free Press, January 8, 2008.

Hill C. (1991), *Sensations: A defense of Materialism*, Cambridge University Press.

Hitchens, Christopher, 'God Is Not Great – How Religion Poisons Everything', Twelve, Hachette Book Group,2007.

Houde, Roland and Mullally, Joseph P. (editors), 'Philosophy of Knowledge – Selected readings', J.B. Lippincot Company, New York, N.Y.. USA, 1960.

Houk, James, T., 'Illusion of Certainty: How the Flawed Beliefs of Religion Harm our Culture', Prometheus Books, New York, 2017.

Hume, D., 'Dialogues Concerning Natural Religion', ed. N. Kemp Smith, Nelson, Edinburgh.

Hume, D., 'Enquiries Concerning Human Understanding', ed. L. A. Selby-Bigge, Oxford University Press, Oxford, 1975.

Hume D., 'A Treatise of Human Nature', ed. L. A. Selby-Bigge and P. H. Nidditch, Oxford University Press, Oxford, 1978.

Indich, William M., 'Consciousness in Advaita Vedanta', Motilal Banarasi Dass, Varanasi, 1980.

Islam, Kazi Nurul, 'A Critique of Sankara's Philosophy of Appearance', Vohra Publishers and Distributors, Allahabad, India, 1988.

Itoh, T., Wakahara, S., Nakano, T., Suzuki, K., Kobayashi, K., & Inoue, O. (2005). 'Effects of Anesthesia upon 18F-FDG Uptake in Rhesus Monkey Brains'. *Annals of Nuclear Medicine*, 19(5), 373–377.

James, W., 'The Principles of Psychology', Dover, New York, 1950.

James, W., 'Psychology: Briefer Course', Harvard University Press, Cambridge, MA, 1984.

James, William, 'Principles of Psychology', Vol. I and II, Pantianos Classics, 1918 (first published in 1890).

Jones, Steve, 'The Serpent's Promise - The Bible Interpreted Through Modern Science', Pegasus Books, 2012.

Kahneman, Daniel, 'Slow thinking, Fast thinking', Penguin Books, May 5, 2012.

Kakigi, R., Naka, D., Okusa, T., Wang, X., Inui, K., Qiu, Y., et al. (2003). 'Sensory Perception During Sleep in 398 Humans: A Magnetoencephalograhic Study'. *Sleep Medicine*, 4(6), 493–507.

Klein, Yossi, 'At the Entrance of the Garden of Eden: A Jew's Search for Hope with Christians and Muslims in the Holy Land', Harper Perennial, June 1, 2002.

Koch, C., 'The Feeling of Life Itself', MIT Press, 2019.

Koenig, Harold G., 'Medicine Religion and Health – Where Science and Spirituality Meet', Templeton Science and Religion Series, Templeton Foundation Press, West Conshohocken, Pennsylvania, 2008.

Koenig, Harold G., 'Spirituality in Patient Care: Why, How, When, and Why, 2nd ed', Templeton Foundation Press, West Conshohocken, Pennsylvania, 2007.

Koenig, McCullough, and Larson, 'Handbook of Religion and Health', 519-22, Oxford University Press, 2000.

Krishnananda, Swami, 'The Mandukya Upanishad' eBook., Sivananda Ashram.

Kroeger, D., & Amzica, F. (2007). 'Hypersensitivity of the Anesthesia-Induced Comatose Brain'. *Journal of Neuroscience,* 27(39), 10597–10607.

Langford GW, Meddis R, and Pearson AJD. 'Awakening Latency from Sleep for Meaningful and Non-Meaningful Stimuli'. *Psychophysiology* 11: 1–5, 1974

Langsjo, J. W., Maksimow, A., Salmi, E., Kaisti, K., Aalto, S., Oikonen, V., et al. (2005). S-ketamine anesthesia increases cerebral blood flow in excess of the metabolic needs in humans. *Anesthesiology*, 103(2), 258–268.

Laura, Judith, 'Goddess Spirituality for the 21st Century: From Kabbalah to Quantum Physics', Booklocker.com, January 2008.

Lindsay, James A., 'Everybody is Wrong About God', Pitchstone Publishing, Durham, North Carolina, 2015,

Llinas, R., Ribary, U., Contreras, D., & Pedroarena, C. (1998). 'The Neural Basis for Consciousness'. *Philosophical Transactions of the Royal Society of London B: Biological Sciences,* 353 (1377), 1841-1849.

Luhrmann, T. M., 'How God Becomes Real – Kindling the Presence of Invisible Others', Princeton University Press, Oct 27, 2020.

Luo, Q., Mitchell, D., Cheng, X., Mondillo, K., McCaffrey, D., Holroyd, T., et al. (2009). 'Visual Awareness, Emotion, and Gamma Band Synchronization'. *Cerebral Cortex,* 19(8), 1896–1904.

Madison, David and Sledge, Tim, 'Guessing About God – Ten Tough Problems in Christian Belief, Book1', eBook on Amazon, July 5, 2023.

Maksimow, A., Sarkela, M., Langsjo, J. W., Salmi, E., Kaisti, K. K., Yli-Hankala, A., et al. (2006). An increase in high-frequency EEG activity explains the poor performance of the EEG spectral entropy monitor during S-ketamine anesthesia. *Clinical Neurophysiology,* 117(8), 1660–1668.

Massimini, M., Huber, R., Ferrarelli, F., Hill, S., and Tononi, G. (2004). 'The Sleep Slow Oscillation as a Travelling Wave'. *The Journal of Neuroscience,* Aug.4, 24(31):6862-6870.

McGrath, Alister, 'The Big Question – 'Why We Cannot Stop Talking About Science, Faith and God', St. Martin's Press, N.Y., 2015.

Mehta, Rohit, 'The Call of The Upanishad', Bhartiya Vidya Bhavan, Chowpatty, Bombay, 1970.

Mikhailov, F. T., 'The Riddle of the Self', International Publishers, New York, N.Y., USA, 1981.

Miles, Jack, 'Religion as We Know it: An Origin Story', W. W. Norton & Company, November 12, 2019.

Nagel, T. (1974), 'What is it Like to be a Bat?' *Philosophical Review*, 83, 435-450.

Oswald I, Taylor A, and Treisman M. 'Discriminative Responses to Stimulation During Human Sleep'. *Brain* 83: 440–453, 1960.

Paley, William, 'Natural Theology or Evidence of the Existence and Attributes of the Deity Collected from the Appearance of Nature', Halliwell, London, 1802.

Parrinder, Geoffrey, 'The Indestructible Soul', George Allen & Unwin Ltd., 1973.

Penrose, R. (1994), 'Shadows of the Mind', Oxford University Press.

Penrose, R. (2004), 'The Road to Reality - A Complete Guide to the Laws of the Universe', New York: Knopf.

Peter Godfrey-Smith, (Oct. 17, 2017), 'Other Minds: The Octopus, the Sea, and the Deep Origins of Consciousness', Farrar Straus and Giroux, N.Y..

Polkinghorne, John, 'Exploring Reality – the Intertwining of Science and Religion', Yale University Press, April 2007.

Portas CM, Krakow K, Allen P, Josephs O, Armony JL, and Frith CD. 'Auditory Processing Across the Sleep-Wake Cycle: Simultaneous EEG and MRI Monitoring in Humans'. *Neuron* 28: 991–999, 2000.

Prothero, Stephen, 'Religious Literacy: What Every American Needs to Know – And Doesn't', Harper One, March 11, 2008.

Raina, B. L., 'Vedanta: What Can It Teach?', B.R. Publishing Corp., A division of D.K. Publishers Distributors, (P) Ltd., Delhi, India -110052, 1995.

Raju, P. T., and Castell, Alburey (Editors), 'East-West Studies on The Problem of The Self', papers presented in the conference on Comparative Philosophy and Culture held at the College of Wooster, Wooster, Ohio, April 22-24, 1965. Martinus Nijhoff, The Hague, 1968.

Ram Kanshi, 'Integral Non-Dualism- A Critical Exposition of Vijnanabhiksu's System of Philosophy', Motilal Banarasi Dass, Delhi, India, 1995.

Rao, V. N. Sheshagiri, 'Vacaspati's Contribution to Advaita', Samuit Publishers, Jayanagar, Mysor, India, 600014, 1984.

Rohr, Richard, 'Immortal Diamond – The search of Our True Self', Jossey-Bass, A Wiley Imprint, www.JosseyBass.com, 2013.

Rosenberg, Alex, 'Atheist's Guide to Reality: Enjoying the Life Without Illusions', W. W. Norton & Company, Dec. 2012.

Rushdie, Salman, 'Satanic Verses', The Viking Press, Feb 1989.

Russel, Peter, 'From Science to God', New World Library, Novato, CA, 2002.

Sarasso, S., Boly, M., Napolitani, M., Tononi, G., Laureys, S., Massimini, M. et al. (2015). 'Consciousness and Complexity during Unresponsiveness Induced by Propofol, Xenon, and Ketamine', *Current Biology,* November 2015.

Scull, Andrew, 'Madness in Civilization: A Cultural History of Insanity, from Bible to Sigmund Freud', from Madhouse to Modern Medicine, Princeton University Press, Aug 29, 2016.

Searle, J. R. (1992), *The Rediscovery of the Mind,* MIT Press.

Shermer, Michael, 'How We Believe: The Search for God in an Age of Science', W. H., Freeman & Company, January 2000.

Shermer, Michael, 'How We Believe: Science, Skepticism, and the Search for God', Holt paperbacks, October 2003.

Shermer, Michael, 'Why People Believe Weird Things: Pseudoscience, Superstition, And Other Confusions of Our Time', Holt paperbacks, September 2002.

Shevrin, H., Snodgrass, M., Brakel, L., Kushwaha, R., Kalaida, N. L., Bazan, A. (2013). 'Subliminal unconscious conflict alpha power inhibits supraliminal conscious symptom experience', *Frontiers in Human Neuroscience,* 7:544 · September 2013.

Silverstein, B., Snodgrass, M., Shevrin, H., and Kushwaha, R. (2013). P3b, 'Consciousness, and Complex Unconscious Processing', *Cortex* 73 (2015) 216 e227.

Singer, Michael A., 'The Untethered Soul, The Journey Beyond Yourself', The Harbinger Publications, Inc., Noetic Books, Institute of Noetic Sciences, 2007.

Smoley, Richard, 'The Dice Game of Shiva: How Consciousness Creates the Universe', New World Library, Novato, CA, 2009.

Solomon, Andrew Solomon, 'The Noonday Demon', Scribner Book Company, January 2002.

Sperry, R. W., 'Some Effects of Disconnecting the Cerebral hemispheres. Noble Lecture, December 8, 1981'. Biosci. Rep 2(5).

Sperry, R. W., 'Cerebral Organization and Behavior: The Split Brain Behaves in Many Respects Like two Separate Brains, Providing New Research Possibilities', Science, 133(3466), 1961.

Sperry, R. W., 'Hemisphere Disconnection and Unity in Conscious Awareness', Am. Psychol. 23 (10), 1968.

Sperry, R. W., Zaidel, E., Zaidel, D., 'Self-Recognition and Social Awareness in Disconnected Minor Hemisphere', Neuropsychologia 17(2). 1968.

Stenger, Victor J., 'God, The Failed Hypothesis: How Science Shows That God Does Not Exist', Prometheus Books, New York, 2007.

Stenger, Victor, J., 'Has science found God', Prometheus Books, April 2003

Stenger, Victor J., 'Not by Design: The Origin of the Universe', Prometheus Books, Buffalo, N. Y., 1988.

Strawson, G. (1994), *Mental Reality*, MIT Press.

Strobel, Lee, 'Is God Real- Exploring the Ultimate Question of Life', Zondervan Book, Grand Rapids, MI, 2023

Sureshananda, Swami (translated by), 'Yoga Vasishta Sara – the Essence of Yoga Vashishtha', Y.S. Ramanan, Tiruvannamalai, 606603, India, 1999.

Tedlock, Dennis, and Tedlock, Barbara (editors), 'Teachings from the American Earth – Indian Religion and Philosophy', Liveright Publisher, N.Y., 1975, 1992.

Tippet, Krista, 'Speaking of Faith – Why Religion Matters – and How to Talk About It', Penguin Books, January 29, 2008.

Tippet, Krista, 'Einstein's God', Penguin Books, N.Y., 2010.

Tobolowsky, Stephen, 'My Adventures with God', Simon and Schuster, 2017.

Tononi, G. (2004). 'An Information Integration Theory of Consciousness'. *BMC Neuroscience,* 5(1), 42.

Tononi, G. (2008a). 'Consciousness as Integrated Information: A Provisional Manifesto'. *The Biological Bulletin*, 215(3), 216–242.

Tononi, G. (2008b). 'Sleep and Dreaming'. In S. Laureys & G. Tononi (Eds.), *The neurology of consciousness* (p. 424). London: Academic Press — Elsevier.

Tononi, G., & Edelman, G. M. (1998). 'Consciousness and Complexity'. *Science,* 282(5395), 1846–1851.

Tononi, G., & Laureys, S. (2008). The Neurology of Consciousness: An Overview'. In S. Laureys & G. Tononi (Eds.), *The neurology of consciousness* (pp. 375–412). Oxford: Elsevier.

Verma, Satya Pal, 'Role of Reason in Sankara Vedanta', Primal Publication, Delhi, 1992.

Ward, Keith, 'Is Religion Dangerous?', William B. Eerdmans Publishing Co., Grand Rapids, MI, 2006.

Warren, Daniel, 'Lies Upon Lies – God, Authority, and How Your Faith is Used to Control You', Kindle edition on Amazon, November 27, 2023.

Wathy, John, C., 'Illusion of God's Presence: the Biological Origin of Spiritual Longing', Prometheus Books, January 12, 2016.

Weinberg, Steven, 'The First Three Minutes: A Modern View of the Origin of the Universe', William Collins, Glasgow, 1977.

Wenneberg, S. R., Schneider, R. H., Walton, K. G., et al., 'A Controlled Study for the effects of the Transcendental Meditation Program on Cardiovascular Reactivity and Ambulatory Blood Pressure', International Journal of Neuroscience, 89, nos. 1-2(1997), 15-28.

Winnick, Pamela R., 'A Jealous God – Science's Crusade Against Religion', Thomas Nelson Inc., January 1, 2005.

Woodruff, M. (2017), 'Consciousness in Teleosts: There is Something it Feels Like to be a Fish', *Animal Senrience.*

Woods, James Haughton (translated by), 'Yoga System of Patanjali – Or the Ancient Hindu Doctrine of Concentration of Mind', Motilal Banarasi Dass, Varanasi, India, 1914.1977 by arrangement with the Harvard University Press.

Connect with the Author

You can reach out to Ramesh K. Kushwaha through the following channels:

Website: www.PhysicalBodyVirtualSoul.org

Email: Rameshkushwaha2279@gmail.com

Your thoughts and questions are eagerly anticipated and warmly welcomed!

www.ingramcontent.com/pod-product-compliance
Ingram Content Group UK Ltd.
Pitfield, Milton Keynes, MK11 3LW, UK
UKHW022256170225
455202UK00012B/613

9 798992 336931